Nelles Guides

... get you going.

TITLES IN PRINT

Australia
Bali / Lombok
Berlin and Potsdam
Brittany
California
  Las Vegas, Reno, Baja California
Cambodia / Laos
Canada
  Ontario, Québec,
  Atlantic Provinces
Caribbean:
  The Greater Antilles
  Bermuda, Bahamas
Caribbean:
  The Lesser Antilles
China
Crete
Cyprus
Egypt
Florida
Greece - *The Mainland*
Hawaii
Hungary
India
  Northern, Northeastern
  and Central India
India
  Southern India
Indonesia
  Sumatra, Java, Bali,
  Lombok, Sulawesi
Ireland

Kenya
London, England and Wales
Malaysia
Mexico
Morocco
Moscow / St Petersburg
Munich *and Excursions to*
        Castles, Lakes & Mountains
Nepal
New York *and New York State*
New Zealand
Paris
Philippines
Prague - Czech Republic
Provence
Rome
Spain, *North*
Spain, *South*
Thailand
Turkey
Tuscany

IN PREPARATION (for 1995)

Israel
South Africa
U.S.A.
  The West, Rockies and Texas
U.S.A
  The East, Midwest and South
Vietnam

TUSCANY
© Nelles Verlag GmbH, 80935 München
  All rights reserved

First Edition 1995
ISBN 3-88618-407-2
Printed in Slovenia

Publisher:	Günter Nelles	**Photo Editor**:	K. Bärmann-Thümmel
Project Editor:	Ulrike Bossert	**Cartography**:	Nelles Verlag GmbH,
Editor:	J.-M. Schneider		Freytag & Berndt
English Editor:	Anne Midgette	**Color Separation**:	Priegnitz,
Translations:	Angelika Funkhauser		München
	Ross Greville, Kent Lyon	**Printed by**:	Gorenjski Tisk

No part of this book, not even excerpts, may be reproduced in any form without the
express prior permission of Nelles Verlag.

TUSCANY

First Edition
1995

TABLE OF CONTENTS

TUSCANY

0   20   40   60 km

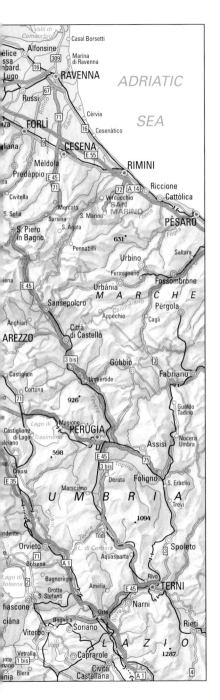

MAP LIST

HISTORY
AND CULTURE

THE LAND OF DREAMS

Tuscany – just the sound of this magical word is enough to make the eyes sparkle and to awake a profound sense of yearning. Tuscany is synonymous with culture, beauty, enjoyment; cities which are themselves enormous works of art, landscapes which seem to imitate paintings. In a word, a Mecca for every art lover, and the destination *par excellence* for romantic dreamers.

The countryside, seductive and full of promise, draws not only artists hoping to draw inspiration from this culture-soaked land, but also many people seeking refuge from civilization, who yearn for the simple life in a still-innocent world.

Three thousand years ago, the Etruscans created the first civilization on the Apennine peninsula. Six hundred years ago, the Renaissance and its ideals of humanism ushered in the modern age. Dante, Boccaccio and Petrarch, Brunelleschi, Arnolfo di Cambio, Nicola and Giovanni Pisano, Ghiberti, Donatello, Giotto, Piero della Francesca, Michelangelo and Leonardo da Vinci – the names are linked forever with cities such as Florence, Pisa, Lucca, Siena, Arezzo in a veritable surplus of art and culture.

And yet there is more. The landscape, shaped by men who knew intuitively where to build their simple stone houses and how most effectively to group their cypresses and pines, is as much a feast for the eyes as any sculpture by Donatello or fresco by Piero della Francesca.

Preceding pages: Tuscan beauty. Landscape of dreams. Annunciation fresco by Fra Angelico in the monastery of S. Marco. Left: Street scene in Florence; detail of a painting by Masolino.

And nature, in Tuscany, has many countenances: there are inaccessible mountainous areas, thick forests where rare species of animals can still be found, lonely river valleys with ancient monasteries and forgotten villages and hamlets, gently rolling hills, sand beaches fringed with pine woods, islands large and small. Anyone seeking untouched nature will find it here, and hikers or cyclists will be in seventh heaven.

If beach life is more to your taste, there's always the coast. There's rest for the weary body in the luxurious thermal spas; and bon vivants can recover here from the effects of dissipate living – only to succumb anew to temptations of the Tuscan cuisine and cellar.

If it is your intention really to get to know Tuscany, a single trip will be woefully inadequate. The visitor who has only seen the main tourist attractions and has ticked off the best-known works of art in his guidebook will have missed a lot of what Tuscany can still offer. If you are interested in the land and the people, you'll have to seek out the small towns with no spectacular monuments to boast of, get off the beaten track.

Chianti, the Maremma, the Crete – every traveller to Tuscany is smitten with these dream landscapes. And many a traveller simply stays. A great many houses here, occasionally whole villages, are owned by foreigners, mostly Germans, Swiss or British. In the 1950s, the rural population began to migrate to the cities, leaving many idyllically situated farmsteads to slow decay; and wealthy foreigners were quick to act. They snapped up these houses, restored them – usually very tastefully, in a traditional style – and proceeded to live there, some for a few weeks each year, others the whole year round.

A dream that every Italy-lover has probably harbored at some time or another – to own a house in Tuscany – has come true. Many of the people who have

taken up permanent residence here try their hands at being vintners, or press their own olives, or keep a few sheep. If they had to make a living this way, they'd have a hard time. Often enough, there follows a rude awakening: disputes with Italian authorities, problems of integration, communication difficulties. Even Italian neighbors sometimes have trouble getting along with these foreign settlers who strive to be more Tuscan than the Tuscans themselves. Still, these foreigners are a sight better than the tourists.

The tourist industry is an important sector of the Tuscan economy, and the main source of income for countless local residents. The flip side of the coin is that the visiting hordes have helped to inflict almost irreparable damage on the works of art which inspired them to descend here in the first place. Tuscany is sick, and drastic measures and a lot of money

Above: Stone Age art. Right: Ewer with equestrian figure – an example of the Bucchero ceramics of the Etruscans.

are called for in order to save what of it can be salvaged, while there's still time.

What do the Tuscans think about all this? People born in Tuscany tend to consider themselves singularly blessed by fate. And one cannot disagree entirely. After all, the Tuscans not only look back on a glorious past; they're also spoiled by the fact that they happen to live in one of the most beautiful places on earth.

And even if, just as in the old days, the Pisans can't stand the Sienese, and the San Gimignans can't abide the Lucchese, and in fact everyone hates everyone else, and the Florentines worst of all, there's one point on which everyone agrees: their homeland is one vast work of art, which their forebears created in the truest sense of the word. Accordingly, they all have a deep awareness of their own and are prepared actively to defend their valuable heritage, while ready, at the same time, to open up to progress.

Fortunately, some recognized the down side of progress early on. People are again giving priority to quality of life, rethinking, and sometimes abandoning, projects based purely on profit motives. But even if an industrial project does besmirch the landscape in a certain area, Tuscany is too large and too multifaceted for it to make a serious dent in its beauty.

So Tuscany, with its art, its landscapes, its mild climate and delightful wines, will continue to be a favorite destination for the tourist hordes. But don't be put off by the crowds; if you'd like to avoid them, simply put off your Tuscany trip until late autumn and winter, when the center of the tourist industry shifts to the southern hemisphere of the globe. In the off-season, Tuscany is virtually deserted: you don't need to stand in line in the museums, hotel staff are friendlier and more obliging, more care and love goes into the preparation of your meals, and everything is more human, warmer, more Italian. The only thing you can't do at this time of year is go for an ocean swim.

THE TURBULENT COURSE OF TUSCAN HISTORY

Early Traces

Traces of the first human settlement in Tuscany date back to the Paleolithic era. Ancient stone tools 30,000 years old have been found in the foothills of the Apennines near Prato, while near Arezzo, excavators have even found the remains of a Stone Age man. The Arno valley and the island of Elba, on the other hand, have yielded up numerous items from the transitional time between the Paleolithic and Mesolithic eras; such finds have, in fact, been made all along the Tyrrhenian coast from Liguria to Sicily.

Permanent settlements with farming and stock-breeding did not, however, develop until the Bronze Age (approx. 1500 to 1000 BC) on the slopes of the Apennines. Finds from this period have included attractive pots with geometrical patterns and countless tools made of stone, metal and bone.

The historical period commences during the transition from the Bronze to the Iron Age. This was the time of the so-called Villanova culture (named after a small village near Bologna), a society which practiced cremation rather than the kind of elaborate tomb interment common in the Bronze Age.

Villanova culture has also furnished the first examples of artistically decorated tools and weapons of bronze, as well as small, stylized figures representing human beings or animals. This culture extended over northern Italy and the region which was later to become Tuscany, and flourished between around 950 to 450 BC. Around 700 BC it was superseded in this area by Etruscan culture, which was to develop into central Italy's first advanced civilization.

The Etruscans

"Once upon a time, a farmer from Tarquinia was plowing his field not far from the town. Thrusting his plowshare deeper

15

than usual into the earth and turning over the clump of sod, he found underneath it a boy with feet like serpents, the countenance of a mature man, and a head of white hair. This was Tages, son of a local deity and grandson of Jupiter. The farmer shouted until people came running from all sides to see what the matter was. His shouts even drew the lucomones, the chiefs of the twelve cities of the Etruscan League. In the midst of this assembly, the wondrous earth-child began to sing his wisdom; and the twelve leaders immediately wrote down every word as he sang it. Thus came to be the Etruscans' "Tagetic books," a body of Etruscan law and learning passed down as a priceless treasure from generation to generation. When Tages had finished singing out everything he knew, he fell back into the earth and was dead."

This, then, is the Etruscan myth of creation. And although more than three

Above: Etruscan grave near Populonia from the 7th-5th centuries BC.

thousand years have gone by since this wonderful event, much is still obscure about the origins of the Etruscans and the development of their nation and their culture. They emerged from the mists of antiquity during the first millennium before Christ, and had returned to obscurity before our written history begins. Even their language, which most authorities do not consider part of the Indo-European linguistic family, still has not been deciphered, although many people have attempted to do so.

The ancient realm of the Etruscans was bounded by the rivers Arno and Tiber, and the Tyrrhenian Sea, a body of water named for the Tyrrhenians, as the Greeks termed the Etruscans. Tyrrhenus was a prince of Lydia who led part of his people to Italy to escape a famine that was ravaging their homeland. The Romans, on the other hand, called them Etrusci or Tusci, and these words gave rise to the later terms Etruria and then Tuscany.

The first physical signs of their presence in what is now the region of

Tuscany go back to the 8th century BC. As to their ultimate origin, there are various theories, and even the scholars of antiquity were not able to agree with one another. In all probability they did come from Lydia, crossing the sea and settling Etruria from the coast, working inland and mixing with the indigenous peoples of the Villanova culture. This, at least, was the hypothesis of the Greek historian Herodotus; and there are many indications to support his theory, from both art and religion.

Another Greek writer, Dionysius of Halicarnassus, postulated in his *Antiquites Romanae* the hypothesis that the Etruscans were an autochthonous people who developed out of the Proto-Italians of the Villanova culture (these terms, of course, are a modern paraphrase).

A third theory, supported by a number of scholars in the 19th century, holds that the Etruscans, who themselves used the name Rasenna (from *Raeti*, the inhabitants of the Rhaetic Alps), are to be counted amongst the groups of Indo-Germanic peoples who migrated across the Alps and onto the Italian peninsula from around 2000 BC onwards. This theory is supposedly supported by inscriptions found in Trentino which bear a certain resemblance to examples of Etruscan epigraphy. Unfortunately these inscriptions date from as late as the 4th century BC, and thus only serve demonstrate that the Etruscans were also present in this area.

Whatever the truth of the matter is, the riddle of the origins of the Etruscans cannot, at present, be solved and it is basically more interesting to examine the ways they developed into a civilization with its own identity and its own, extremely advanced, culture.

There is no disputing the fact that the Etruscans, starting from the cities of Vetulonia and Populonia on the coast and their early inland settlements of Volterra and Chiusi, spread into Umbria and Latium. They founded cities and settlements, put the land to the plough, drained the swamplands of the Maremma with their ingenious drainage systems, and mined the ores and minerals of the wooded (and aptly named) Colline Metallifere ("metal-bearing hills").

Etruria was organized into city-states on the Greek model, and ruled on the basis of an aristocratic constitution, with a priest-king, the lucomon, at the top. The cities themselves were autonomous. In the 6th century the twelve most important cities, which included Arezzo, Cortona, Volterra, Chiusi, Roselle and Vetulonia, joined into a loosely-knit federation for defensive purposes. At the same time, the Etruscans extended their dominion northwards beyond the Apennines as far as the plain of the Po, and founded the cities of Adria and Spina on the Adriatic coast.

The Etruscans were also a seafaring people. As pirates they were feared, as trading partners valued. Allied with Carthage, the fleet of the League of the Twelve Cities (also called the dodecapolis) defeated the Greeks off Corsica in 540 BC. After this, the Etruscans effectively held sway over the entire northwestern Mediterranean, and their maritime trading activities were secured.

Between the 7th and the 5th centuries Etruscan art and culture blossomed as never before. Strong Greek influence can be detected in their writing, their religious pantheon and in their coinage. The Etruscans also looked to Greek models in their art, something that can be seen, for example, in their vase painting; nonetheless, their works had a unique, distinctive flavor. In their small-scale sculptures, they simplified and stylized shapes, which gave their works a lifelike vividness of expression quite removed from the distant, enlightened serenity you see in Greek sculptures.

Another feature of their art which is to be seen almost exclusively in cult objects is the excellence of technical quality. Working with gold, the Etruscans were

masters of highly developed granulation and filigree techniques; they developed a high degree of mastery in such artisan skills as working metals into basins, mirrors and candleabras, carving ivory, or in the production of *bucchero* ceramics (bucchero is a brilliant black substance similar to clay).

Characteristic of this people who had such a love of life was, paradoxically, their preoccupation with the next world, the afterlife, and a very distinctive cult of the dead. The Etruscans furnished their necropolises, which lay outside the city walls, with everything that made life and living pleasant. The tombs were built like dwellings or homes amidst a network of roads and lanes modeled on the city of the living. Inside, the tomb walls were decorated with gaily-colored frescoes depicting scenes of life and death. Costly grave goods were provided so that the de-

Above: Alabaster figure of a dead man (Etruscan Museum, Chiusi). Right: Etruscan-age doorway arch in Volterra.

ceased need lack for nothing in the hereafter. The vaulted tombs and cottage tombs consisted of multiple levels and rooms, and there was space enough for successive generations of a family. In the north of Etruria these necropolises were built of stone blocks, while in the south they were hewn in their entirety out of the volcanic limestone, or tuff. The tombs were designed for eternity, unlike the homes and temples of wood and terracotta tiles which have not survived the millennia.

Contemporaries of the Etruscans found their rituals strange, especially as their religion was otherwise basically Hellenistic; it was particularly marked by a strong dependence on the involvement of the gods in their fate. In accordance with the procedures laid down in the *Etrusca disciplina*, the Etruscans observed natural phenomena, the flight of birds and the innards of animals, and their priests interpreted what they saw. Essentially, if the gods were to be pleased, their will had to be clearly understood. These methods of

soothsaying were later taken over by the Romans, as were the Etruscans' music, theater and gladiatorial games.

A thorn in the side of patriarchal societies such as those of Ancient Greece and Rome would very probably have been the fact that Etruscan women clearly enjoyed a position of equality with the men, as well as a broad spectrum of matriarchal rights. As priestesses, they had an important role to play in the spiritual leadership of the people and could even participate in feasts and banquets, and in contests and competitions.

The Etruscans were thus "a people who don't resemble any other, either in their language or in their customs," as Dionysius of Halicarnassus summed up his experiences.

Then began their decline. They lost a sea battle to the Syracusan fleet in 474 BC, and this ushered in a gradual loss of their power over the seas. In addition, a rival culture was beginning to expand. This was Rome, which initially was very much under the influence of the Etruscan

aristocracy, and had become rich and powerful very rapidly under the seven Etruscan kings of legend (Romulus, Numa Pompilius, Tullus Hostilius, Ancus Marcus Tarquinius Priscus, and Tarquinius Superbus). The conquest of Etruria can be said to have started with the fall of Veii in 396 BC after a siege that had lasted ten years. One by one the city-states fell under the rule of Rome, until the last of them, Volsinii (Bolsena on the Lago di Bolsena) surrendered definitively in 265 BC, whereupon the Romans deported all of its inhabitants.

The fact that the Etruscans play such a subordinate role in Roman historiography seems to indicate that there must have been a certain degree of Roman jealousy of this highly-civilized people. This may also be a reason why so few written testimonies of the Etruscans have been handed down to us. Accordingly, scholars who attempt to decipher their language have only their relatively short grave inscriptions and a small number of manuscript fragments to go on. On the

other hand, numerous examples of their architecture still survive in Tuscany. We may instance the remnants of city walls in Roselle, Vetulonia, Populonia, Cortone, Fiesole and Volterra (the last being where the Porta dell'Arco, the famous gate with the Etruscan heads, still stands) and also the necropolises with their precious grave goods which can be seen in many museum collections today. The most important ones in Tuscany are the Museo Archeologico in Florence and the Museo Etrusco Guarnacci in Volterra.

Roman Etruria

The Romans were skilled at handling the peoples they had conquered. Cities were permitted to retain a certain degree of formal autonomy while the entire corresponding region was incorporated into a system of federation. This is why a

Above: Roman amphitheater in Fiesole.
Right: Bronze statue of Charlemagne, c. 870.

number of Etruscan cities in the north – Arezzo, Cortona and Perugia – actually accorded the Romans a friendly reception. During the Punic Wars and in the battles with the Celts, the Etruscans fought alongside the Romans as allies, and in 91 B.C. they were granted Roman citizenship.

During the first century of Roman rule, the region initially continued to flourish. Roman colonies were founded and wide roads were built to connect Rome and Etruria. The first of these roads, the *Via Aurelia*, which follows the coastline, was started in 241; then came the *Via Clodia*, which leads from Veii to join the Aurelian Way at Roselle, in 225. From around 220 Rome and Fiesole were connected by the *Via Cassia*, and the year 187 saw completion of the *Via Flaminia*, which passed through Arezzo and over the Apennines into Emilia.

Not very many buildings or works of art from the Roman era have survived in Tuscany; most traces were destroyed in the Middle Ages and Renaissance. Occasionally, however, remnants of the typical Roman range of civil works can still be seen: amphitheaters (in Luni, Volterra and Fiesole), temples (in Fiesole) and thermal baths (in Pisa and Fiesole). To this we may add the remains of Roman patrician villas on Mount Argentario near Porto Santo Stefano and on the island of Giannutri.

The last century of the Roman Republic meant the final downfall for Etruria too. Parts of the region were used as battlefields in the Civil Wars, which resulted in the destruction and devastation of wide tracts of land.

As malaria spread more and more along the coastline, land here had to be abandoned and the people fled inland. No longer was it worth growing corn locally, as cheaper grain was being imported from Asia, Egypt and Sicily. The same applied to the mining of ore.

Emperor Augustus tried to improve the dismal economic situation in the country and in the course of an administrative reorganization of Italy, Etruria was declared the VIIth Region, the borders of which were the river Magra and the Apennines in the north and northeast respectively, the Tiber in the southeast and the coast as far as the mouth of the Tiber in the west.

During the 3rd century, under the emperor Diocletian, the country – which was now called Tuscia – went to Umbria. A *corrector* took over the office of chief administrator, and had his residence in Florentia, the Roman veterans' colony on the Arno, which had been founded in the days of Caesar.

The Period of the Barbarian Migrations

The insurgence of the barbarians resulted in Tuscia's political and economic downfall. The country was destroyed, and some cities, particularly those located on the major highways leading to

Rome, never recovered. After the Alamanni and the Ostrogoths, there was a brief upswing under the Byzantines (553-569), but the Lombards, who settled principally on the Po plain, had only a military interest in Tuscia, which had been virtually destroyed and thus had little to offer. Fortified settlements went up along the Apennines and from the Garfagnana via the Mugello into the Chiusi region as a protection against the Byzantine Empire.

The Lombards made Tuscia an archduchy, subdividing it into smaller duchies. The most important city at the time was Lucca, which was probably the first city to be conquered by the Lombards when they invaded the country via the Cisa pass in the north. The next city to be taken was Pisa, which was still involved to a certain extent in maritime trade, and from where the Lombards sailed to conquer Sardinia and Corsica. The other cities, such as Pistoia, Fiesole, Florence and Arezzo, at this time were in a state of utter decay. Siena was involved in a cen-

R exRoGAT ABBATem: MATbILDIOn SupplicAT ATR;

tury-long dispute with Arezzo involving the ownership of certain parishes, and Chiusi was threatened by the spread of the marshlands of the Chiana valley.

In the year 774, with the conquest of Pavia, Charlemagne brought the kingdom of the Lombards into the kingdom of the Franks. Under Charlemagne, who no longer regarded Tuscia as an enemy territory to be exploited, there began a new era of recovery. Commerce flourished once more, prosperity increased, and cities gained in importance. Lucca, Siena, San Gimignano and Colle di Val d'Elsa profited from the newly built *Via Francigena* (the Frankish road) which extended though the interior of the country, connecting Pavia and Rome. Pilgrim hostels were built, as well as business centers and monasteries, such as, for example, the Abbazia di San Salvatore on

Above: Emperor Henry IV with the Margravine Matilda before his Journey to Canossa (book illumination, 1114). Right: Dynastic towers in Lucca (14th-century illumination).

Monte Amiata. Other cities, however, which had once benefited from their location on the Roman consular roads, such as Florence, Arezzo and Chiusi, were now too far removed from the new trading and pilgrimage routes to participate in this economic recovery. At this time, the population living near the coast was being forced to flee into the mountains to take refuge from the raids of both Normans and Saracens.

During the 9th century, Tuscia became a margravate, and in 934 the name *Tuscana* first appeared in a document. At this time, a feudal system had already been established with both ecclesiastical and secular lords in the feudal pyramid. The landed aristocracy had built numerous castles for itself, while the monasteries were becoming even richer and more powerful. However in the cities the middle classes were gaining self-confidence due to their successes in commerce and were exerting more and more political influence. Back in the 9th century, there had already been popular assemblies held to decide on administrative and building measures, and in the 11th century the first consuls were already ruling in Pisa and Lucca.

The Gregorian church reforms had a strong following in many of the episcopal cities, particularly in Pisa, Lucca and Florence; this movement later developed into the strife between the Papacy and the Empire. The new burst of religious zeal demanded stricter morals and more discipline within the church, and led to the founding of new orders everywhere. In Tuscany the orders of the Vallombrosans and the Camaldolensans dominated.

The Era of the Communes

The Margravine Matilda, on whose family estate in Canossa Henry IV had knelt before Pope Gregory VII, died in 1115, bequeathing all her worldly possessions to the Church. This bequest in-

tensified the conflict between the Pope and the Emperor. The cities exploited the dispute to undermine the power of the bishopric and the margrave, thereby winning more independence for themselves. In the 12th century, the larger cities were to all intents and purposes autonomous and were developing into independent communes, although they continued to be governed by the aristocracy.

As a result of the crusades and the trade in the eastern Mediterranean, Pisa had in the meantime experienced a rapid ascent. It was in Pisa that the crusaders were provided with transportation, military escorts and provisions. Thus Pisa remained the most important city in Tuscany throughout the 12th century. But a sudden economic upswing was also felt in the other cities. The banks and money-lenders in Siena had connections which extended as far as Rome, northern Italy and France; Lucca and Florence made a modest start to their textile industry, and in Florence this soon brought with it a flourishing activity in banking.

The demand for unrestricted commerce without road tolls led to the gradual dissolution of the feudal system. Minor landed aristocrats were encouraged or forced to take up residence in the cities. Only the larger families such as the Guidi, the Aldobrandeschi and the Malaspina were able to maintain the traditional system for some time yet. The struggle against the feudal lords continued throughout the 12th century. At the same time Pisa, Lucca and Florence started to fight for supremacy over their neighbouring, and rival, cities. The first victim was Fiesole which was razed to the ground by Florence in 1125.

But soon everyone was fighting everyone else, in alliances which were as quickly dissolved as made. Florence and Pisa were especially bitter rivals, as Florence required unimpeded access to the sea for its booming wool trade. But Florence had also been in conflict with Siena for years, as Siena was rich and thought to be an especially dangerous competitor in this particular line of trade.

Guelphs and Ghibellines

The incessant disputes between the Pope and the Emperor served as a pretext for these battles, the real purpose of which clearly was the struggle for supreme power. The Emperor's supporters called themselves the Ghibellines after the Swabian city of Waiblingen, the home of the Hohenstaufen dynasty, and were primarily members of the aristocracy which expected the old order to be upheld and maintained by the power of the Emperor. The new upper strata of the middle class, which included wealthy merchants and bankers who were not very interested in a return to the old order, were adherents of the Guelph party (named after the Guelph king crowned as emperor Otto IV by Pope Innocence III) and they expected greater trading possi-

Above: Romanesque capital in S. Antimo, Maître de Chambestany. Right: First flowering of Tuscan painting – Cimabue, Madonna and Child Enthroned (1272-74).

bilities as a consequence of the Church's extensive connections. Social tension grew within the cities and feuds developed between the different parties, finding visible expression in the fortress-like towers that the various noble families were erecting everywhere.

The cities' wealth manifested itself at this time in the construction of many great monuments. In Florence, the church of S. Minato al Monte was built and the Baptistery took on its present form; Pisa developed a style of its own which blended northern architecture with oriental elements. The Duomo and the Baptistery are outstanding examples of this type of architecture, but it's also reflected in cathedrals in Prato, Pistoia and along the coast up to Carrara. In Lucca, the Pisan style found an additional, typically Lucchese variant, and a mixture of the two was realized in the cathedrals of Volterra and Massa Marittima.

Siena and Arezzo, on the other hand, continued to maintain a style of their own. In Siena, in particular, there are few relics of Romanesque architecture. However, the abbey of Sant'Antimo, in the south of the region, is one of the most exquisite Romanesque churches in all of Tuscany.

Alongside the great ecclesiastical buildings there arose in the cities the palaces of the temporal governing powers, such as the Palazzi del Popolo and the Palazzi del Podestà, which resembles a fortress. A very fine example of this is the Bargello in Florence. From this era Prato can still boast a special edifice of a type that is otherwise only found in Apulia and Sicily: the Castello Imperiale, Emperor Frederick II's imperial castle.

During the 12th century, Pisa became the center for Tuscan sculpture, the city where the great sculptor Nicola Pisano made his first mark. The field of painting saw the development of marvelous wooden painted crucifixes, which demonstrate a strong Byzantine influence. A masterwork of this art, a wooden cross painted in 1138 by Guglielmo, who was probably from Lucca, is today on display in the cathedral of Sarzana.

Active at the end of the 13th century was Cimabue, who also worked in Rome, Assisi and Pisa, and who is considered one of the most important painters in the development of Tuscan art, and a major forerunner of Giotto. Over in Siena, Duccio di Buoninsegna was at work, the first outstanding master of the Sienese School in whose art one can already detect Gothic elements.

At the beginning of the 13th century, the outcome of the struggle for regional supremacy was gradually becoming clear. Pisa had dissipated its energy in its endeavor to obtain supremacy in the Mediterranean and did not have the strength to secure its hinterland. Siena was defeated repeatedly by Florence and was forced to concentrate its interests on the south of the country, which economically was nowhere near as lucrative as the area between Siena and Florence.

At this time, Florence was the center of Guelph resistance to Emperor Frederick II. However, he expelled the Guelphs from the city. But the Ghibelline faction was not able to maintain its dominance and in the constitution of the so-called *primo popolo* (1250) the people organized themselves against the Ghibelline aristocracy and summoned the Guelphs to return. This first popular regime lasted some 10 years. At its head was the *capitano del popolo* (captain of the people) who was supported by a council of twelve elders. Under the parallel authorities of the Commune (headed by the *podestà*) and the people, the city experienced a decade of strong economic and political growth. In 1252, the first gold florin was minted, a visible sign of the power of Florence and a coin which was soon highly regarded all over Europe.

In the battle of Montaperti (1260), Guelph Florence and its *primo popolo* was crushingly defeated by its great rival Siena, which had entered an alliance with

the banished Ghibellines one last time. This, however, meant only a temporary postponement of Florence's supremacy in Tuscany.

The Guilds

In order to counterbalance the all-powerful nobility, which continued to keep a firm grip on the reins of political power, the merchants, bankers and craftsmen started to join together in guilds (*arti*). Membership in these associations was on a voluntary basis, but anyone who did not join had to make do without a whole series of benefits, as the guilds not only defended professional interests at the commune level but also protected their members from the demands of their employees. Wages and salaries were specified in a special ordinance, and the

Above: Relief representation of the architects' guild on Orsanmichele, Florence.
Right: Dante Alighieri, painted by Michelino.
Far right: Giotto's Campanile.

guilds can thus be seen as an early form of the trade union.

The guild members were industrious and clever and often controlled the markets of entire areas. They gradually gained in influence until they finally pushed the nobility out of city governments. After the late 13th century, it was the guilds who essentially controlled the political arena. They made the appointments to the political and military offices and by keeping a close watch on and frequently changing government positions made sure that no one could obtain absolute power.

At the same time, the guilds played an important role in the artistic and cultural development of the cities. Constantly competing with each other, they demonstrated their power and greatness by commissioning magnificent works of art.

At this time, Florence had consolidated its predominance over the other Tuscan cities, and Prato, Pistoia, Arezzo, Colenle di Val D'Elsa, San Gimignano, Volterra and Cortona already came under its

sphere of influence. The expansion of this sphere of influence was not always accomplished by military force; in many cases, it was accompanied by the jingle of coins.

Florence was also the center of a flourishing cultural life. It's no coincidence that Italy's greatest poet, Dante Alighieri, who was the first to wrtie in the Italian vernacular, was a Florentine; after 1340, the celebrated poet Boccaccio also lived in the city. The painter Giotto, whose style influenced art all over Italy, and many of whose students and followers were also to attain renown, was from Florence. It was here that the monumental cathedral was built to the design of Arnolfo di Cambio, who was also responsible for the Franciscan church of Santa Croce. Next to this cathedral, the campanile is visible proof of Giotto's architectural genius. This period also saw the building of Santa Maria Novella.

But such development wasn't unique to Florence; there are outstanding cultural monuments dating from the 14th cen-

tury in other parts of Tuscany, as well. Siena's Palazzo Pubblico epitomizes Sienese pride, as do the great families' palazzi in typical Gothic-Sienese style. Exceptional monuments were erected elsewhere in Tuscany, such as the Camposanto and the church of Santa Maria della Spina in Pisa. Pisa and Siena were the leading cities for sculpture (Giovanni and Andrea Pisano), and in painting the Sienese school stood alongside the Florentine (in particular, Simone Martini and Pietro and Ambrogio Lorenzetti).

It is astonishing that such a vast amount of excellent art could be produced at a time that was so marked by internal and external calamities. In Florence in 1378 there was an uprising of the *ciompi* (wool-combers); a similar rebellion broke out in Siena; there were grave bank crises, and in 1348 a severe outbreak of the plague devastated Europe, wiping out two-thirds of the country's population.

But none of these blows meted out by fate could block the rise of Florence. The

27

only cities that had not yet capitulated to her dominance were Pisa, Lucca and Siena. And by 1406 the Republic of Pisa, too, succumbed and entered the official Florentine domain.

The Medici

The Florentine conquest of Pisa meant that the city had finally gained access to the sea. It also meant that Lucca was now the only city in northern Tuscany that was still independent; in the south, Florence's strongest rival Siena was able to maintain its independence until 1555. The city was forced to surrender after a 10-year siege in which troops of Charles V took part. Four years later Siena and all its possessions fell under Florentine rule.

In the meantime a wealthy merchant family had worked its way up to hold the

Above: Guild emblem of the woollen trade. Right: Cosimo de' Medici (il Vecchio) receives the model of the church S. Lorenzo from Brunelleschi and Ghiberti.

highest positions in Florence's government. As far back as the ciompi uprising a member of the then-obscure family, one Silvestro de' Medici, attained public office. The poor had rebelled when the Guelph party did not accept the election of this democratic Medici as the *gonfaloniere* (or "standard-bearer," a kind of tribune or supervisor of the judicial authority) of the city. The people stormed the Palazzo Vecchio and actually managed to remain in power for several weeks. Then the "people's government" was forced to surrender, as the upper middle class reacted with an immediate lock-out, which would have meant starvation for the workers who depended on them.

After the rebellion had been suppressed, the aristocracy once more assumed their position at the top. This upper class was actually a mixture of the nobility and upper middle-class families who had gradually made their way into the upper echelons of society on account of their wealth. The facade of democracy obscured the fact that power actually rested in the hands of just a few families. The administration of the expanded territory necessitated a vast body of civil servants, and of course the positions were only filled by people of whom these families approved. This inequitable system of patronage and favoritism led to social tensions that ultimately resulted in overt crisis.

The hour of the Medici had come. Cosimo de' Medici (1389-1464), later known as *il Vecchio* or "the Elder," managed, as the leader of the popular party which formed the opposition, to come out on top against the Albizzi family. Following quarrels over the conduct of a campaign against Milan, Rignaldo degli Albizzi had sent Cosimo into exile for ten years in 1433, but the pro-Medici signory called him back in 1434 and he was enthusiastically welcomed home by the crowds. Even though the Medici family technically shared the reins of govern-

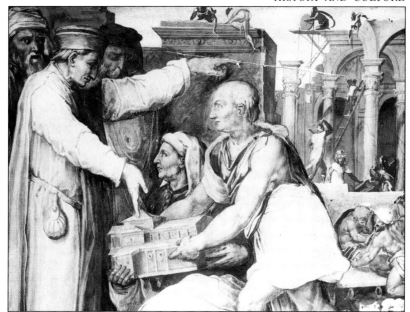

ment with several other families, it was Cosimo who was most conspicuous and made his power felt. Cosimo's mantle later passed on to his son Piero, with the approval of the city's most influential citizens. Thus began the reign of a dynasty which was to last for three centuries.

The Medici were from the Mugello and belonged to the guild of Florence's cloth merchants and money-lenders, called the Calimala, the oldest and most respected guild in the city, which had branches all over Italy and throughout Europe. It was as bankers that the Medici family had amassed its immense wealth, which in turn brought them to such a position of power that even foreign ruling houses depended on them.

Ultimately, it was Cosimo's goal to consolidate further the power of the aristocracy. Occasionally he even implemented his own private political strategies, such as when he cultivated a friendship with Francesco Sforza, whom he helped become Duke of Milan when

Filippo Maria Visconti died. This meant a long war against the Viscontis which ended with the Florentines' victory at the battle of Angihiari (1440) and subsequently the alliance between Milan and Florence in 1450.

Cosimo was a skilled and clever ruler. He exerted unrestricted control over the city government and at the same time was careful not to openly violate the republican-democratic way of doing things. Churches and monasteries received generous financial support from him, and due to his close affiliations with powerful contemporaries, it even came about that Pope Eugene IV resided in Florence for extended periods of time and that the 17th General Council convened here in 1439.

Florence as the Cultural Center of Europe

Cosimo's rule initiated a new era for the arts and sciences as well. He provided patronage to the artists and had palaces

built, the first one for himself in the Via Larga (today's Via Cavour). Typical of Cosimo's reserved style is the wise way he eschewed making the building simply an ostentatious display of power. It was designed by Michelozzo, Cosimo's favorite architect, who worked on many other palaces and churches with Leon Battista Alberti. A new style evolved that transcended the Gothic style and incorporated architectural elements of antiquity.

This new era of the Renaissance was a true Golden Age for Florence, and saw the city reach a cultural zenith. Brunelleschi, who had studied the monuments of antiquity in Rome, completed the cathedral cupola, which at that time was considered a wonder of the art of building, and which formed an unmistakeable part of the city skyline. The churches of San Lorenzo and Santo Spirito were built, as

Above: View of Florence, around 1490.
Right: Lorenzo il Magnifico, with Florence in the background (16th-century painting).

were the Capella Pazzi and the portico of the Ospedale degli Innocenti, the Palazzo di Parte Guelfa, the Badia Fiesolana and the Palazzo Pitti in its original form.

Meanwhile, such talented painters as Fra Angelico, Masaccio, Andrea del Castagno and Filippo Lippi were breaking new ground with their painting techniques, their realistic representations of people and landscapes in exact, measured perspectives. Famous sculptors included Donatello, the most outstanding artist of his time, Lorenzo Ghiberti (who created the doors of the Baptistery), and terracotta artists Andrea and Lucca della Robbia. It was at this time that Leon Battista Alberti penned his *Ten Books of Architecture*.

Many of these Florentine artists were of humble origin. Only through commissions from wealthy guilds at the beginning of the century, and later through the generous patronage of Cosimo and his grandson Lorenzo the Magnificent, were they able to develop and unfold freely as artists; and the result of their

growth can be seen not only in Florence, but also in other cities throughout Tuscany.

Lorenzo the Magnificent

The grandson of Cosimo, Lorenzo the Magnificent (born in 1449) ruled from 1469 to 1492. He had been preceded by his father, Piero the Gouty, who had died only five years after succeeding his father. Lorenzo, unlike his predecessors, was obsessed with absolute power, the consequence of which was that tensions within the ruling class mounted and this ultimately resulted in 1478 in the conspiracy of the opposition family, the Pazzi. Lorenzo escaped assassination, but his brother Giuliano was killed.

Pope Sixtus IV, who had gained cognizance of the planned assassination in advance, was not uninterested in the downfall of Lorenzo. With all the means at his disposal he tried to break the unwholesome power of the Medici. But Lorenzo resisted his attacks. In 1480, he set up the so-called Council of Seventy in Florence, which consisted of the most influential families in the city. They were thus given a certain amount of authority, including important administrative positions and even the signory (the priories and the gonfaloniere) was placed under their authority, although it now actually only carried out a formal function.

Lorenzo put to work his diplomatic skills outside of Tuscany, too; in this way he managed to establish close relations with the Count of Milan and the Kingdom of Naples. Ultimately he even secured an advisory position with Pope Innocence VIII, who had succeeded his old enemy Sixtus IV. This new accord between the Church and the House of Medici was reinforced by the marriage of one of Lorenzo's daughters to the son of the Pope. The alliance thus formed with southern Italy and the Church was naturally entirely in the economic interests of the city.

The growing power of the aristocracy was the reason why so many palaces

31

were built and decorated by famous architects and artists. Scholars and scientists, poets and artists met in the Medici villas around Florence. Pico della Mirandola and Marsilio Ficino, Angelo Poliziano, Verocchio, Sandro Botticelli, Benozzo Gozzoli, Ghirlandaio and the architect Giuliano da Sangallo were among Lorenzo's illustrious guests. But he was not only interested in intellectual discourse and the arts but also was actively involved in the promotion of general education. Accordingly, he had the public schools extended and in 1472 the Florentine university was founded in Pisa, although its doors were only open to the social elite.

At this point, too, Florence reached the zenith of its power in Italy. Yet patriotism in today's sense of the word did not as yet exist. The great politician and writer Niccolò Machiavelli (1469-1527)

Above: Niccolò Macchiavelli (painting by S. di Tito). Right: Savonarola's execution on the Piazza della Signoria in Florence.

was one of the few people at this time who was capable of looking beyond his own horizons.

After Lorenzo's death, Florence was forced to relinquish pride of place Rome in terms of the magnificence of its arts and culture. Lorenzo's blundering son Piero was expelled from the city in 1494 because of his involvement in the dispute between the Church and Ludovico il Moro of Milan. Piero had initially opposed Ludovico's ally, the French king Charles VIII, but soon gave into him when the latter had some military success, and handed over to the king Pisa, Livorno and a number of other cities. The Florentines were disgusted at this and would not let him into his own palace when he returned to the city.

One important figure of this period was the Dominican monk Girolamo Savonarola, prior of the monastery in San Marco, who gave inflammatory sermons calling for the Florentines to return to a more ascetic form of Christianity. Against the background of an increasing clamour for a change in the constitution, his political sermons which were extremely influential when the new constitution, founded on the old republican principles, was drawn up. But because of his attacks on the increasing secularization of the Church, on church corruption and often on the Pope himself, Savonarola fell into disgrace with Pope Alexander VI. He was excommunicated, and finally, in 1498 hanged in the Piazza della Signoria and then burned at the stake. His republic survived him until 1512.

The Grand Duchy of Tuscany

In the course of changes in the European political power structure, Italy became a target for French and Spanish attempts at conquest, which ultimately led to all of Italy coming under Spanish control. The discovery of the New World by the Spanish and Portuguese meant that

sea trade routes were shifted to the west. This ushered in a period of decline for Italy; Tuscany, too, felt the effects.

In 1512, the Medici returned to Florence. In the conflicts between France and Spain the city had sided with the French, against Pope Julius II and the Spanish; after the French were defeated, Florence was unable to defend itself, and the republic was overthrown. But the far-sighted Lorenzo de' Medici had already entered into an alliance with the Church (in 1489 his 13-year old son Giovanni was appointed Cardinal), and his fore-thought now paid off: the Pope returned Tuscany to the Medici. In 1513, Giovanni was elected to the papal throne and became Leo X; his brother Giulio succeeded him as Pope Clemens VII (1523-1534). Both popes distinguished themselves through their nepotism, distributing all manner of ecclesiastical offices, and therewith political power, to their friends and relatives.

In Florence, Cardinal Giulio had the Medici's favorite church, San Lorenzo, extended by Michelangelo with the New Sacristy; construction started in 1520. Another Medici commission was the Biblioteca Laurentiana, which Michelangelo designed a few years later.

Because of Clemens VII's pro-French politics, and his dispute with Emperor Charles V, Rome was finally conquered by the Emperor's mercenaries in 1527 in the infamous *Sacco di Roma.*

Florence's citizens seized on the weaknesses of Papal and Medici power to drive the Medici once again from the city and to proclaimed a new republic. In 1528, however, this toppled when the Pope used armed force to effect a Medici return. In 1531, Alessandro was proclaimed Duke of Florence. He abolished the democratic procedures which his predecessors had at least gone through the motions of observing for appearances' sake, and introduced a monarchical system of government. In 1537, Alessandro was murdered by his nephew Lorenzino, and succeeded by Cosimo, who came from a cadet line of the family.

Cosimo I was an autocrat. He transferred his seat of government to the Palazzo della Signoria and renamed it the *Palazzo Ducale*. The city of Florence was no longer his prime concern – he was principally interested in bringing about the political unification of Tuscany. Thus he conquered Siena at the battle of Marciano in 1555, and this city and its surrounding territories were annexed into his duchy in 1559. Ten years later, he was anointed as Grand Duke of Tuscany by Pope Pius V.

Now almost all of Tuscany was unified in the Grand Duchy. The only exceptions were Lucca, some parts of the Garfagnana, a portion of the Lunigiana, the so-called Stato dei Presidi (on Argentario and on Elba), Piombino and the Principality of Santa Fiora which was then sold to the Medici by the counts of Sforza-Cesarini in 1633.

Above: Pope Leo X (by Raphael). Above right: Duke Cosimo I Medici (by J. Carrucci). Right: Michelangelo Buonarotti.

But the political unification did not entail an administrative unification. Cosimo I and his successors made sure that customs barriers divided the old state and the new state economically for two hundred years. The state that suffered most was Siena, whose economy was based on arable and pastoral agriculture: the Grand Duchy would only grant it a limited concession for one of its most important sources of income, the cultivation of cereals. Florence was still a city of craftsmanship, if not to the extent that it once had been, and continued to stand superior to other cities.

Cosimo I had public buildings erected in Florence with a view to demonstrating his power. The Uffizi, as their name suggests, were built to house the administrative offices of the Grand Duchy and the interiors of the Palazzo Ducale were completely refurbished. Cosimo's favorite architect, Giorgio Vasari, built the corridor that connected the Uffizi to the Palazzo Pitti. Cosimo's wife, Eleanor of Toledo, had acquired the palace in 1549 and now was also having it redesigned and extended. When the Grand Duke subsequently chose the Palazzo Pitti as his residence, the Palazzo Ducale was rechristened the Palazzo Vecchio (or Old Palace).

During the reign of the Medici, not only civil architecture but also military works gained greatly in importance. Accordingly, it was during Alessandro's rule that the vast complex of the Fortezza da Basso went up, whose real purpose was to keep conquered cities cowed.

Italy's greatest artists, such as Michelangelo, Ammanati, Benvenuto Cellini, Sansovino, Giambologna, and many others, were active in Florence at this time. The Santa Trinita bridge, destroyed by a flood, was rebuilt by Ammanati in a masterwork created with the help of Michelangelo, who had a consulting role. At the beginning of the 16th century Michelangelo had already set new standards for the art of sculpture with his statue of David which was set up in front of the Palazzo Vecchio, and surpassed even these standards with his monuments for the Medici tombs.

On the cultural side, Cosimo's rule was a glorious period for the academies which were being inaugurated in almost every city. One of the most important ones, which still exists today, was the *Accademia della Crusca*, which concerned itself with the care of the Italian language. In 1612, it published the first Italian dictionary, based on the dialects of the language used by Dante, Boccaccio and Petrarch, and thus elevating Florence's Tuscan to Italy's standard language.

In Siena, the *Collegio Tolomei* was founded for scientists and students from all over Italy to work together. Cosimo was also the first ruler to recognize the important role which the printing press could play in political power. He had a ducal printing works established which was only allowed to print works for which he had given his imprimatur.

Independent Lucca was the only city that had so far been able to assert itself against Florence; it was also the only city where the seeds of Luther's reformation fell on fertile soil and took root. In the rest of the Grand Duchy, the Church and the secular powers were able to nip in the bud any movements in this direction. But soon it was feared that the Grand Duke would use Lucca's tolerant attitude as a pretext for annexing the Luccan state. Fearing this, and the repression which would ensue, many families began to emigrate and settle abroad, mainly in Geneva.

After Cosimo's death in 1574, his son Francesco succeeded him on the throne. Francesco left government in the care of his civil servants, preferring to devote his own time and energy to scientific studies.

The next Medici, Ferdinando I (1587-1609), Francesco's brother, had a greater impact on Tuscany. All of the subsequent successors to the throne, including the last of the Medici, Gian Gastone, who died in 1737 without leaving an heir,

The Reign of the Hapsburg-Lorraines

At the beginning of the 18th century, the question of succession in the Grand Duchy of Tuscany was a matter of major concern for all of Europe. Finally in 1735 it was decided, during the preparations for the treaty of Vienna, that Francis of Lorraine, the future consort of Empress Maria Theresa and later emperor of Austria, should succeed to Tuscany, provided he gave up Lorraine in return. However, Francis was too busy with other affairs to be bothered with his newly-acquired Grand Duchy. He appeared there once in 1739, but otherwise he passed on the administration of the state to his regents.

His son and successor, Pietro Leopoldo, actually lived in Tuscany, residing in the Palazzo Pitti after 1765 until he left Florence again after 25 years in order to return to Vienna as emperor. During his capable rule he implemented major reform policies, mainly in agriculture, impelling Tuscany to emerge from the dull lethargic state into which it had sunk under the last of the Medici grand dukes.

were distinguished by their obedience to Spain and the Church.

Anna Maria Ludovica, Gian Gastone's sister, died in 1743. She bequeathed the entire Medici estate to Florence and hence ensured that the family treasures would not be scattered to the four winds.

Even if the Medici dukes – apart from the two outstanding personalities of Cosimo I and Ferdinando I – were on the whole unexceptional, they did all the same devote themselves to a greater or lesser extent to an extremely important project, the extension of the harbor of Livorno. Under Ferdinando in particular the city, which was being renovated in accordance with a single unified plan, enjoyed a new period of prosperity. And since Livorno was a port for international trade, it was also a gateway for foreign settlers of every nationality and religion. It soon became the second-largest city in Tuscany, and remains so to this day.

Above: Leopold I, Grand Duke of Tuscany.
Right: Napoleon Bonaparte on Elba.

One example of these new policies was the establishment of the *Accademia dei Georgofili* (1753), the first European academy of agriculture, whose members included well-known names from the Tuscan patrician classes and the bourgeois intelligentsia. The Academy tried to develop scientific methods of farming and stock-breeding; for the first time, agriculture became a focus of attention in Tuscany. Hitherto, interest had mainly concentrated on crafts and commerce.

The rule of the Hapsburg-Lorraines began under Pietro Leopoldo, who was in power until 1790, and gave Tuscany its first real autonomy. Tuscany became a model state in which peace, order and progress prevailed. The reform policies of the Grand Duke included innovations in the field of the economy, in the administration, in jurisdiction and in the school system, which was founded on the prin-

ciples propagated by the European Enlightenment. A new constitution was even considered. The entire country profited from these reforms and along with Lombardy was one of the most progressive regions in Italy.

The Napoleonic Interlude

Napoleon's troops brought revolutionary ideas into Tuscany in 1799; but these didn't seem to have much effect. Only in Livorno, Pisa and Florence were there a few Jacobites who greeted the French revolutionaries with open arms; the majority of the people, especially the rural population, was content with the *status quo*. Around Arezzo and Siena, in fact, the peasants were so infuriated by the intruders, particularly their atheistic attitudes, that bloody skirmishes ensued.

Fifteen years of Napoleonic rule followed the French occupation of Florence in 1799. Pietro Leopoldo's son and successor, the Grand Duke Ferdinando III, was forced to leave, and Tuscany once

again fell into foreign hands. First, the so-called King of Etruria Lodovico I, prince of the house of Bourbon-Parma, took control, followed by his son, Carlo-Lodovico (or Charles Louis), under the regency of his mother, Maria-Luisa of the Spanish Bourbon house. In 1808, Napoleon took over Tuscany anew, incorporating it into the Departements of the Arno (with Florence as its capital city), the Mediterranean, and Umbria. A year later, however, the Grand Duchy was brought back into existence for the benefit of Napoleon's sister, Elisa Bonaparte Baciocchi. During her rule, Tuscany acquired an ostensible autonomy, but in reality it was entirely dependent on Paris.

Elisa Bonaparte Baciocchi, like her predecessors, resided in the Palazzo Pitti, which she had ornately refurnished in the Empire style. The French furniture which she brought in from Paris influenced the local style; and neo-classicism, which found its true expression in Canova's paintings of Napoleon and his family, was the trend of the next few decades.

37

After the defeat of Napoleon and his banishment to Elba in 1814, the congress of Vienna (1814-1815) restored the Grand Duchy to Ferdinand III who returned to an enthusiastic reception.

The Risorgimento in Tuscany

At the time of Ferdinand's return to Tuscany, it comprised the former Stato dei Presidi, the principality of Piombino and the island of Elba. The only territories which were not integrated into Tuscany were the duchy of Lucca, under Maria Luisa of Bourbon, and the duchy of Massa Carrara, which was unified with Modena after the marriage of Maria Beatrice Cybo and Francesco IV from the house of Hapsburg-Este. The congress of Vienna did however guarantee that Lucca should at some future date be reincorporated into Tuscany.

Above: Plebiscite in Tuscany about the unification of Italy, March 1860. Painting by E. Gamba (1861).

Ferdinand III and his successor Leopold II (1824-1859) resumed the reform politics of Pietro Leopoldo which had been interrupted by the French occupation. While he reinstated the old legislation, Ferdinand did not abolish any of the reforms that had been introduced during his exile. In the prevailing liberal climate of the period, Florence became a meeting-place for the leading figures of the Italian intelligentsia. Center of these meetings was the *Gabinetto Vieusseux* of Jean-Pierre Vieusseux, a forum for lectures and discussions. The main organ of this liberal spirit was *L'Antologia*, at that time the most progressive newspaper in Italy. *Archivo storico italiano*, first published in 1841, was another important journal of science and culture.

Because of the climate of tolerance that characterized Ferdinand's reign, the country became a haven for political refugees, mainly from Southern Italy. Many other foreigners, particularly the English, drawn by the pleasant atmosphere, came to stay – sometimes for the

rest of their lives. In Florence, along the coast of Versilia and in Livorno, a nascent tourist industry got underway.

Under Leopold II, however, the government's anti-liberal tendencies and increasing dependence on Vienna became more and more apparent. In 1833, the *Antologia* was shut down. When, during the critical year of 1848, democratic liberalism moved into the foreground with revolutionary agitation, the Duke left Florence. He did return, but continued to pursue his reactionary politics, and the chasm between him and his subjects became wider and wider. When the Second War of Italian Independence broke out in 1859, the Duke was put under pressure to grant a constitution and join the Sardinians in a looming second ware against Austria. He felt unable to do so, whereupon the Florentines expelled him. He left the country hoping to be able to return when things calmed down.

But he did not return. A referendum was taken in March of 1860, and the majority of Tuscans decided in favor of a unified Italy. Against the separatist efforts of a minority that wished to maintain Tuscany's regional independence, the unification movement was pushed forward, mainly by the energetic efforts of Baron Bettino Ricasoli. From now on Tuscany was no longer a grand duchy but shared its history with the Italian state.

Tuscany in a Unified Italy

Florence was the capital of unified Italy for six years (1865-1871) and Victor Emmanuel II resided in the Palazzo Pitti. Florence's function as capital of the country meant that housing was required for the multitudes of civil servants and state officials. Old palaces, which now were used for accommodating the ministries, underwent rebuilding and additions. When the Papal State was captured in 1871 and Rome was declared the capital, Florence turned into nothing more than a major drain on the state's finances.

Following its final years as a grand duchy, the appearance of Tuscany and its

della Repubblica and its unattractive and bombastic buildings. The cathedral's new facade with overly ornate statues was completed, and the Santa Croce Church was given a neo-gothic campanile and a marble facade.

In the countryside agriculture was still based on the traditional sharecropping or *mezzadria* system (the landlord provides capital and equipment, the tenant labor, and they divide the harvest between them) but industry was now beginning to develop. Shipbuilding, for example, started up in Livorno, the wool industry took hold in Prato and the mining of minerals on Elba. The working class, especially in smaller towns such as Colle di Val d'Elsa, Sesto Fiorentino, Empoli and Piombino, and also in the upper Arno valley, formed socialistic organizations.

The intellectual life of the cities remained, as ever, the preserve of the upper middle class. After the expulsion of the Hapsburg-Lorraines from Florence in 1859, *La Nazione* was established: initially moderate, this newspaper became with time ever more conservative. In 1866, the *Nuova Antologia* first appeared, a journal which concerned itself with current affairs and was highly respected throughout Italy. At around this time the *Istituto degli Studi Superiori* was founded, finally being made a university in 1924.

cities gradually started to change. New roads and railways were built. Florence gained a railway station. Guiseppe Poggi, a Florentine, had the old city walls torn down and replaced by wide avenues. He built the Viale dei Colli on the south bank of the Arno and designed the Piazzale Michelangelo as a terrace offering a panoramic view over the city. The downtown area filled up with pavement cafés, shops and arcades, and at night gas lanterns lit the streets. The first public transportation – a horse-drawn omnibus – entered service in Florence in 1865, and towards the turn of the century the first streetcars appeared.

But progress also had negative ramifications: in the course of redevelopment of the town center, one of the liveliest and most beautiful sections in Florence, the Old Market and its immediate vicinity, was levelled to make space for the Piazza

Towards the end of the 19th century, Tuscany stood only a little behind Rome, Milan and Naples in intellectual importance. The only literary event of international significance was the publication of Carlo Lorenzini's *Pinocchio*, the tale of the wooden puppet with the long nose and one which will also amuse the adult reader. The Sicilian artist Emilio Grecco created a monument in Collodi to commemorate the puppet.

At the beginning of the 20th century, intellectual life in Tuscany experienced a revival. A number of newspapers, including *La Voce*, *Il Regno* and *L'Unità*, ap-

Above: Victor Emmanuel II. Right: Pinocchio, brainchild of Florentine Carlo Collodi, has been around for more than a century

40

peared and the great Italian publishing houses Le Monnier, Barbera, Sansoni, Salani, Olschki and Nerbini were founded in Florence.

The First World War took place at a time when Tuscany was experiencing an industrial boom, which initially was stimulated even more by the war. But after the war came a crisis with workers' and peasants' uprisings and strikes in protest against the high cost of living and unemployment. This helped prepare the ground for fascism in Tuscany as well. Between 1920 and 1922, the new fascist movement launched attacks against not only the socialist-communist movement but also even the Popular Party, which had a large Tuscan following. The international economic crisis after 1929 hit Tuscany with full force, especially in the areas of industry and mining. The government tried to combat unemployment by means of public works, such as the construction of the autostrada from Florence to the coast and the Florence-Bologna railway.

Between the two world wars, Florence was also a cultural leader in Italy. More publishing houses and magazines were founded and launched, the music festival *Maggio Musicale Fiorentino* was initiated, the painters Ottone Rosai and Ardengo Soffici created new styles. Other Tuscan artists making their mark included Marino Marini, a gifted sculptor from Pistoia, and Amedeo Modigliani from Livorno and Lorenzo Viani from Viareggio, who are among the most important painters of the first half of the 20th century. Works of architectural importance that date from the 1930s include the stadium in Florence and the new train station Santa Maria Novella.

During the Second World War, Tuscan cities too suffered grievously from the bombing. Particularly hard-hit were Livorno, Pisa and especially Florence, which at the end of the war was partially destroyed by the retreating Germans. All bridges leading across the Arno were blown up, except for the Ponte Vecchio which was only saved because a German

Increasingly, the landscape of Tuscany is undergoing change as a result of industrialization, especially the areas of the Arno valley and to the west of Florence, in Val d'Elsa and along the Tyrrhenian coast. But gradually, even in Italy, people are becoming aware of the dangers of pollution and the destruction of the environment. Tuscany has become a trendsetter for a more environmentally-conscious type of tourism. Since the 1980s, the tourist and gastronomic industries have participated in demonstrations with the Green Party and environmental protection associations. Their motto: a clean sea, clean coasts and a ban on the use of pesticides in farming.

Tuscany is also ahead of other regions when it comes to urban renewal projects. Since 1987, the town center of Florence – not just its historical core – has been closed to automobiles because it has been recognized that this is the only way that unique and irreplaceable works of art can be protected from being destroyed for ever. Siena made this decision even earlier than Florence: cars have been banned from its Old Town since 1956.

officer had the courage to ignore his orders. Instead, many of the old houses at the approaches to the bridge were demolished, making it difficult for the allied troops to cross the river. The resistance also had many members in Tuscany, and the reprisals they had to suffer were frequent and severe.

Not only the old town centers have been damaged in Tuscany. Since the 1950s, when the great emigration from the countryside started and more and more farmers quit their hard life as leaseholders to move to the cities, drab suburbs have been springing up around the historical centers of the old cities.

Tuscany Today

In 1946, a referendum was held and Italy abolished the monarchy and became a Republic, although it was a near thing: the vote was 13 million for and 11 million against. In Tuscany, however, a majority of cities favored the Republic, and since then the region has been ruled for the most part by the parties of the left. The only exception is Lucca: the city that has always played a special part in Tuscan history votes Christian Democrat.

But ambitious large-scale plans such as Firenze 2000, a project for a state-of-the-art city of apartments and offices north of town, met with fierce resistance. Some fear that the projected area will become a ghetto for the 35,000 people who are to live and work there. Furthermore, a area of barely 500 acres that otherwise could be used for recreational facilities would be covered over with pavement. Failure to reach a compromise has resulted in the whole project being put on ice. Whether it will ever be realized is uncertain.

Above and right: Tourists – marvelling at the sights, or worn out from the shops.

43

POWER, WEALTH, AND BEAUTY

FLORENCE, THE FLOWERING

AROUND FLORENCE

MUGELLO / SIEVE VALLEY

PRATO

PISTOIA

FLORENCE, THE FLOWERING

When the French writer Stendhal visited Florence on his journey to Italy some two hundred years ago now, he was so overwhelmed by the beauty of the city that he genuinely fell ill. To this day, there are still repeated instances of tourists having to be hospitalized because they have the "Stendhal syndrome": so great is the abundance of cultural monuments which people think they absolutely must see before they leave that many are driven into a state of hysteria bordering on nervous breakdown. To this phenomenon, it seems, only Italians appear to be immune; so, at least, demonstrated a scientific study made in 1987.

It's simply impossible to "see," or truly to get to know, Florence in a matter of a few days – indeed, weeks and months are hardly adequate to the task. The city is so inexhaustibly rich in sights – and not just cultural ones – that it is definitely a better idea to take your time and limit yourself to those works of art which come closest to your own particular, personal tastes

Preceding pages: View of Florence from the Piazzale Michelangelo. Lungarno degli Acciaioli. Left: Terracotta relief (1475) by Andrea della Robbia; the frame includes symbols of the masons' and carpenters' guilds.

and interests. In addition, you should let the flavor of the city and its life work on you, and, last but not least, reserve some time for shopping, as in this last respect Florence is also seductive in the extreme.

In the restricted space at our disposal here, it will, of course, be impossible to provide exhaustive information about Florence. There are plenty of detailed studies available for those who want to immerse themselves in the history, art and culture of the city, and some of these titles are listed at the back of the book. We will therefore limit ourselves to an overview of the most important works of art and buildings.

The City's Early History

Back in the time of the Etruscans, there was already a settlement on the banks of the Arno; and it was here that the Romans established a veterans' colony for former legionnaires in 59 B.C, in other words at the time of Caesar. The colony was called *Colonia Florentia*, the blossoming colony – maybe because the fertile Arno valley has such an abundance of flowers. There are a number of theories about the true origins of the name, but none of them is really convincing.

Because of its exposed location on the river in the midst of the hilly Tuscan

49

landscape, the settlement was hardly suitable as a military base, so we can assume that right from the start it had primarily an agricultural function. Its defense was secured by the hilltop town of Fiesole, just a few miles away, an old stronghold of the Etruscans, in whose shadow the *Colonia Florentia* had a fairly insignificant existence for quite some time.

The earliest ground plan of the city on the right bank of the Arno formed an almost perfect rectangle, the outlines of which still largely correspond to the heart of the Old Town today. Because of its favorable location on the Via Cassia, which ran from Rome through Florence and went on to Lucca, and because of the connecting roads to the other most important cities of what was then the province of Etruria, Florence rapidly developed into an important trade center in the first two hundred years after its foun-

dation. A freshwater harbor on the river Arno meant that goods could be transported down to the Mediterranean; and the traders from the East who started settling here brought with them Christianity, which began its steady progress after 300 AD. The 4th century saw the construction of the first two Christian churches: San Lorenzo, which at that time was located outside the city walls, and Santa Felicità, on the opposite bank of the Arno. As early as the year 313, the first bishop was appointed under the Emperor Constantine.

Under the Romans, marble palaces and temples dominated the cityscape, while an aqueduct brought water down from Monte Morelli to supply the city's residents with drinking water and fill the public baths. A huge amphitheater was built during the 2nd century; you can still detect its outlines in the curving facades of the houses on the Via de' Bentaccordi and the Via Torta.

Florence in the Middle Ages

This first flowering, which may have seen the city's population swell to almost 10,000, came to an end in the confusion of the great barbarian migrations. Florence was attacked and devastated by the Ostrogoths, the Byzantines and the Lombards in turn. After the fall of the Roman Empire, traders and merchants stayed away, as the new power constellation meant that trade routes had shifted west and east of the Arno Valley. When the Western Roman Empire fell in the 5th century, the inhabited part of Florence had shrunk to a small area around the old Roman forum, which lives on today, in shape and size, in the form of the current Piazza della Repubblica.

The only event of importance for the art historian during this period was the first phase of construction of the Santa Reparata, the church which preceded the cathedral. Work may well also have

Above: Cathedral, campanile, and Baptistery in Florence. Right: S. Miniato al Monte.

started on a forerunner of the present Baptistery.

Not until the Franks under Charlemagne conquered large parts of Italy and proclaimed Tuscany a margraviate did the economy begin to take off again. In 854, Lothar I combined the two duchies of Florence and Fiesole and established Florence as the seat of government, which brought with it numerous privileges for the city. Prosperity increased; Florence's population rose to 20,000; and soon the city had spread to take over the left bank of the Arno, as well. The churches of San Lorenzo and Santa Reparata were expanded, and with the construction of the monastery and the basilica of San Miniato, as well as the Baptistery, we have the first manifestations of the Florentine Romanesque style. In 978, Willa, the widow of the margrave Umberto, founded the *Badia fiorenta* and thereby the first monastery in the city.

The clergy, already endowed with large estates, now began to strive for more and more political power, and ecclesiastical offices were sold off to the highest bidder. The monk Giovanni Gualberto protested against the increasing immorality of the Church, but found little response from the Florentines. He left the city to live as a hermit in the Vallombrosa forest, where he founded the order of the Vallombrosans.

The 11th century was a period marked by the increasing self-confidence of the middle class. Craftsmen, artisans and merchants were gaining in influence. Their struggle for autonomy was, moreover, supported by the margravine Matilda of Canossa, who to protect church from secular intervention took the Pope's side in the struggle between the Pope and the Emperor. After her death in 1115, Florence proclaimed a government of its own, which was officially recognized by the Emperor in 1183.

The Period of Communal Constitution

When the empire temporarily lost its grip on Italy after the death of Henry V

51

(1125), nothing more stood in the way of Florence's rise to independence. The conquest and destruction of Fiesole marked the start of Florentine domination of the surrounding territories, a domination which continued to expand. Commerce and trade were growing inexorably, and the city spreading rapidly. Contacts with Pisa facilitated sea trade with countries in the eastern Mediterranean.

In the 12th century, Florence proclaimed a communal constitution in which the power of government lay with the aristocracy and leading members of the merchant classes. The social preeminence of the nobility was expressed in unmistakable terms by the dynastic residential towers which once dominated the city's skyline. During the savage feuds that raged in the 12th century between various aristocratic families, these towers turned into regular fortresses.

Outside the city, too, there were bloody feuds with the feudal lords, who were gradually subjugated and stripped of their autonomy.

Disputes between the noble families led to a change in the communal constitution. The business of governing was taken over by a *podestà*, a professional politician who regulated public affairs on the basis of newly-developed legal standards.

A typical feature of public life in Florence at that time was the formation of various associations, which then proceeded to develop active, and often bitter, rivalries between one another. This resulted in a state of political instability which, however, proved greatly beneficial to the city's cultural development. Since each party was attempting to outdo the next, they all commissioned new buildings which were intended to demonstrate the status and greatness of the group in question. This was the heyday of the Romanesque style in Florence, a style characterized by clear lines, balanced proportions, a restrained use of color and

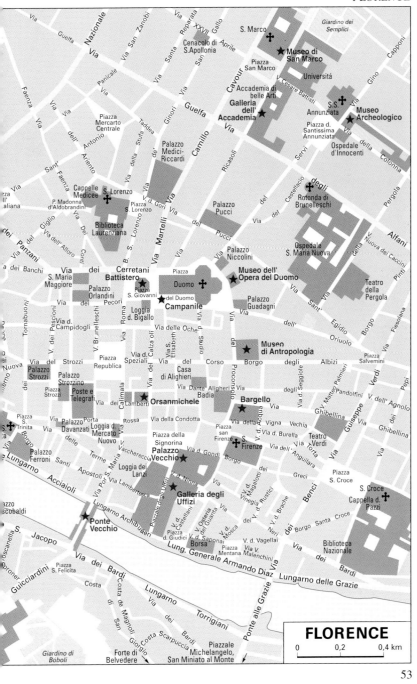

FLORENCE

0   0,2   0,4 km

materials (mainly white and green marble), and geometric patterns.

Another major influence on the city's art and culture was exerted by the monastic orders, which had been settling in Florence since the beginning of the 13th century. The Franciscans built a small church on the site of what was later to be the basilica of Santa Croce; the Dominicans established themselves on the western outskirts of the city, where Santa Maria Novella was built towards the end of the century. Both of these churches functioned as schools which soon came to enjoy an international reputation; Dante, in fact, was a pupil here. The squares in front of the churches were arenas for festive celebrations or the competitions that were so popular with the Florentines.

In addition to these two mendicant orders, numerous other religious com-

Above: Image of the blacksmiths' guild on Orsanmichele in Florence. Right: Ponte S. Trinità over the Arno.

munities settled in Florence and built their monasteries there. One rather unusual order was the Humiliates who had immigrated from Northern Italy and were later to prove of great economic importance for Florence, turning their hands to the cloth-weaving and dyeing trades and maintaining their own workshops.

The Guilds

By far the most important of all the associations and organizations which formed in the 13th century were the guilds (*arti*), associations of merchants and craftsmen. Not only did these guilds control trade and commerce, but they also wielded considerable political power and put up money for major artistic projects.

The oldest and most influential guild was the Guild of the Calimala, whose trade connections extended from northern Europe to the Near East. Its members were cloth traders, but they were also active as money-changers right from the

start, and were soon handling not only the banking business of their trade partners but also of entire aristocratic families. This close affiliation between manufacturing, trade and financial matters was a trademark of Florence's economy and the secret of its tremendous success. The concrete symbol of this ascent to financial power was the florin, a gold coin which was first minted in 1252.

The power struggle between the Guelphs, the followers of the Pope, and the Ghibellines, who were loyal to the Emperor, continued to divide the city until finally the Guelphs got the upper hand after the death of Emperor Frederick II in 1250. One of the victims of this feud was Italy's greatest poet, Dante Alighieri, a Ghibelline who was banished from his home town in 1302 and died in exile in Ravenna 19 years later, a bitter and lonely man.

The prosperity and growing self-confidence of Florence's middle class during the 13th century was expressed in a new need to beautify the city. Numerous plazas were enlarged and new streets built, which, according to the government's plan, were to be attractive, wide and straight. The Santa Trinità bridge was built; in 1296, work started on the Duomo, or cathedral, and the Palazzo Vecchio was begun a mere three years later.

The 14th century, by contrast, was characterized by internal and external conflicts, natural catastrophes and economic collapse. In 1333, a huge flood devastated the city; in 1348 more than a third of the population died after an outbreak of the plague; in 1378 the city's poor rebelled in the so-called uprising of the *ciompi* (wool-carders), who stormed the Palazzo Vecchio and forced the election of Salvestro de' Medici as *gonfaloniere*.

After this "proletarian revolution" the city was governed by the lower classes, but soon they had to relinquish their power to the great families who were becoming stronger and stronger, until finally the Medici took over.

The Medici

Despite the external difficulties and political instability, the middle class did still manage, even in this turbulent period, to maintain and indeed improve its standard of living, and to continue the beautification of the city.

When the Medici, a successful family of bankers and merchants, came to power in the city with Cosimo the Elder, there began an period of cultural flowering which reached its zenith under Cosimo's grandson Lorenzo the Magnificent, a n era known as the Florentine Renaissance. Names such as Botticelli, Ghirlandaio, Leonardo da Vinci and Michelangelo come to mind when one thinks of this epoch, which also was the acme of Florence's political power in Italy.

Rivalry among other patrician families came to a head with the Pazzi conspiracy

Above: What would the strict Savonarola say about all this modern graffitti (right)...

in the Duomo on April 26, 1475, in the course of which Lorenzo's brother Giuliano was killed. Even though this attempt to overthrow Medici rule failed, Florence ultimately relinquished its leading position in the arts to Rome. The inflammatory machinations of the puritanical monk Girolamo Savonarola, who condemned the immoral ways of the Renaissance aristocrats, ultimately led to the Medici's expulsion from Florence. Savonarola prepared a new republican constitution which remained in effect until 1512. But his sermons against the increasing secularization of the Church attracted the wrath of Pope Alexander VI, and he was burned at the stake in 1498 on the Piazza della Signoria.

The Medici returned to power in 1512, and several members of the family became popes during the course of the century. Wealth, power and education were at this time in the hands of the aristocracy, who built majestic palaces for themselves and commissioned great works of art. Other Renaissance masterpieces were also commissioned by the guilds, including Brunelleschi's dome atop the cathedral.

In 1530, Alessandro de' Medici was appointed the Grand Duke of Tuscany by Emperor Charles V; Florence and Tuscany were to remain under the absolutist control of the Medici until 1743. When the last member of the dynasty, Gian-Gastone, died, the duchy was transferred to Francis of Lorraine, the husband of Empress Maria Theresa of Austria. The Hapsburg-Lorraines governed Tuscany until 1859 – with a fifteen-year interruption between 1799 and 1814 when the French, Napoleon's sister Elisa among them, ruled Florence and held court in the city.

In 1859, the Grand Duke Leopold II was expelled from Florence, and in 1860 Tuscany relinquished its century-old independence in favor of a unified Italy. Florence was the capital of the Kingdom

of Italy from 1865-1870, until Victor Emmanuel II moved to Rome.

Florence Today

During the Second World War, Florence was devastated by Allied bombing raids and by the German troops who destroyed all of the bridges over the Arno when they retreated in 1944, with the sole exception of the Ponte Vecchio.

During the catastrophic floods of November 4, 1966, when the Arno rose with extreme rapidity to 17 feet (5.2 m) above its normal level, many precious works of art were damaged or destroyed. The people of Florence pitched in selflessly, aided by countless helpers from all over the country, to save whatever could be saved.

The last major calamity suffered by the city was the car bomb that went off in front of the Uffizi on May 27, 1993, which killed five people and injured 50 others, as well as grievously damaging a number of works of art.

Today, Florence numbers almost half a million inhabitants, and continues to expand upriver along the Arno. In order to protect the old center of the city from the corrosive effects of exhaust fumes, private car traffic was banned there in 1988. There are attended parking lots around the edge of the downtown area and on the other side of the Arno. Since most sights are relatively close to one another, they can be reached comfortably on foot.

A tip to aid in orientation: Florence's system of house-numbering can be, to say the least, confusing. Shops and restaurants have red house numbers (the address includes a red R), while private residences and hotels have black. The red and the black are two independent series of consecutive numbers.

And another tip: Watch out for pickpockets! Don't carry your purse or handbag on the street side. Be alert when you are in large groups, especially when groups of gypsy women or children come begging and you are jolted or pushed. This distracts you for a minute, and when

you look down again you may well find your wallet has disappeared.

The City

For a first view out over the city of Florence, drive up the beautiful winding road to the **Piazzale Michelangelo**, which was built for this very purpose by Guiseppe Poggi between the years 1867 and 1875.

Located 160 feet (50 m) above the city on the south side of the Arno, the square offers a spectacular view which takes in the palaces, the towers, the dominating dome of Brunelleschi, the hills which enclose everything on three sides, the river flowing westward to the plain and its bridges. The view is particularly stunning at dusk, when the sky goes a soft bluish green and the first lights start to come on in the city below.

Above: World-famous designs from a couple of different centuries. Right: Juggler on the Piazza del Duomo.

If you want to avoid the unfortunately inevitable crowds of tourists thronging this observation terrace, drive to the Forte di Belvedere at a slightly higher elevation, where the view is just as beautiful, if not more so, and the crowds are smaller. As a bonus, from here you can even see the hilly landscape of Chianti to the south.

When you have drunk your fill of this picturesque view of the Duomo, the Campanile, the towers of the Palazzo Vecchio and Badia, Orsanmichele, Santa Maria Novella and Santa Croce – to name just a few of the most impressive sights – clothe yourself in equanimity and patience and plunge into the crowds of tourists that choke the streets of Florence from March to October. Florence, after all, has an enormous number of works of art – only Rome has more – in a very small area. If you keep you eyes open, however, and dare to venture into the little side streets away from the main tourist routes, you can still experience a taste of real Italian ambience.

Cathedral, Campanile and Baptistery

These three monuments form the spiritual center of the city. They are located on a narrow space which had to be cleared by hand before they could be built. Perhaps the best place to get a full view of them is the **Loggia del Bigallo**, located between the Via dei Calzaiuoli and the Via Roma, which was built in the 14th century as the seat of the *Misericordia*, a charitable institution that is still in operation today.

The **Duomo**, or **Santa Maria del Fiore**, was begun in 1296. Arnolfo di Cambio, the architect, situated it where the Santa Reparata church used to stand (remains of which can be seen inside the present edifice). After di Cambio's death, the work was continued by the best architects of the time (Giotto, Andrea Pisano, Francesco Talenti and Giovanni Ghini). While the church was consecrated in 1436, the dome which crowns it was not completed until 1461. Building it was perhaps the greatest challenge ever faced by the architect Brunelleschi. He determined to build it without using scaffolding, tile by tile, and working from the outside in. Technically this was an enormously difficult undertaking, which was finally completed in the face of every conceivable kind of obstacle. After Brunelleschi's death, Michelozzo made the lantern according to his design, while Verrocchio topped it off with the golden ball you see today. Cracks were recently discovered in the roof of the dome, but these were probably there right from the start.

The walls are encased in marble, green from Prato, white from Carrara and red from the Maremma; the intricate and somewhat overelaborate facade decorated with figures was not created until the 19th century.

The gloomy, stark interior covers an area of 27,000 square feet (8,300 sq. m) and can accommodate up to 25,000

people. Of interest is the clock above the main door, whose hands run counterclockwise; the canonical sacristy with a terra-cotta *Ascension* by Luca della Robbia over the door; the New Sacristy with its bronze door by Michelozzo and Maso di Bartolomeo, through which Lorenzo the Magnificent fled from the assassins of the Pazzi conspiracy in 1478; and finally, in the left transept, the metal plate in the floor which has been used for astronomical measurements since the 15th century.

Another notable work of art is a remarkable equestrian painting by Paolo Uccello (1436) of Sir John Hawkwood – Giovanni Acuto to the Italians – who was the leader of the English mercenaries that fought alongside the Florentine army at the end of the 14th century. Its complicated perspectives make it an important example of Renaissance painting. A painting of Dante (on the same wall) standing in front of a mediaeval Florence is a Florentine tribute to the greatest Italian poet, as well as a gesture of atone-

The **Baptistery**, like the Duomo and the Campanile, is clad with polychrome marble and is one of the oldest buildings in Florence. There is still some dispute as to exactly when *Il bel San Giovanni* – as Dante referred to the church where he was baptized – was built. It is assumed that its structure dates from the 11th or 12th century and that it was erected on the site of an older building from the 4th-6th century. The octagonal church, which is reminiscent of ancient Roman buildings, is crowned by a white pyramidal roof which conceals the cupola beneath it. Its interior is lined with late 13th-century mosaics representing the medieval concept of Heaven, Hell and Purgatory. On the right of the apse is the tomb of the antipope John XXIII, designed jointly by Donatello and Michelozzo (1425).

ment for the fact that he was banished from his home town.

Next to the cathedral is one of the most magnificent towers in the world, Giotto's **Campanile**. The construction of this Gothic masterpiece, which is almost 280 feet (85 m) high, was started in 1334. After Giotto's death it was completed by Andrea Pisano and Francesco Talenti between 1336 and 1359.

The base of this fine and seemingly weightless tower is decorated with two rows of bas-reliefs by Andrea Pisano and Luca della Robbia (the originals are on display in the cathedral museum). The ogival windows in the tower actually get larger the higher you go up, and convey an almost filigree lightness to the tower. From its top, which you reach after climbing 414 steps, there is an impressive view of the dome of the Duomo and the surrounding buildings.

The most beautiful aspect of the Baptistery is, however, the three famous bronze doors which are a highlight of Western sculpture. The **South Door**, oldest of the three, was created by Andrea Pisano and for us represents the sunset of Gothic sculpture in Florence. The **North Door** was started by Lorenzo Ghiberti seven years later, following a competition in which his proposed design was selected over those of Brunelleschi and Jacopo della Quercia. It took 21 years to complete this work, executed with the participation of such other great artists as Masolino, Donatello, Paolo Uccello and Michelozzo. The **East Door**, or **Gate of Paradise**, which faces the cathedral, was Ghiberti's masterpiece. He started it in 1425 and took 27 years to complete it. "It was executed with great patience and effort. Of all my works it is the most remarkable... it was executed with great skill, in the right proportions and with understanding," he said, with accuracy if not overmuch modesty. In fact, these relief panels depicting scenes from the Old Testament, with rich architectural and natural backgrounds, demonstrate at once exact perspective and a truly lifelike

Above: Doors of Paradise on the Baptistery.
Right: The Singer's Pulpit by Luca Della Robbia in the Cathedral Museum (detail).

quality. In his work the artist included a portrait of himself to be preserved for posterity (left-hand door, right-hand side, fourth head from the top). The panels containing the reliefs are gradually being restored and replaced by copies. The originals are in the Cathedral Museum.

The **Cathedral Museum** is located at the rear of the Duomo, across from the apse. It contains works of art from the Duomo, the Baptistery and the Campanile which are stored here to save them from decay. Artistic highlights include the two choir-gallery pulpits by Luca della Robbia and Donatello; the *Pietà* by Michelangelo, which he started when he was already of advanced age and which was completed by his student Calcagni; and Donatello's wood carving of Mary Magdalene.

From the Piazza Duomo to the Signoria

From the Piazza Duomo, the Via de' Calzaiuoli, lined with elegant shops, leads to the Piazza della Signoria. Halfway along, the Via degli Speziali turns off to the right to the **Piazza della Repubblica**, a large square that occupies the site of the Roman forum and for which the Mercato Vecchio and countless historical buildings were ruthlessly demolished towards the end of the last century. Only the attractive old cafés that surround the square are really worth visiting here.

A few steps more will bring you to the peculiar **Orsanmichele** Church (the abbreviation for *San Michele in Orto*), which was originally a granary built in the 13th century by Arnolfo di Cambio in place of an oratory for Saint Michael. But a painting alleged to work miracles attracted so many worshipers that the grain was first moved up to be stored in one of the upper floors and finally the whole building was converted into a church. The interior includes the famous marble tabernacle of the *Madonna delle Grazie* by Andrea Orcagna, on which lovely reliefs illustrate the life of Mary. Of par-

ticular interest on the outside of the building are the pilasters with canopied niches containing the statues of the patron saints of the guilds. Fourteen niches or tabernacles are distributed around the building like a kind of outdoor museum of first-rate Renaissance sculptures, some of which have been replaced by newer works over the course of the years.

Piazza della Signoria

Signoria means rule or power, and this piazza was and still is the political center of the city. It was the site of the first public assemblies, and it was where the Dominican monk Savonarola was hanged and then burnt at the stake (a small granite plaque next to the Neptune Fountain commemorates him). The Palazzo Vecchio was originally the residence of the

Above, right: Ammanati's Neptune on the Piazza della Signoria wasn't, and isn't, to everyone's taste – but all are agreed about Michelangelo's David.

city's councils and administrative offices; then the residence of Duke Cosimo I Medici, and from 1865-1971 housed Parliament and the Foreign Ministry. Today, it is the seat of the municipal government and residence of the mayor.

The different names the palace has been given over the years reflect the course of the city's history. Originally it was called the Palazzo dei Priori; at the time of the oligarchy it was called the Palazzo della Signoria; when Cosimo I resided there, it was the Palazzo Ducale; and finally, when the duke moved to the Palazzo Pitti, it assumed the name of **Palazzo Vecchio**, the Old Palace.

It is the largest communal palace in Florence (designed by Arnolfo di Cambio in 1298), a forbidding, fortress-like building of irregular blocks of rough-hewn, light brown ashlar, and crowned by the rectangular battlements of the Guelphs. The 310-foot (94 m) tower with the swallow-tail crenellations of the Ghibellines and steep bronze roof rises high above the Palazzo. And it's no accident that the city hall resembles a fortress: its original purpose really was to protect the civil servants and defend their independence and autonomy.

For the same, defensive reasons, the entrance gate on the west side was kept small. It leads into the courtyard, which is surrounded by high porticoes. In the center is a fountain with putti and dolphin by Verrocchio. Not all sections of the palazzo's interior are open to the public. Most of the rooms date back to the 16th century and are decorated with numerous frescoes, paintings and statues.

The **Piazza della Signoria** resembles an open-air sculpture museum. Michelangelo's *David* takes pride of place in front of the main entrance to city hall, although what you see here is a copy (the original, which was created between 1501 and 1504, is on display in the Galleria dell'Accademia). The Florentines claimed that this work represented the

victory of democracy over tyranny. Opposite stands the marble group *Hercules and Cacus* by Bandinelli (1533), which Cellini is said to have referred to as a sack full of pumpkins.

The *Marzocco* Lion (which derives its name from the fact that the lion is said once to have stood at the plinth of a column of Mars) with the coat-of-arms of Florence is the emblem of the city; it is modelled on a sandstone original by Donatello (now in the Bargello). Defeated enemies of the Florentines supposedly had to kiss the lion's hindquarters... In 1980 a copy of Donatello's bronze sculpture of *Judith and Holofernes* was placed alongside it.

In the southwest corner of the Palazzo is the Neptune Fountain with its sea-god by Ammanati, which is to have inspired the following remark from his contemporaries: "*Ammanato, Ammanato, che bel marmo hai rovinato*" (...what beautiful marble you have ruined). The equestrian statue to the left of the fountain is by Giambologna and represents Cosimo I

(1594-1598). The reliefs in the plinth depict him being crowned archduke by Pope Pius V.

On the southern edge of the piazza is the **Loggia dei Lanzi**, built between 1376 and 1382 by Benci di Cione and Simone Talenti, probably based on a design by Orcagna. It was named after the German mercenaries (*Landsknechte*, or *lanzichenecchi*) who acted as guards here for Count Alessandro I de' Medici. Today, the loggia houses a collection of statues, among them the famous sculpture *Perseus and the Head of Medusa* by Benvenuto Cellini (around 1550).

To the left of the loggia, which served as an architectural model for the Feldherrnhalle in Munich, we continue on to the **Uffizi**, the former "offices" of the archducal administration, located between the Palazzo Vecchio and the Arno. Vasari built this edifice between 1560 and 1574, and it houses one of the richest museums in the world. Famous masterpieces include works by Botticelli (*Birth of Venus, Allegory of Spring, Adoration*

of the Magi), Piero della Francesca (*Duke of Urbino*), Filippo Lippi (images of the Madonna), Michelangelo (*Holy Family*), Raphael (*Madonna of the Goldfinch*), Titian (*Venus of Urbino*), Andrea Mantegna (*Adoration of the Magi*), and so many others that it would take much more than just one visit to see them all.

The two parallel sections of the building are connected by an open loggia on the south side. A corridor, built by Vasari in 1565, leads from the Uffizi across the Ponte Vecchio to the Palazzo Pitti, thus ensuring a private, safe and discrete connection between the two buildings.

Bargello and Santa Croce

Passing the memorial to Cosimo I, continue on through the Via de' Gondi to Piazza San Firenze. At the far end of this piazza is the **Palazzo del Podestà** or

Above: Botticelli's "Spring" alone is worth a visit to the Uffizi. Right: Open-air staircase in the inner courtyard of the Bargello.

Bargello. This plain battlemented castle, a symbol of the victory of Florence's bourgeoisie over the squabbling aristocracy, was begun in 1255, half a century before the Palazzo Vecchio, and is therefore the oldest secular building in Florence. It started out as the official residence of the city leader, then of the *podestà* – i.e. the city government – and finally became a courthouse and prison (*bargello* = police captain). Today, it contains the National Museum, and is therefore home to the best collection of Florentine Renaissance sculptures in existence.

The impressive interior court (14th century) has a circular arcade and a magnificent flight of steps leading up to a loggia. Right next to the octagonal fountain in the courtyard stood the arena for public executions, until the Grand Duke Leopold abolished the death penalty in 1782.

Across from the Bargello is the **Badia**; this building's pointed tower is a memorable characteristic of the skyline of Florence. This church, a part of the oldest and most important monastery in the city, has frequently been extended and rebuilt during the course of the centuries. Inside there are a number of works of art, among these a masterpiece by Filippo Lippi and the tomb of the Tuscan margrave Ugo (died 1001) by Mino da Fiesole. The atmospheric cloister is called *Chiostro degli Aranci* (of the orange trees).

Right next to the Badia is the Via Dante Alighieri and **Casa di Dante**, the house where Dante is said to have been born. Within the building are displayed various mementoes commemorating the greatest Italian poet.

The Via dell'Anguillara leads to the Franciscan church of Santa Croce and the **Piazza S. Croce**, one of the most attractive squares in Florence, lined with old mansions and palaces. It's here that the traditional *Calcio in Costume*, a historical football match between the city's different *quartieri*, is held every year in June.

S. Croce is the largest and most beautiful of the Franciscan churches, which was begun, possibly by Arnolfo di Cambio, in 1294, and finally consecrated in 1443. The polychrome marble facade and the Neo-Gothic campanile were added to this Gothic church during the 19th century. The cruciform interior is a kind of pantheon of Florentine notables: the mendicant monks required financial support for its building, and the return for a pious contribution was a final resting-place within the church itself. Here you will find tombs or monuments to men of genius such as Michelangelo, Dante, Machiavelli, Foscolo, Rossini, Alberti, Cherubini, Galileo Galilei, and many more. Even more striking than the tombs are the works of art that were donated by the families of the dead. Standing out in particular are Donatello's relief of the Annunciation and his famous wooden crucifix, of which Brunelleschi said that the artist had nailed a peasant to the cross. Then there are Rosselino's *Madonna and*

Child, the octagonal marble pulpit by Benedetto da Maiano, or frescoes by Maso, Taddeo Gaddi and Giotto. In passing, one may note that Santa Croce houses the largest organ in Italy.

To the right of the church, in Santa Croce's first cloister, Brunelleschi created one of the very first Renaissance buildings, the **Pazzi Chapel**. The museum of Santa Croce is located in the former refectory of the convent and adjacent rooms, and contains a collection of masterpieces of Florentine art.

South of the convent of Santa Croce is a huge complex that extends down to the Arno, the **Biblioteca Nazionale.** Built at the beginning of this century, it houses a vast collection of manuscripts, incunabula, drawings and prints from the collections of the Medici, the Palatine electors, and the Lorraines. Since 1875, a copy of every book published in Italy has been deposited here. The catastrophic flood in 1966 severely damaged innumerable objects both in the National Library and in Santa Croce.

**Santa Maria Novella
and San Marco**

The second church of the mendicant order in Florence is **Santa Maria Novella,** situated near the train station (which bears its name). This mighty building dominates the Piazza Santa Maria Novella, to clear space for which the city bought up a number of old buildings and then had them demolished. The church was built in 1279, the facade – the lower part of which is Romanesque-Gothic – was not completed in the Renaissance style by Leon Battisti Alberti until the 15th century.

The triple-naved interior is a masterpiece of the Florentine Gothic style. The side altars accommodate the graves of notable Florentines, and are decorated with paintings and frescoes. The famous fresco of the *Trinity* by Masaccio in the

Above: S. Maria Novella. Right: The Accademia offers plenty of material for aspiring artists.

left nave was discovered behind an altar together with a painting by Vasari in the 19th century. Reflecting the new conception of the importance of man that was central to the philosophy of the early Renaissance, the fresco is organized according to strictly applied rules of perspective; the portraits of donors at the sides of the painting are on the same scale as the holy figures, rather than on a smaller scale, as they would have been in the Middle Ages to reflect their lesser importance.

The frescoes in the choir, executed by Domenico Ghirlandaio, represent the people, customs and taste of the period in a precise and yet carefree manner. They are thus an invaluable document which allows insights into, for example, life in the home of an aristocratic family at the time of Lorenzo the Magnificent (just look at the fresco of the *Birth of Mary* on the left wall).

The celebrated crucifix carved by Brunelleschi stands on the altar of the Gondi Chapel, which Donatello unselfishly praised as being much more beautiful than his own crucifix in Santa Croce. Another masterpiece is the painted crucifix by Giotto in the sacristy.

To the right of the church is an old cemetery where members of leading Florentine families are buried. To the left of this is the entrance to the cloisters of the former Dominican monastery. The first one, the so-called Green Cloister, derives its name from the various shades of green on its walls in the shady figures which are all that has survived of Paolo Uccello's frescoes of the story of the Creation. But you can still make out the images; those of *The Deluge* and *Noah's Sacrifice* are especially striking.

Opening off the cloister is the Spanish Chapel, where you can see 14th-century frescoes by Andrea da Firenze depicting the missionary works and triumphs of the Dominican Order. People, in these frescoes, are symbolically represented as

sheep, guarded by black and white dogs – *domini canes*, or "dogs of God," or Dominicans – while the wolves being torn apart by the dogs represent the heretics (Cathars and Waldensians) who enjoyed a considerable following in Florence at that time.

San Marco, another Dominican monastery in Florence, is situated on the piazza of the same name, which you can reach by the Via Cavour or Via Ricasoli from the cathedral square. If you opt for the Via Ricasoli, you will see, on the right-hand side just before the Piazza San Marco, the **Galleria dell'Accademia**, which since 1910 has housed the original of *David*, as well as other works by Michelangelo.

The **San Marco** monastery was built by Michelozzo for Cosimo the Elder between 1437 and 1452. The monks' cells on the upper floor are today a Fra Angelico museum: this is where the "Blessed" Fra Angelico painted frescoes on the walls of his fellow monks' cells to inspire them to meditate. The most fa-

mous fresco, the *Annunciation*, is opposite the staircase leading to the first floor. At the far end of the right corridor is the cells that belonged to Savonarola when he was the prior of the monastery. A large bell by Donatello, the *Piagnona* or Bell of Lamentation, is set up in the cloister. It was rung to assemble the followers of this hypermoral monk, whose aim was to turn all of Florence into a monastery. After his execution the bell was temporarily removed so that its sound would no longer remind people of this unpopular reformer.

Besides the frescoes in the cells, San Marco contains other famous paintings by the blessed Fra Angelico, such as the *Descent from the Cross* and the famous *Tabernacle of the Linaioli* (the flaxworkers) in the pilgrims' hospice, it also displays a *Last Supper* by Ghirlandaio in the refectory, as well as works by Fra Bartolomeo. The library, also by Michelozzo, contains precious manuscripts, missals and bibles, some of which are on display.

Santissima Annunziata and San Lorenzo

Continuing along the Via Battisti, you come, after a short walk, to the **Piazza Santissima Annunziata**, a broad square surrounded by stately loggias. The equestrian statue of Ferdinand I in the center of the piazza is Giambologna's last work and was completed by Tacca, who also created the two curious fountains.

What is most impressive about this harmonious piazza, which resembles a huge cloister, is Brunelleschi's 15th-century facade of the **Ospedale degli Innocenti** (Foundlings' Hospital) with its resplendent loggia and the charming majolica reliefs of terra-cotta babes in swaddling clothes by the great Andrea della Robbia.

One hundred years later, Antonio da Sangallo and Baccio d'Agnolo created

Above: Images of foundlings on the loggia of the Ospedale degli Innocenti. Right: Inner courtyard of the Palazzo Medici-Riccardi.

the portico for the Servite Order on the opposite side of the square, and at the end of the 16th century the piazza was rounded off with the portico of the basilica of Santissima Annunziata on the north side.

A few steps beyond the Piazza SS. Annunziata, in the Via della Colonna, is the entrance to the **Archaeological Museum** in the Palazzo Crocetta. The museum – unjustly neglected by most visitors to Florence – contains Greek and Etruscan masterpieces, which can provide a good insight into the art of antiquity.

Continue now along the Via dei Servi in the direction of the Duomo to Via dei Pucci, the extension of which is Via de Gori, which leads right to Piazza San Lorenzo. At once corner, right across from San Lorenzo Church, is the **Palazzo Medici-Riccardi**, which Michelozzo built for Cosimo the Elder in the 15th century. The great palace, built of solid blocks of ashlar and with iron grilles over the windows on the ground floor, looks more like a fortress than the city

residence of a wealthy family. Today it houses a Medici museum. In the house chapel on the upper floor, you can see precious frescoes by Benozzo Gozzoli, which are supposed to include representations of members of the Medici family as well as their illustrious guests.

Brunelleschi's **San Lorenzo** church, commissioned by the Medici family, was built on a building from the 4th century which had been destroyed by fire. Michelangelo's design for the facing of the brick facade was never carried out. The interior of this triple-naved church projects an air of harmony, calmness and serenity. The rich decor, of great artistic note, includes two bronze pulpits by Donatello as well as one of the most important works of Filippo Lippi, the *Annunciation* (over the altar).

The **Old Sacristy** (enter from the left-hand nave) is by Brunelleschi. In its architectural perfection, it became a model for the ideals of European architecture. The interior was decorated by Donatello and contains a tomb and a sar-

cophagus for members of the Medici family, both works of Verrocchio (1472). The cloister is a picturesque garden court which leads to the renowned **Biblioteca Laurenziana** by Michelangelo, which contains, in addition to its marvelous staircase, one of the most comprehensive collections of manuscripts in the world.

You can reach the **Medici Chapel** and the **New Sacristy** from the Piazza Madonna degli Aldobrandini. The octagonal **Medici Chapel** (1604) serves as a funerary chapel for six Medici princes. It is imposing, austere and cold, unlike the **New Sacristy**, a funerary chapel built for the Medici family by Michelangelo, which also contains his famous tombs. This masterpiece of the High Renaissance manages ingeniously to combine sculpture and architecture. The two tombs which were actually realized – Michelangelo had originally projected six – rise up from the wall which, with its strict lines and clear geometric divisions, has an almost three-dimensional effect. Within the tombs are interred Lorenzo II,

69

grandson of Lorenzo the Magnificent, and Giuliano, one of his sons. In niches above the tombs stand statues of the dead, while resting atop the sarcophagi themselves are the allegorical figures of Dawn and Dusk, Day and Night.

On the Piazza San Lorenzo, and spilling over into the alleys around it, there's a colorful street market. It is, unfortunately, rather heavily geared towards tourists, so locals frequent the **Mercato Centrale di San Lorenzo**, the great market hall whose two floors are also a mecca for Florentine gourmets. The ironwork construction of this 19th-century building is reminiscent of Parisian train stations, and definitely worth a look. The colorful stalls are a feast for the eyes and the unbelievably varied selection will make your mouth water.

And speaking of food, try one of the simple restaurants behind the market

halls if you want to have a really good lunch. These eateries have small kitchens, staffed by perspiring cooks and rather limited menus offering only one or two simple dishes, but what you get is likely to represent the very best of plain Florentine fare. These places tend to be crowded, and you may have to wait a while for a table, but your patience will generally be rewarded.

Art connoisseurs will find two treats near San Lorenzo. The first one is in the refectory of the former Franciscan convent of **San Onofrio** at Via Faenza 42 (ring the custodian's bell and press 5,000 lire into his hand): the *Last Supper* by Perugino, painted in 1445-1450 and one of the most famous depictions of the Last Supper in all of Florence.

The second delicacy is located in the monastery of **Sant'Apollonia** in Via XXVII Aprile No. 1, situated between the Piazza dell'Independenza and Piazza San Marco; on your way there make a slight detour through the Via Nazionale, where you can admire, near the train sta-

Above: Variety in the market hall of San Lorenzo . Right: Please touch: the bronze boar as a symbol of good luck.

tion, the largest remaining fountain by Della Robbia that is still extant in Florence. In the refectory of the old Benedictine monastery there is a museum that contains the most important works of the Renaissance painter Andrea del Castagno, including the Last Supper, captivating because of its realism, exact perspectives and powerful presentation.

The Right Bank of the Arno

From the Piazza della Signoria, continue on westwards through the Via Vacchereccia to the **Loggia del Mercato Nuovo** (16th century) where gold and silk merchants used to meet. Today, it's a great place for anyone looking to purchase samples of Florentine artisanship. On the south side is the famous **Fontana del Porcellino** by Tacca (early 17th century). The "piglet" is actually a full-grown bronze wild boar which replaced a marble original in the Uffizi. Touch it and throw a coin into the fountain, both of which actions are supposed to bring

good luck. Certainly the brightly polished spots on the statue's nose indicate that many people are willing to give it a try.

Not far from here, in the Via Porta Rossa, is the **Palazzo Davanzati**, where the museum of the Old Florentine House has been located since 1956. The collection of furniture and objects for everyday use from the Middle Ages, Renaissance and Baroque periods provide an interesting look into the highly civilized daily life of Florence's middle classes, and the precious furnishings of their homes.

Continue on to Via Tornabuoni, one of Florence's most attractive and elegant streets, and the **Piazza Santa Trinità** where stands the eponymous **Santa Trinità Church**. The column which supports the statue of Justice by Tadda (16th century) is a granite monolith that originally stood in the Baths of Caracalla in Rome.

The Gothic church of Santa Trinità, which dated back to the 11th century, was extended in the 13th and 14th cen-

71

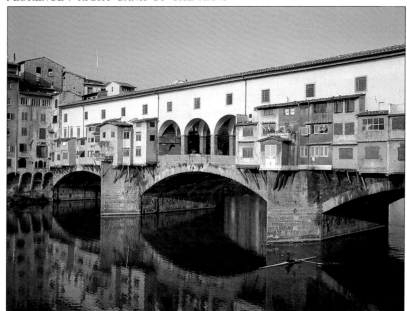

turies, and fitted out with a Baroque facade by Buontalenti in 1593-1594. The fine interior was financed by aristocratic families who had built their palaces nearby; two of these *palazzi*, in fact, are located directly on this piazza.

Better-known than either of these, however, is the **Palazzo Strozzi**, which stands a little further away, on the corner of Via Tornabuoni and Via Strozzo. Filippo Strozzi had it built by Benedetto da Maiano in 1489 and it was completed in 1536 by Cronaca. Legend has it that the wealthy merchant Strozzi did not want to upset the most powerful man in Florence, Lorenzo the Magnificent, by building this opulent city palace. He therefore had a rumor spread to the effect that he was putting shops in on the ground floor to finance the expensive building with the rents. Lorenzo was dismayed at the idea of his beautiful city being thus disfigured,

Above and right: The Ponte Vecchio, Florence's most famous bridge. Here, only goldsmiths' shops are allowed.

and quickly granted Strozzi a free hand in building his palace. The result was one of the loveliest Renaissance palaces in Florence. Today, it's home to various scientific institutions, and sometimes hosts major exhibitions.

If you continue on towards the Arno along the Via Tornabuoni, you will come across one of Florence's most attractive bridges, the **Ponte Santa Trinità**. The bridge (1567-70) was blown up by the retreating German Army in 1944, but then rebuilt from the rubble retrieved from the Arno. Thus Ammanati's masterpiece, which was based on a design by Michelangelo, was preserved.

Strolling further down the Arno, you'll pass the **Palazzo Corsini** with its splendid private collection of paintings (the entrance is on the Via del Parione) and come to the Piazza Goldoni. Here, the Via della Vigna Nuova turns off sharply to the right. On the left side of the street is the palace and the chapel of the Rucellai family, both designed by Leon Battista Alberti.

Also starting at the Piazza Goldoni is the Borgo Ognissanti, which will bring you to the square of the same name and the **Ognissanti** (All Saints) **Church**. Founded during the 13th century, it was remodelled in 1627 by Bartolomeo Pettirossi into the first Baroque church in Florence. It contains important works of art, in particular the *Madonna* by Domenico and Davide Ghirlandaio, the *Last Supper* by Domenico Ghirlandaio (in the refectory), *Saint Augustine in his Study* by Botticelli, and a *Saint Jerome* by Ghirlandaio.

Contrasting to the Baroque Ognissanti, the nearby **Ospedale San Giovanni di Dio** probably dates back all the way to the 14th century.

Across the Ponte Vecchio to the left bank of the Arno

The **Ponte Vecchio** is the oldest and most famous bridge in Florence. It's very likely that the Etruscans built a bridge at this point over the Arno; and it's certain that the Romans did. When the German Army was retreating from the city in 1944, Hitler ordered that all bridges over the Arno be blown up. Yet the Ponte Vecchio was spared, thanks to a brave officer who dared to disobey orders and, rather than blowing up the bridge, simply blew up the houses at either end to block access. Thus this masterpiece was saved for posterity.

In the Middle Ages, it was the butchers who had their shops on the bridge, and threw their waste directly into the Arno. In 1539, however, the Grand Duke Ferdinand passed an ordinance that only goldsmiths were to be allowed to operate shops on the bridge – and so it's remained to this day.

In the center of the bridge, between the two rows of shops, there is an open terrace from which you have a beautiful view of the Arno, Florence and the surrounding hills. On the right side the goldsmiths have erected a bust of Benvenuto Cellini (1900), one of Florence's most celebrated goldsmiths.

Above the left-hand row of shops runs the enclosed walkway which Vasari built for Cosimo I so that he could move freely between the Palazzo Vecchio and the Uffizi and his residence in the Palazzo Pitti, unobserved by his subjects.

Before turning to the Palace itself, turn right and walk parallel to the river until you come to the Piazza and church of **Santo Spirito**, which Brunelleschi designed for rich Florentine families in 1428. In the course of construction, which continued throughout the entire century, the design underwent many changes. From outside, the church seems rather plain; in fact, its facade was an addition from the 18th century. The triple-naved interior, however, with its semicircular side chapels and Corinthian columns, makes Santo Spirito one of the most brilliant creations of the Florentine Renaissance. This church, like most of

Above: Popular with photographers – Bacchus in the Boboli gardens. Right: Interior of S. Miniato al Monte.

the other major churches, also contains many famous works of art, including pieces by Filippino Lippi (*Madonna and Child with Saints and Donors*), Perugino (rose window on the facade) and Giuliano da Sangallo (entry hall and sacristy).

Somewhat further on, along the Via S. Agostino and Via S. Monaca, you'll come to the church of **Santa Maria del Carmine**, which was levelled by fire in 1771 and rebuilt in the Late Baroque style. Luckily the **Brancacci Chapel** in the right transept was spared by the flames, preserving the sublime frescoes by Masaccio (*The Tribute Money*) and his teacher Masolino. The frescoes were started during the 15th century and completed by Filippino Lippi.

The neighborhoods of Santo Spirito and San Frediano, where these two churches are located, are two old, homey quarters where there are still plenty of artisan workshops that produce and restore paintings, furniture, and musical instruments, as well as executing a number of other typical Florentine crafts.

**Palazzo Pitti
and the Boboli Gardens**

The Via de Serragli, which divides these two neighborhoods, leads south from the Arno, past the Giardino Torrigiano, to the **Porta Romana**, one of Florence's medieval gates, through which you leave Florence to reach Siena and Rome. From here you can walk back to Ponte Vecchio along the Via Romana, which is lined with magnificent palaces.

Opening out after Piazza S. Felice is the gradual upward incline of the Piazza Pitti, which is dominated by the **Palazzo Pitti**. The palace is 650 feet (200 m) long and is built entirely of blocks of ashlar. Brunelleschi designed it, and construction began in the mid-15th century. The original client was the wealthy merchant Luca Pitti, but eventually Cosimo I chose it as his residence. Later, when Italy had become a kingdom, Victor Emmanuel II moved in and in 1919, Victor Emmanuel III bequeathed it and its contents to the state.

The Palazzo Pitti contains one of the most famous collections of paintings in the world, the Galleria Palatina, as well as the Museo degli Argenti, the Museum of Crafts, a collection of costumes from various epochs, magnificently decorated apartments with paintings, tapestries and precious furniture, and the Galleria d'Arte Moderna, which contains art and objects from the 18th and 19th centuries. Ammanati's great courtyard behind the palace was originally used as an impressive open-air stage; and performances are still occasionally put on here today.

On the hill behind the palazzo, Cosimo I laid out the grandiose **Boboli Gardens**. Winding, shaded paths lead up to terraces from which one has a beautiful view out over Florence. Fountains, grottoes, statues and a coffee house (from 1776) make the gardens into a kind of open-air museum. Logically enough, therefore, an admission charge of 10,000 lire has recently been introduced for (foreign) visitors. (However, you can still walk in the large popular park of **Le Cascine** on the other side of the Arno, west of the train station, free of charge).

On the other side of the Boboli Gardens is the **Forte di Belvedere**, a beautifully-renovated fortress was built by Buontalenti for Ferdinand I during the 16th century. From the fortress walls (which themselves house major exhibitions) you can also enjoy a stunning panoramic view of Florence and the hills behind the city.

San Miniato al Monte

The classic beauty of the Romanesque marble facade of **San Miniato al Monte** can be seen from all over the city. St. Mi-

nias's first church was established during the reign of Charlemagne, and that monarch bequeathed vast estates to it. Eventually, however, it fell into a state of disrepair, to be built anew in the 11th century.

San Miniato and its baptistery are the most precious examples of Romanesque architecture in Florence. The interior, like the facade, is also decorated with colorful marble; geometric patterns predominate in this beautifully clear space. The raised presbytery with beautiful choir screens stands on a crypt where, within an altar from the 11th century, the bones of St. Minias are kept. At the end of the nave is an exquisite tabernacle by Michelozzo. Note the wonderful inlaid marble floor and the marble pulpit from the 13th century.

To the right of the church is the Episcopal Palace, formerly the summer residence of Florence's bishops. From the square in front of the church, you have a beautiful view of the city, which is actually preferable to that from the crowded Piazzale Michelangelo.

AROUND
FLORENCE

Fiesole

One of the most popular excursions for visitors to Florence has always been **Fiesole** to the north of the city. As the Roman settlement *Faesulae*, it once overshadowed Florence on account of its favorable location high above the Arno and Mugnone valleys. Even before Roman times it was one of the twelve cities of the Etruscan Confederacy – remains of the city walls near the Roman amphitheater date from this period. Under the Romans, the city also boasted, as well as this theater, a forum, a capital, temples and baths. Fiesole was the center of the region, wealthy and powerful. The era of the great migrations came and went without leaving any major traces. But then, in 1125, Fiesole was conquered and destroyed by its strengthened rival, Florence, and it never managed to recover fully from this blow.

After the 15th century, wealthy Florentine families, notably the Medici, started having summer residences built on the hills of Fiesole. These villas are situated amid beautiful surroundings on a steep, terraced slope just under the town, anc command a spectacular view of Florence and the Arno valley. If you follow a winding road, the *Via Vecchia Fiesolana*, it will take you up to the church and monastery of the little village of **San Domenico**, where the painter monk Fra Angelico was a novice before he moved to San Marco in Florence. The Altar of the Madonna in the church, in the first chapel on your left, is his work.

Not far from San Domenico is the **Badia Fiesolana**, which was the cathe-

Left: Fiesole's steep streets will keep you in shape.

dral church of Fiesole until the 11th century, after which its monastery was turned over to the Benedictines. During the Renaissance, the abbey was enlarged and rebuilt. In the facade of the church, which was never quite completed, you can still see the light and dark stones of the old Romanesque facade. The interior is appointed in the style of Brunelleschi. To the right of the church is the entrance to the former convent.

Between the Badia and Fiesole's city center is the **Villa Medici** – also referred to as *Belcanto* or *Il Palagio di Fiesole*. This villa was built by Michelozzo for Cosimo the Elder between 1458 and 1461. It was here that Lorenzo the Magnificent entertained his literary friends, such as Poliziano, Pico della Mirandola and Landino. Today, the villa is privately owned, and not open to the public.

Center of Fiesole is the **Piazza Mino da Fiesole**, located on the site of the old Roman forum. To the north of the piazza lies the Romanesque cathedral, the **Dom San Romolo**, with its high crenellated campanile. A few steps further is the entrance to the **Roman Theater** and the archaeological excavation site. The theater, which had a seating capacity of 3,000 people, dates back to the first century B.C., as do the remains of bathing facilities and of a temple, which were discovered in a lower level. The north boundary of the excavation site is formed by remains of the Etruscan wall. Every year, the *Estate Fiesolana* (Fiesole summer) stages theater performances and concerts in the Roman theater.

The **Museo Civico**, a building that resembles a temple, is immediately to the right of the entrance to the theater. Exhibited here are finds from the days of the Etruscans and Romans, as well as medieval artifacts. A little further on is the small but interesting **Museo Bandini**, which displays Florentine paintings from the 13th-15th centuries as well as Della Robbia terra-cottas and wood carvings.

The lovely 14th-century City Hall on the east side of the square is quite charming, adorned with numerous coats of arms. On the other side, adjacent to the 11th-century Bishop's Palace, the steep Via di San Francesco leads up to the **Franciscan Monastery**. You can enjoy a beautiful view of Florence from the square in front of the monastery.

From Fiesole you reach Poggio Gherardo by way of Mariano. In 1348, Boccaccio and ten young Florentine aristocrats are supposed to have retreated to the **Villa di Poggio Gherardo** in the face of an outbreak of the plague in Florence. To pass the time, they exchanged ribald stories, which became the ostensible basis for Boccaccio's famous collection of novellas, the *Decameron*. Continuing on, you'll come to **Ponte a Mensola** and the church of San Martino, which contains a triptych by Taddeo Gaddi. Nearby

Above: Illustration for Boccaccio's Decameron (F. di Stefano, 15th century). Right: La Petraia – the Medici summer palace.

is the **Villa I Tatti**, which today houses Harvard University's Center for Renaissance History, as well as a valuable art collection. The road leads on toward Settignano by way of Coverciano. Just past Coverciano come the villas of Porziuncola and Capponcina, where Eleanora Duse and her lover Gabriele D'Annunzio lived at the beginning of this century.

Settignano was home town of such famous sculptors as Desiderio, the Rossellinos, and Bartolomeo Ammannati. Not far off, near Terenzano, is one of the most beautiful Renaissance villas in Italy, the **Villa Gamberaia**. Heavily damaged during World War II, it was restored according to the original plans. It is principally noted for its magnificent park which contains statues, fountains and waterworks. You may be able to visit this park if you contact the owners (tel. 055/697205).

The Medici Villas around Florence

Some of the most famous villas built by the Medicis are on the northern out-

skirts of Florence. On the road that leads up to the slopes of Monte Morello and the mountains of Calvana, for example, you can find the **Villa Medicea di Careggi**. Today, this is part of the huge hospital complex of the Florence Medical School. The villa, renovated by Michelozzo for Cosimo the Elder, is supposed to have been the Medici's favorite villa. It's here that Cosimo founded the Platonic Academy during the 15th century, which became a meeting-place for celebrated writers, philosophers and artists.

Within a radius of a few miles, there are three other famous villas. First, there's the **Villa Corsini** with its Baroque facade. To the left of this, the Via della Petraia leads to the **Villa Medicea della Petraia**, a former palace of the Brunelleschi family which was purchased by the Medici in 1530. Ferdinand I then had the building magnificently redesigned and renovated by Buontalenti.

The gardens were laid out by Niccolò Pericolo, known as Tribolo, who also created the elegant fountains of Venere-

Fiorenza with a statue by Giambologna. The terraces of the hanging gardens command a beautiful view of the city.

From Villa Corsini, continue along the Via di Castelloto to the **Villa Medicea di Castello**. In the 14th century, a fortified castle stood upon this spot. Lorenzo and Giovanni di Pierfrancesco de' Medici acquired the estate in 1477, and Cosimo I had it turned into an exquisite Renaissance villa. Here, too, it was Tribolo who was responsible for the layout of the beautiful park and for the fountain, which depicts Hercules battling the giant Antaeus. The renowned *Grotta degli Animali* (grotto of the beasts) at the end of the central path was also designed by Tribolo and fitted out with animal representations in different colors of marble by Ammannati and others (today, the bronze birds created by Giambologna can be seen in the Bargello Museum).

Since 1974, the Villa di Castello has been the headquarters of the *Accademia della Crusca*, an Italian language academy founded in 1583, which has been concerned with maintaining the purity of the Italian language ever since.

EXCURSION TO THE MUGELLO AND THE SIEVE VALLEY

If you want to see a part of Tuscany that's not overrun by tourists, take a trip into the Mugello and the Sieve valley, the area east of the Bologna-Florence expressway. For this trip, start out on the old road that leads over the Apennines toward Bologna, the SS 65, running through a landscape dotted with villas and gardens. First town you'll come to is Pratolino, a spot famous for its **Villa Demidoff** (as it is called today) which the Grand Duke Francesco de' Medici had built for his mistress (later his wife), Bianca Cappello, back in the 16th century. The villa is surrounded by a wonderful park with numerous fountains, grottoes and statues, including the huge Apennine Statue by Giambologna. The park is open to visitors from Friday to Sunday.

Continue on to **San Piero a Sieve** in the Sieve valley, which is dominated by the impressive Medici fortress of San Martino. Immediately after San Piero a Sieve comes the fortress-like edifice of the **Villa Medicea di Cafaggiolo**, which was built by Michelozzo for Cosimo I as a summer residence. Lorenzo the Magnificent used it later as a hunting lodge.

A few miles further on, a small road turns off to the right and leads off to the Franciscan monastery of **Bosco ai Frati**, which Cosimo's architect, Michelozzo, who also designed the nearby **Castello di Trebbio**, practically rebuilt from scratch. A precious wooden crucifixion carved by Donatello is on display in a diminutive *Museo d'Arte Sacra* in the chapter-room of the monastery.

The route continues past Barberino di Mugello and leads over the Futa Pass (2,950 feet/903 m), where one of the largest cemeteries for German soldiers in

Italy was laid out between 1962 and 1965. Five miles (8 km) further on, the road intersects with the SS 503, which takes us back to San Piero a Sieve by way of Firenzuola and the Giogo di Scarperia.

Firenzuola or Little Florence, a spa town and tourist center that lies 1,390 feet (422 m) above sea level, was founded by the Florentines during the 12th century so that they could control the road to Bologna. During World War II, it was almost completely destroyed, but later it was rebuilt according to the original rectangular ground plan.

Scarperia is one of the more important towns in the Mugello. The medieval center of the town, which was founded by the Republic of Florence during the 12th

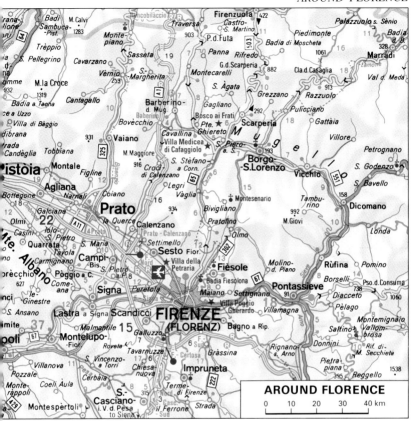

AROUND FLORENCE

0   10   20   30   40 km

century to control the pass road through the Apennines, is still very well preserved. The facade of the Palazzo Pretorio with its high, turreted campanile, is adorned with coats-of-arms of stone and ceramic. There is a tabernacle ascribed to Andrea della Robbia contained in the oratory of the Madonna di Piazza, where the curates once swore their oath of allegiance upon taking up office.

The Mugello race track (3.3 miles/5.3 km long) is on the outskirts of Scarperia. It was built by Florence's Automobile Club in 1974; it was recently modernized to such an extent that Formula 1 motor-racing can now be held here every year.

Borgo San Lorenzo, Mugello's capital, is a center of agriculture and industry,

particularly brickmaking and artistic ceramics. The church of San Lorenzo dates back to the 13th century; its hexagonal campanile, built entirely of brick, is from the same period. The facade was severely damaged during an earthquake in 1919, but it was rebuilt, using the old material, during the 1920s.

From Borgo San Lorenzo, continue following the Sieve valley downstream for about 4 miles (7 km) to the village of **Vicchio**, the birthplace of Fra Angelico (ca. 1387-1455). On the square named after the painter Giotto (who was born in the neighboring village of Vespignano) stand the Palazzo Pretorio, which houses the Museo Beato Angelico, displaying sacred art from the Mugello.

The town of **Dicomano**, at the intersection with the SS 67, the *Tosco Romagnola*, was already established in the days of the Romans, and has always served as a transportation hub, and therefore as a trade center, of the Sieve valley. It's for this reason that the little city was spared by the Florentines when they conquered all of the castles in the area during the 14th century. Dicomano suffered severe damages during several earthquakes, the last of which was in 1919. It was rebuilt during the 1940s, but unfortunately hardly anything is left of the old town.

Rufina, renowned for its good wine, is on the way to Pontassieve. There's a wine museum located in the cellars of the 16th-century Villa di Poggio Reale. Call the owner to make arrangements if you'd like to visit the villa (tel. 055/836948).

From Pontassieve, an old trade center at the confluence of the Sieve and Arno

Above: Michelozzo's famous exterior pulpit on the cathedral in Prato. Right: "Salome Dancing" by Fra Filippo Lippi, Prato.

rivers, you can drive the 12.5 miles (18 km) back to Florence.

PRATO

Prato lies on the plain between Florence and Pistoia at the beginning of the Bisenzo valley. Excavations have shown that there were already settlements here during the early Stone Age. Later, Prato came under Roman rule and subsequently developed into a larger settlement during the Lombardian period. In the 12th century it became a free imperial city. This ushered in a burst of economic development, which wasn't even slowed down when the city came under the sway of the ubiquitous Florentines in 1350.

Since the Middle Ages, Prato has had the weaving and cloth industry to thank for its exceptional prosperity. The development of a modern textile industry since the 19th century has made this city – which after World War II even started making money by recycling rags into cheap new garments – into a kind of "Manchester of Tuscany". In the city's countless mills and factories, all manner of wool and woollens are processed into finished products each and every day. Today, Prato, with its approximately 170,000 inhabitants, is accounted one of the wealthiest cities in Italy.

Around 600 years ago, the local merchant Francesco di Marco Datini not only invented money exchange as a means of making payments without cash, but also came up with double-entry bookkeeping. And yet, for all their love of cash and commerce, the business-minded Pratese have by no means overlooked art and culture. The old center of the city demonstrates a wealth of old buildings, and even modern Prato has managed to maintain a feeling for the arts.

Center of the hexagonal downtown area, encompassed by a 14th-century city wall, is the Piazza Communale with its medieval city hall and the **Palazzo**

Pretorio, which houses the valuable art collection of the municipal museum.

From here, Via Mazzoni leads to the cathedral square and the **Cattedrale di Santo Stefano**, an excellent example of Romanesque-Gothic architecture. From outside, the cathedral displays a typically Tuscan exterior with stripes of pale white and green serpentine marble. Over the main portal is a relief by Andrea della Robbia, while on the right side of the facade projects the famous **outdoor pulpit** built by Michelozzo in 1434-1438, which Donatello furnished with magnificent bas-reliefs of dancing children (the originals can be seen in the Cathedral Museum, located in the Bishop's Palace). From this pulpit, the *Pergamo del Sacro Cingolo* (Pulpit of the Holy Girdle), the faithful are several times a year given a chance to glimpse a belt said to have belonged to the Virgin Mary, which was brought to Prato in 1141 by a local crusader when he returned home.

The interior of the cathedral consists of a Romanesque nave, flanked by massive columns of green serpentine marble, and a Gothic transept. The marble pulpit is by Mino da Fiesole and Rossellino, while the main altar bears a wooden crucifix by Ferdinando Tacca. Most impressive, however, are the choir frescoes by Fra Filippo Lippi, a masterpiece of the early Renaissance. Particularly successful is the Dance of Salome (on the right), one of the series of frescoes illustrating scenes from the life of John the Baptist. Legend has it that the painter monk, who was not at all indifferent to the pleasures of the flesh, depicted in Salome his mistress, the nun Lucrezia Buti, who bore him two children. Their son, Filippino, later followed in his father's footsteps and became a famous artist.

Another church worth seeing is **Santa Maria delle Carceri** in the Via Cairoli, a beautiful domed building that was erected by Sangallo between 1485 and 1492. The church stands on the remains of an old prison (*carceri*), on the wall of which was painted an image of Mary said to have miraculous properties. The marble exterior of the church was never completed, but the building's architectural proportions are magnificent. The interior contains a beautiful majolica frieze by Andrea della Robbia.

Across from the church is the **Castello dell'Imperatore,** the emperor's fortress, which Frederick II had built in the 13th century on top of the old castle of Duke Alberti. The mighty walls and towers with their swallow-tail merlons are reminiscent of the Hohenstaufen castles in Apulia and Sicily. Because of Frederick's death in 1250, the courtyard was never completed, but it's used today as an open-air stage for plays and concerts.

Not far from here is the **Palazzo Datini** in the Via Rinaldesca, which Datini, the wealthy banker and merchant mentioned above, had built for himself. In 1870, 460 years after Datini's death, numerous accounts ledgers, insurance policies, partnership contracts and business letters were discovered in a hiding place beneath the staircase. Today, this valuable historical material is kept in the archives in the palace.

Examples of modern art in Prato can be found on the Piazza San Marco on the east side of the old town center, where there's an impressive white marble sculpture by Henry Moore. If you depart from the Piazza San Marco and head south, you will pass through the modern sections of the city (the Institute for Textile Technology and the Textile Museum, founded in 1886, are both located on the Viale della Repubblica) before coming to the **Museo d'Arte Contemporanea Luigi Pecci** (1988) which houses a museum of modern art, a research center and an archive (CID).

If you leave the old city center in a northerly direction by way of the Piazza Mercatale, you'll come to a bridge spanning the Bisenzio, which could be your

Right: The campanile of the cathedral of Pistoia.

point of departure for an excursion into the countryside around Prato.

The Bisenzio Valley

From Prato, the highway SS 325 heads northward to Bologna, parallel to the expressway and railway tracks. It follows the **Bisenzio valley** to the border of Tuscany and Emilia, between the rough slopes of the Monti della Calvana and the wooded ridge of the Apennines. Ever since the age of industrialization, the valley has always been densely settled, as the Bisenzio river supplied the countless textile factories, mills, paper factories and copper plants with water.

In a green hollow full of olive groves lies **Vaiano**, center of the modern textile industry. During the Middle Ages, this town was an important military outpost for Prato.

The 11th century saw construction of the **Badia di San Salvatore**, of which the church, with an impressive campanile dating back to the 13th century, remains today. The triple-naved interior of the church is reminiscent of Prato's cathedral. The sacristy with wooden inlays from the 18th century is of interest, as is the cloister (14th century) with its colonnaded portico and loggia.

Further north, the ruins of **Rocca Cerbaia**, which was a castle of the Alberti family in the 12th century, perch on a steep cliff. To get there, you have to walk up a small path which begins just past the little medieval bridge and ends at Montecuccoli, a village on the ridge of the Calvana (2,069 feet/633 m).

From Mercatale di Vernio, at the confluence of the Fiumenta and Basenzio rivers, a steep road leads up to the fresh-air resort of **San Ippolito** (1,357 feet/415 m), a town famous for its *carnevalino* (carnival and fair) on Ash Wednesday. Another road leads across the Bisenzio and through the lofty town of Lucciana to **Cantagallo**, where you can depart on a

lovely hike up to the Pacini hut on the Pian della Rasa (3,273 feet/1,001 m).

After Mercatale, you come to the mouth of the 12.5-mile (18 km) train tunnel that cuts through the Apennines, and, once past this, you will arrive at **San Quirico di Vernio** in the Fiumenta valley, above which looms a fortress with remnants of the old castle. On the first Sunday in Lent, the traditional Sagra della Polenta is held here (the polenta is made using chestnut flour).

A steep climb brings you to one of the more easily traversable Apennine passes, which brings you over into Emilia and onto a sunny plateau where sits the pretty little fresh-air resort of **Montepiano**; like many mountain towns, this is also a good point of departure for a number of different hikes along well-marked trails.

PISTOIA

Pistoia, like Prato, also stands in the cultural and political shadow of the more important cities of Florence, Lucca and Pisa. But it should not be neglected for this reason, as its old town center has a number of important works of art that bear comparison with other, more renowned ones in Tuscany.

Pistoia goes back to the Roman era, when it was a fortified village on the Via Cassia. But it had its heyday during the 12th and 13th centuries, when it declared itself a free municipality. It was in this period that the buildings went up which still grace the historic part of town.

The best starting point for a walk through the old town – which is based on a rectangular ground plan and is still surrounded by the remains of a 14th-century city wall – is the picturesque **Piazza del Duomo**, which is lined with a number of important buildings.

On the southeast side of the piazza rises the **Duomo San Zeno**, whose 220-foot (67 m) campanile, the lower part of which resembles the tower of a fortress, is the trademark of the city. The Romanesque-Pisan church (12th/13th centuries) was built on the site of another church

which dated from the 5th century. Its well-proportioned marble facade, with a porch supported on fine, slender columns, is decorated with a relief of the Madonna and majolica tiles by Andrea della Robbia. Among a number of notable art works in the interior, the most famous object is the **Silver Altar of St. Jacob**, a masterpiece of Florentine silversmithing which took almost 200 years to complete (from 1287 to 1456).

Next to the cathedral, the medieval **Bishop's Palace** forms the south side of the square. Adjoining it is the octagonal **Baptistery**, built in the 14th century according to designs by Andrea Pisano.

On the west side of the piazza is the **Palazzo Pretorio** (14th century) with painted and sculpted armorial bearings and an attractive interior courtyard, which serves as a courthouse today.

On the northeast side of the piazza and

Above: The "7 Works of Mercy" on the majolica frieze of the Ospedale del Ceppo.
Right: Pulpit in S. Andrea by G. Pisano.

to the left of the cathedral is the **Palazzo Comunale**, a massive sandstone building which was begun during the 13th century and finally, after many interruptions, completed in the 14th century. A 17th-century wing joins it to the cathedral. On the ground floor, the facade is divided into five loggias, while arched window openings create the division in the three upper stories. Over this, the facade sports the Medici coat-of-arms and the papal keys in honor of the Medici Popes, Leo X and Clemens VII. Next to the central window, you can make out a head carved in black marble; no one is quite sure as to the significance of this image. The palace houses the **Museo Civico**, which has an attractive painting collection.

If you leave the Piazza del Duomo and head northeast, the Via Pacini will take you to the **Ospedale del Ceppo,** named for the hollow tree-stump (*ceppo*) where alms were collected. Built in the 13th or 14th centuries, the hospital, which is still in use today, was adorned with a beautiful portico in the 16th century. The facade sports a magnificent majolica frieze from the school of Della Robbia, depicting the Seven Works of Mercy.

The church of **Sant'Andrea,** architecturally an interesting building in the Pisan style, contains a special treasure: the **Pulpit** by Giovanni Pisano, which was built between 1298 and 1301, or, in other words, before his pulpit in the cathedral at Pisa. The relief panels show scenes from the life of Christ; the dramatic representation of the Massacre of the Innocents is particularly impressive.

Another architectural masterpiece is the church **San Giovanni Fuorcivitas** in the Via Cavour, south of the Piazza del Duomo. A particularly notable feature of this church is its outer side wall, which is beautifully decorated with stripes of light and dark marble and geometrical patterns. Over the entrance is a terra-cotta relief by Gruamonte from Como, while the church's interior contains a stoup by Giovanni Pisano and a terra-cotta relief of the *Visitation*, which is ascribed to either Luca or Andrea della Robbia.

Things are more modern in the **Pallazo Tau** on Via Garibaldi, devoted to modern art. Displayed here is a collection of sculptures and drawings by Marino Marini, who was born in Pistoia.

Ice machines and snow cannons

Pistoia's convenient location between Florence, Pisa and Lucca is not the only reason one might want to choose to stay longer in this area. Another enticement is the beautiful countryside behind Pistoia, ideal for long excursions, by foot or on horseback. An attractive wooded landscape, medieval villages, old traditions and festivals are all reasons to get to know the Pistoian Apennines and their nature parks. One specialty of the region are the so-called *ghiaccai*, devices which in the 19th and early 20th centuries were used to keep cool ice which had been "mined" in the mountains and transport

it down to the cities on the plain. Until the invention of artificial ice, this was the sole source of income for many families in the Reno valley; you can see a few of these devices displayed in Le Piastre, about 14 miles/20 km from Pistoia).

And Pistoia's back country isn't only popular during the summer. In winter, the ski area around **Abetone** becomes a paradise for all manner of winter sports (recently, snow cannons have made it possible to ski no matter what the snow conditions are).

Baths, Flowers, and a Wooden Scamp

The renowned health resort of **Montecatini Terme** is one of the most elegant thermal spas in Italy, and its waters were probably known and valued even in Antiquity. Since the late 18th century, palazzo-like edifices have been built over the eleven springs, which are said to be especially good for people suffering from liver disorders and rheumatism. With beautiful parks; large hotels, and tidy or-

ganization, this town is an ideal place for anyone looking for a way to combine the necessity of a "cure" with pleasant surroundings. It is not, however, so interesting for anyone looking for the "real Tuscany." The same holds true for nearby **Monsummano**, which offers natural steam baths in caves. The hot and healing steam from the bowels of the earth can be enjoyed in the natural Grotta Giusti or in the artificial Grotta Parlanti.

There are a number of different excursions which could enliven a "cure." Take the medieval villages of Montecatini Alto and Monsummano Alto; or Valdinievole in the north, with its old mountain villages and villas; or the neighboring town of **Pescia**, with its famous flower market.

A few miles past Pescia is the village of **Collodi**, a name which Carlo Lorenzini, the author of *Pinocchio*, adopted as a *nom de plume*. In addition to Pinocchio Park, which boasts life-sized wooden

Above: The healing waters of Montecatini.
Right: Monks' cells in Certosa del Galluzzo.

figures from the tales of the long-nosed puppet, this medieval village along the slope of a hill includes the Villa Garzoni, which has truly beautiful gardens.

LOWER ARNO VALLEY AND MONTALBANO

The drive from Monsummano on the SS 436 leads through the marshy areas of Fucecchio, with its unusual flora and fauna, to the Arno valley, where the town of **San Miniato** extends along a mountain ridge on the south side. Because of its strategic location high above the valleys of the Arno, the Elsa and the Egola, the town was of military significance even during the Roman era. During the reign of the German emperor Otto I it became the seat of the imperial vicariate in Tuscany. Today, San Miniato is a quiet little town that only becomes lively in autumn, when it hosts a popular truffle festival (the third Saturday in October). And in November, a market for white truffles is held here every weekend.

One noteworthy sight is the castle that Frederick II had built high above San Miniato. Below this, on the tree-shaded Prato del Duomo, is the 13th-century cathedral with its forbidding tower, actually a leftover from the old fortress.

Between San Miniato and Empoli, on the highway leading from Livorno to Florence, a small road turns off to the left, which will take you across the Montalbano ridge to Pistoia. This winding, yet extremely lovely scenic road passes through dense olive groves on its way to **Vinci**, birthplace of none other than Leonardo. There's a museum devoted to him in the old castle, while the house where he is supposed to have been born is actually a bit outside of town near Achiano, almost hidden behind olive trees and cypresses. Here, too, you can see exhibits and reproductions of some of his works.

Above the town, the road continues through lovely forests, and on the other

side of the hill a view opens out over the densely populated basin extending from Pistoia through Prato to Florence. At Casalguidi, a road leading off to the right will take you via Quarrata and Olmi to the straight road from Pistoia to Florence, the SS 66. The famous wine town of Carmignano is situated on the slopes of Montalbano to your right. At about the latitude of Prato, you'll reach **Poggio a Caiano** with its beautiful **Medici villa** which Lorenzo the Magnificent had redesigned in Renaissance style by Guiliano da Sangallo. Especially attractive is the facade with its majestic entry loggia and majolica relief by Andrea Sansovino. The villa contains a museum, and is surrounded by a beautiful park.

A brief detour from Poggio a Caiano leads you to another Medici villa, the **Ferdinanda of Artimino**. Ferdinand I had it built by Buontalenti in 1594 as a hunting lodge. The roof of this castle-like villa, with its lovely open-air staircase and a loggia, is adorned with countless chimneys of various shapes.

Certosa del Galluzzo

South of Florence, high above the road to Siena and surrounded by a high wall, stands the **Certosa del Galluzzo**, the Carthusian monastery of Galluzzo. This was founded in the 14th century by the Florentine statesman Niccolò Accaiuoli for the Carthusian order. Florentine patrons gave generous donations, and in the course of time the monastery was expanded and furnished with precious works of art, many of which can be seen today in the painting gallery in the Palazzo Accaiuoli. A large part of the original collection was stolen by Napoleon's armies in 1810.

The monastery consists of a collection of little buildings – actually the cells of the monks, whose order dictates a life of strict seclusion, – as well as common rooms for prayers and church services. The only way to see the monastery is to join a guided tour conducted by a Cistercian monk; these are available throughout the day.

FLORENCE
(Telephone area code 055)

Accommodations
LUXURY: **Excelsior**, P.za Ognissanti, 3, tel: 264201. **Regency**, P.za M. d'Azeglio, 3, tel: 245247. **Brunelleschi**, P.za S. Elisabetta, 3, tel: 562068. **Minerva**, P.za S. M. Novella, 16, tel: 284555. **Relais Certosa**, Via di Colle Ramole, 2, tel: 2047171. *MODERATE:* **Ariele**, Via Magenta, 11, tel: 211509. **Basilea**, Via Guelfa, 41, tel: 214587. **Beacci Tornabuoni**, Via Tornabuoni, 3, tel: 212645. **Calzaiuoli**, Via Calzaiuoli, 6, tel: 2112456. **Cavour**, Via del Proconsolo, 3, tel: 282461. **Corallo**, Via Nazionale, 22/A, tel: 496645. **David**, V.le Michelangiolo, 1, tel: 6811695. **Villa Liberty**, V.le Michelangiolo, 40, tel: 6810581. *BUDGET:* **Alessandra**, Borgo SS. Apostoli, 17, tel: 283438. **Apollo**, Via Faenza, 77, tel: 284119. **Ariston**, Via Fiesolana, 40, tel: 2476980. **Bologna**, Via Orcagna, 50, tel: 678359. **Capri**, Via XXVII Aprile, 3, tel: 215441. **Le Vigne**, P.zza S. M. Novella, 24, tel: 294449. **Liana**, Via Alfieri, 18, tel: 245303.
CAMPGROUNDS: **Italiani e Stranieri**, Viale Michelangiolo, 80, tel: 6811977, closed Nov. to March. **Villa Camerata**, Viale A. Righi, 2-4, tel: 610300, open year-round.
YOUTH HOSTELS: **Villa Camerata**, Viale A. Righi, 2-4, tel: 610300.

Restaurants
La Baraonda, Via Ghibellina 67/r, tel: 2341171. Friendly trattoria, light, typical Florentine specialties, and good quality for the price. Closed Sun. **Cibreo**, via dei Macci, 118/r, tel: 2341100. Typical Tuscan specialties, prices reflect the quality. Closed Sun. and Mon. **Dino**, Via Ghibellina, 51/r, tel: 241452. Closed Sun. and Mon. **Enoteca Pinchiorri**, Via Ghibellina, 87, tel: 242777. One of Italy's leading restaurants; prices are high, but you get what you pay for. Closed Sun. **Le Fonticine**, Via Nazionale, 79/r. tel: 282106. Good, affordable cooking; lots of homemade specialties. Closed Sun. and Mon. **Alle Murate**, Via Ghibellina, 52/r. tel: 240618. Specialties from different regions of Italy. Closed Mon. Ruggero, Via Senese, 82/r. tel: 220542. Typical Florentine trattoria, reasonable prices. Closed Tue. and Wed. **Burde**, Via Pistoiese, 6/r, tel: 317206. One of the last old-style trattorias in Tuscany. Marvellous home cooking. Closed evenings and holidays.

Cafés
Caffetteria Gilli, P.zza d. Repubblica, 39/r, tel: 213896. A real "must" in Florence. **Paszkowski**, P.zza d. Repubblica, 3/r, tel: 210136. Lovely sidewalk café, great ice cream. **Rivoire**, P.zza d. Signoria, 5/r, tel: 214412. Wonderful chocolate delicacies.

Museums
Uffizi, P.le degli Uffizi, Tue-Sat 9 am-7 pm, closed holidays.
Palazzo Pitti (includes Galleria Palatina, Appartamenti Monumentali – currently closed for renovations – Galleria dell'Arte Moderna, Galleria del Costume, Museo delle Porcellane, Museo degli Argenti), Tue-Sat, 9 am-2 pm. Closed holidays.
Galleria dell'Accademia, Via Ricasoli, 60. Open Tue-Sat 9 am-2 pm, closed holidays.
National museum Bargello, Via del Proconsolo, 4. Tue-Sat 9 am-2 pm. Closed holidays.
Museum San Marco, Piazza San Marco, 1. Tue-Sat 9 am-2 pm. Closed holidays.
Museum Palazzo Davanzati, Via Porta Rossa, 13. Open Tue-Sat 9 am-2 pm, closed holidays.
Archaeological Museum, Via della Colonna, 36. Tue-Sat 9 am-2 pm, closed holidays. **Medici Chapel**, P.zza Madonna degli Aldobrandini, Tue-Sat 9 am-2 pm. Closed holidays.
Palazzo Vecchio and Quartieri monumentali, P.zza della Signoria, Mon-Fri 9 am-7 pm, Sun and holidays 9 am-noon, closed Sat.
Palazzo Medici-Riccardi, Via Cavour, 1. Open weekdays 9 am-12:30 pm and 3-6:30 pm, Sundays and holidays 9 am-noon, closed Wed.
Museo di Santa Maria del Fiore (Cathedral museum), Piazza Duomo, 9. Opening times: Summer (March 1-October 31) 9 am-8 pm, winter 9 am-6 pm. Closed Sundays.
Museo dell'Opera di S. Croce, P.zza S. Croce, 16. Opening times: Summer (March 1-Oct 31) 10 am-12:30/3-6:30 pm. Winter 10 am-12:30/3-5 pm. Closed Wed.
Museo di Storia della Scienza (Museum of the History of Science), P.zza dei Giudici, 1. 9:30 am-1 pm/2-5 pm. Sat 9:30-1 pm. Closed Sun and holidays.
Museo Marino Marini, Piazza San Pancrazio, opening hours: 10 am-1 pm/3-6 pm, closed Tue.
Museum Stibbert, Via Stibbert, 26. Opening hours: weekdays 9 am-1 pm, holidays 9 am-12:30 pm. Guided tours every half hour.
Pinacoteca della Certosa, Certosa del Galluzzo. Opening hours: Summer, 9 am-noon and 3-6 pm. Winter 9 am-noon and 3-5 pm. Closed Mon.
Museo di Storia della Fotografia F.lli Alinari (Alinari Photography Museum), Via d. Vigna Nuova, 16. Open 10 am-7:30 pm, closed Wed.

Sights
CHURCHES: Most churches are open mornings and afternoons, with a midday break between 12:30 and 3:30 pm. The Cathedral is open throughout the day; the dome can be climbed 10 am-5 pm. Closed Sun and holidays**.** The **Baptistery** is open 1-6 pm, holidays 9 am-1 pm. Access to the **campanile:** 8:30 am-7 pm (summer) and 9 am-4:30 pm (winter).

VILLAS: You can only enter the Medici villas with written permission from the responsible authorities. Admission fees are charged to visit the gardens.

Tourist Information
Tourist Information Office (APT), Via Manzoni, 16, tel: 23320. Province of Florence: Via Cavour, 1/r, tel: 2760382.

Guarded parking lots/garages
Fortezza da Basso, hourly rate: L. 1,500. **Stazione S.M.N.** (underground garage): L. 2,000, each additional hour L. 3,000. Other parking lots: Mercato Centrale, Lungarno Torrigiani, Lungarno Zecca Vecchia, Piazza della Libertà, on the ring road.

Taxi
Radio taxis SO,CO.TA. tel: 4798, **CO.TA.FI.** tel: 4390.

Emergencies
Police: tel: 113. Traffic police: tel: 36911. **ACI:** tel: 24861.

Hospitals
Arcispedale Di S. M. Nuova, P.zza S. M. Nuova, 1, tel: 27581. **Careggi**, Viale Morgagni, 85, tel: 4277111.

FIESOLE
Accommodations
LUXURY: **Villa San Michele**, Via Doccia, 4, tel: 59451. **Villa Aurora**, P.zza Mino, 39, tel: 59100.
MODERATE: **Villa Bonelli**, Via F. Poeti, 1, tel: 59513. **Bencistà**, Via B. da Maiano, 4, tel: 59163.
BUDGET: **Villa Baccano**, Via Bosconi, 4, tel: 59341. **Villa Sorriso**, Via Gramsci, 21, tel: 59021.

Restaurants
Le Cave di Maiano, Via delle Cave, 16, tel: 59133. Traditional cuisine in rustic surroundings. Prices are acceptable.
Pizzeria San Domenico, San Domenico, tel: 59182.

Museums
City Museum - Roman Theater, Via Portigiani, 1. Opening hours in winter: 10 am-4 pm, summer: 9 am-7 pm.
Museo Bandini, Via Duprè, 1. Open in winter 10-1 pm/3-6 pm, summer 9:30 am-1 pm/3-7 pm. Closed Tue.
Antiquarium Costantini, Via Portigiani, 9. Open in winter 10 am-4 pm and in summer 9 am-7 pm. Valuable collection of ancient ceramics.

Sights
Observation terrace Parco della Rimembranza. Church and museum of **S. Francesco**, Via S. Francesco. Opening hours in winter 10 am-noon and 3-5 pm, in summer 10 am-noon and 3-6 pm.

Tourist Information
Information office, Piazza Mino, 37, tel: 598720.

PRATO
(Telephone area code 0574)
Accommodations
LUXURY: **Art Hotel Museo**, V.le della Repubblica, tel: 5787. **Palace**, Via Piero della Francesca, 71, tel: 592841.
MODERATE: **Flora**, Via Cairoli,, 31, tel: 20021. **Villa S. Cristina**, Via Poggio Secco, 58. tel: 595951.
BUDGET: **Stella d'Italia**, Piazza Duomo, 8, tel: 27910, **Il Giglio**, P.zza S. Marco, tel: 37049.

Restaurants
Il Piraña, Via Tobia Bertini, tel: 25746. Very modern decor, high prices, and excellent fish dishes. Closed Sat. and Sun.
Trattoria Lapo, P.zza Mercatale, 141, tel: 23745. Rather uncomfortable, but very rustic. Closed Sun.

Sights
Palazzo Datini, Via Ser Lapo Mazzei, 9 amnoon/3-6 pm, Sat 9 am-noon, closed Sun and holidays. **Textile Museum**, tel: 570352, open weekdays 9 am-noon. Closed Sun. **Museum of contemporary art "Luigi Pecci,"** open daily exc. Tue 10 am-7 pm. **Medici Museum** in **Poggio a Caiano**, Tue-Sat 9 am-5:30 pm, Sun and Mon 9 am-2 pm.

Tourist Information
Tourist Information Office Prato, Via Cairoli, 48/ 52, tel: 24112..

PISTOIA
(Telephone area code 0573)
Accommodations
MODERATE: **Leon Bianco**, Via Panciaticci, 2, tel: 26675. **Patria**, Via F. Crispi, 6, tel: 25187. **Villa Vannini**, Villa di Pitecchio, Pitecchio, tel: 4203. **Il Convento**, Via S. Quirico, 33, Loc. Ponte Nuovo, tel: 452651.

Restaurants
Cucciolo della Montagna, Via Pancaticchi, 4, tel: 29733. Closed Sun. eve. and Mon. **Lo Spuntino**, P.zza dell'Ortaggio, 12, nice trattoria, good food, low prices. Closed Sun.

Museums
Museo Civico, open 9 am-1 pm and 3-7 pm. **Palazzo Tau**, opening hours as Museo Civico. **Villa Garzoni in Collodi**, open 8 am-sundown, lunch break 1-2:30 pm. **Pinocchio Park**, 8:30 am-sundown. **Museo Vinciano**, (in the Vinci castle), open 9:30-noon, 2:30-5:30 (in summer 3-10 pm). Closed Wed.

Tourist Information
A.P.T. Pistoia, Via Toma, 1, Palazzo dei Vescovi, tel. 21622.

CHIANTI

WINE COUNTRY
VIA CHIANTIGIANI
VIA CASSIA
SAN GIMIGNANO
VOLTERRA

WINE COUNTRY

The word Chianti awakens associations even in those who have never been to Tuscany. It conjures up images of rolling hills, silvery olive groves, cypresses and, of course, vineyards. And nearly everyone has tasted Chianti wine at one time or another. In the 1960s and 70s, you could buy it in supermarkets for next to nothing in the famous *fiaschi*. Today, these straw-wrapped bottles are largely obsolete, and quality and prices have increased substantially.

Glossy photographs in magnificent coffee-table volumes and large-sized calendars show a Tuscany that is mostly limited to Chianti, as if Tuscany were best represented by this small region. And it's true. This landscape between Florence and Siena, between the Upper Arno Valley and the valley of the Elsa, is breathtakingly beautiful. In addition to the famous wine, it boasts historic towns rich with art, monasteries and castles, fortified villages and solitary farmsteads amidst vineyards and olive groves.

No other part of Tuscany can boast such a variety of attractions; no other part

Preceding pages: An evening mood in Chianti. Left: In May, irises transform the area around S. Polo into a sea of flowers.

is visited by as many tourists. The down side is inevitable as well: it is more expensive and more crowded here, especially in the towns, which everyone wants to have seen. The "real" Tuscany frequently loses out and what the tourist gets to see is an artificial preparation of *Toscanità*, which is only out to bleed him for as much money as it possibly can.

It is well worth your time, then, to deviate from the well-travelled main roads, and dare to explore the narrow valleys and bumpy country lanes, winding and difficult as they may be. You'll be rewarded with splendid views, majestic solitude and sometimes unforeseen encounters.

Geography and History

Geographically, Chianti is located within the triangle formed by the Arno Valley between Florence and Arezzo, the road between Arezzo and Siena, and the Siena-Florence expressway. The Chianti region, which is home to the famous "Gallo Nero," however, is limited to the townships of Radda, Castellina, and Gaiole. The area was inhabited by the Etruscans as early as the 7th and 8th centuries BC; and it's they who are thought to have first brought viticulture to Tuscany. For many years, the rival cities of Florence

95

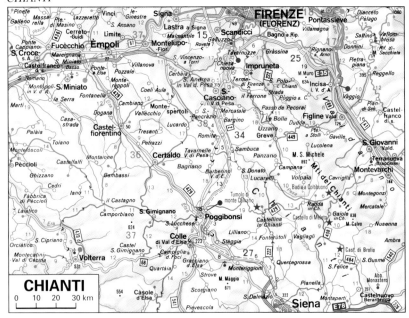

and Siena fought over this fertile region, until it was finally won by Florence in the 13th century. According to an old legend, this came to pass in a rather unusual manner: both cities were to send out a rider at the first crowing of the cock. At the point where the two riders met up, the new border would be drawn. The clever Florentines, however, starved their black cock, who was so hungry that he started to crow well before dawn. Naturally, the Florentine rider was able to cover a much greater distance than his Sienese colleague, and thus the Chianti region was won for Florence. The black cock was incorporated into the coat-of-arms of the so-called *Lega del Chianti* (League of Chianti), formed by the three cities of Radda, Gaiole and Castellina under Florentine jurisdiction.

As well as its "historic" core, the name Chianti also applies to the wine region

Chianti, which is divided into seven zones, plus the Chianti Classico, which, in accordance with a law from 1929, is made up of approximately 175,000 acres (70,000 ha) of vineyards. Only wines made here may carry the name *Vino Chianti Classico Gallo Nero.*

To get to know Chianti, we recommend two routes. One follows the Via Chiantigiana (SS 222), which leads from Florence via Greve to Siena; the other, the Via Cassia (SS 2), runs a little further west, parallel to the Florence-Siena expressway.

VIA CHIANTIGIANA

Leaving Florence, follow the historic arterial road into Chianti by taking the Via di Ripoli toward Grassina. Grassina is a small town of little importance, where the mountain river of the same name flows into the river Ema. If you are travelling during the month of May, you might, however, want to consider an excursion to S. Polo in Robbiana.

Right: The wine festival in Greve, in the wine country of Chianti, takes on something of the character of a harvest Thanksgiving.

96

A Sea of Blue Blossoms

In Grassina, turn left into the Via Tizzano. The road passes a number of scattered estates and churches, leads through the village of Capannucia, and, after about 7 miles (10 km), comes to the town of **San Polo in Robbiana**, one of the centers of iris-growing. In May, the hills around San Polo are covered with this flower's purply-blue blossoms, and the air is filled with the intensive aroma of spring violets, which, people say, you can even detect in the bouquet of some Chianti wines.

Even today these flowers, of which the medicinal and cosmetic values were already appreciated in the days of Hippocrates, are planted, harvested and processed by hand. The roots are powdered and used as a basis for perfume production on the international cosmetic market. Unfortunately, the irises bloom for only one short week in May. If you happen to be in the area during that time, however, you should really try to make certain not

to miss out on this singularly enchanting sight, even if you have to make a detour.

Impruneta

If it doesn't happen to be iris season, take the main road out of Grassina, past the *Golf dell'Ugolino*, which is considered one of the most beautiful golf courses in Italy. Coming over a range of gently rolling hills which separates the Ema Valley from the Greve Valley, you reach Strada in Chianti, a village of little charm. At a junction just before Strada, you turn right to **Impruneta** (4 mi/6 km), a town renowned for its ceramics, which are shipped all over the world. As early as the 14th century, the town began to produce its famous Cotto tiles. Most of the workshops are family-owned even today; a few of them have gone over into a more industrial kind of production. In any event, it's well worth your time to visit the various workshops. Everyone is friendly and perfectly happy to let you observe the craftsmen at work. And if

97

you feel the urge to adorn your balcony with some particularly well-formed ceramic pots, don't hesitate to make the investment: the prices for hand-made pottery here are high, but they are still cheaper than they would be back home.

From a cultural historical perspective, Impruneta is of interest for its image of the Madonna, which is believed to perform miracles; it hangs in the **Basilica di S. Maria**. Because the Florentines had such a profound veneration for the *Madonna dell'Impruneta*, which was borne to Florence in solemn religious processions in times of war, plague, droughts and other catastrophes, Impruneta became, in the Middle Ages, a religious center of the whole Northern Chianti region. Also dating from the Middle Ages is the festival of San Luca, held annually in mid-October with horse races, a fair, and general to-do.

Above: For centuries, Impruneta has been a center for ceramics. Right: Under the arcades on the main square of Greve.

From Impruneta you can get back to the Via Chiantigiana by way of Il Ferrone, either by driving to Strada and continuing on through Chiocchio, or by opting for the somewhat longer route over the Passo dei Pecorai to Le Bolle, where both roads converge. Just past the "Shepherds Pass," the SP 3 leads off to the 10th-century **Castello di Vichiomaggio**, sitting atop a hill overlooking Le Bolle. Only one tower, dating back to the 13th century, remains of the original structure. The rest was converted into a villa during the 16th century.

The Chiantigiana continues on toward Greve, past the castles of Verrazzano and Uzzano. The **Castello di Verrazzano** once belonged to the family of the seafaring Giovanni di Verrazzano, who was the first person to explore the Atlantic Coast of North America in 1524. Of the old 13th-century mansion, only a turreted tower now remains. Today, Verrazzano is one of the most prized vineyards of Chianti.

The same goes for the **Castello di Uzzano**. It sits like a crown atop the mountain overlooking the terraced vineyards, which produce the "Niccolò di Uzzano." This castle, too, belonged to an aristocratic family, one scion of which was the eponymous Niccolò; the Uzzani played an important role during the days of the Republic in Florence.

Greve in Chianti

Greve is not a particularly attractive town; the only thing worth seeing is the arcaded marketplace, the Piazza Giovanni da Verrazzano, which lies at the center of town like an extended triangle. Located at the point where the road from Florence intersects with the one connecting the Greve Valley with the Upper Arno Valley, Greve has been an important trade center from the very beginning. It is particularly well-known for its wild boar delicacies, which you can buy in

pretty shops beneath the arcades. At one end of the marketplace stands **Santa Croce**, a church rebuilt in neoclassical style in the middle of the 19th century. It contains a triptych by Bicci di Lorenzo and a 14th-century *Annunciation* of the Florentine School.

A small road leads from Greve to the castle **Montefioralle**, which is nestled amidst cypresses, vineyards ands olive trees about a mile (1.5 km) outside town. If you wish to end your Chianti trip here, you can take the 13-mile (19 km) long road running between Greve and Figline Valdarno, which takes you through the Arno Valley back to Florence.

From Greve to Radda

Two roads lead from Greve to Radda in Chianti. One takes you on the Via Chiantigiani through oak forests, olive groves, and vineyards to **Panzano** (4 mi/6 km). This little town has its roots in the days of the Etruscans; it was later an arena for the contests and strife between Guelphs and Ghibellines. During the 1950s, it developed into a favorite home away from home for the British, who fell in love with Panzano's dream location high above the valley and the truly magnificent surroundings. Today, however, you'll find that the Germans and Swiss have edged them out.

A little ways past Panzano, a road branches off to the left to **Pieve di San Leolino**. This beautiful Romanesque church was first mentioned in a manuscript in 982. During the 12th and 13th centuries it was enlarged, again in the Romanesque style. In the 16th century it was further decorated with the beautiful portico, which rests on five sandstone pillars. The inside of the church is ornamented with works by Sienese painters.

Just past Panzano, the SP 2 turns left and leads past Lucarelli and the Castello di Monterinaldi to Radda (7 mi/10 km).

The other way to get from Greve to Radda is certainly longer, but particularly attractive for its beautiful scenery. Just

outside of Greve, turn left (toward La-mole), and follow the road past vin-eyards, olive groves and beautiful estates until you get to the **Villa di Vignamag-gio** (16th century). It's said that this was once the home of the Monna Lisa del Giocondo, whose mysterious smile was made world-famous by Leonardo da Vinci. Through pine avenues and chest-nut groves, the road continues on to the pretty village of Lamole, and from there to **Volpaia**, once a fortified medieval town with a castle believed to have been built around the year 1000.

For centuries, this town had to suffer in the fighting between Florence and Siena, both of which valued it for its strategic location atop a hill right on the border of the two city-states. When the Republic of Siena fell in 1555, Volpaia lost its mili-tary importance. Today, Volpaia still boasts some of its old city walls and sev-eral beautifully restored medieval build-

Above: A Chianti winery. Many vintners take in paying guests.

ings. The most important of these is the 15th-century **Commenda di S. Eufro-sino**, today a venue for exhibitions and other cultural events.

Radda in Chianti

From Volpaia, it's 4 miles (6 km) to Radda in Chianti, which lies on a hill 1,743 feet (533 m) above the valleys of Pesa and Arbia. Today, Radda is home to the headquarters of the *Consorzio del Gallo Nero*. The town is quite small and lives from viticulture and the wine trade, as well as the tourist trade that's spurred by its incredibly beautiful surroundings. Radda has managed to maintain much of its medieval character. As the seat of the Chianti League's *Podestà* (since 1415) it attracted the aristocracy of the surround-ing area, who built elegant homes around the dignified **Palazzo del Podestà**. The palace, which was built early in the 15th century and expanded again later, is adorned with the coats-of-arms of the various city fathers.

From Radda to Siena

From Radda it is 7 miles (10 km) to **Badia a Coltibuono**. Formerly a Benedictine monastery, this site is endowed with a beautiful, albeit heavily restored, Romanesque church. Nowadays, the adjacent monastery hosts cultural events, as well as furnishing a home for the winery. Right next to it, you can find a fine restaurant with a magnificent view of the surrounding forests.

At the junction of the road to Montevarchi, if you follow the SS 408, the so-called "Castle road of Chianti," to the right you'll come to Gaiole in Chianti, a little wine-making village surrounded by hills covered with grapevines. Long ago, the **Castello di Meleto** (2 mi/3 km) controlled the access roads to Gaiole from its lofty vantage point. Of all the fortifications in the Chianti League, these here are the best-preserved original structures.

Just past Meleto, a left turn onto a small road leads to the **Castello di Brolio**. Built in its present form in the latter part of the 15th century, this edifice belongs to the well-known family Ricasoli Firidolfi, who have ruled this region since the 12th century. One of their ancestors, Bettino Ricasoli, created the original formula for Chianti wine. Near Brolio, in the little village of S. Regolo, there's a charming *trattoria* that serves good local cuisine. A connecting road leads in a westerly direction back to the SS 408, which will bring you to Siena (20 mi/30 km).

Castellina in Chianti

Another road from Radda to Siena leads through Castellina in Chianti, which is situated atop a hill high above the valleys of Arbia, Elsa and Pesa. The town was once part of the defensive fortifications which Florence had erected in a line from the Elsa to the Arno Valley. After a turbulent history against a backdrop of power struggles between Florence and Siena, Castellina lost its strategic importance when the Republic of Siena finally fell, and the fortifications were gradually incorporated into residential buildings.

Today this town, like most Chianti mountain villages, suffers from a decline in population caused by migration into the cities. Although it hasn't been altogether spared architectural modifications, it's been able to retain at least parts of its original structure. In the center of town stands the medieval castle, which today houses the city's administration. A little ways out of town you'll find a large Etruscan grave site, the **Tumulo di Monte Calvario**, which is thought to date back to the 7th century BC and is among the most interesting excavations in the Chianti region. The grave is testimony to the former importance of the spot due to its geographical location between the Arno Valley and Volterra.

VIA CASSIA

The Via Cassia (SS 2) runs parallel to the Florence-Siena expressway, and, since it touches upon a larger number of towns than the Chiantigiana, there tends to be more traffic on this route. The old Roman Road mostly follows the mountain crests and offers one magnificent panoramic view after the other.

Leave Florence by taking the Via Senese in the direction of Poggibonsi. Between Certosa del Galluzzo and San Casciano in Val di Pesa, just past the "Florence American Cemetery and Memorial" (built by American architects in 1959), a little road leads off to the right toward **Sant'Andrea in Percussina**. There, in the Villa Albergaccio, Niccolò Machiavelli sat in 1513 and brooded over his great treatise, *Il Principe* (*The Prince*). The Osteria which this great political author once frequented continues to serve commendable cuisine to this day.

The little town of **San Casciano Val di Pesa** owes its importance to its location at the intersection of two important thoroughfares: one connecting Florence with Rome, the other connecting the Pesa and the Greve Valleys. As well as the ruins of the medieval fortress, the village contains remnants of its old city walls. Interesting buildings to visit here include the collegiate church of S. Francesco and the Chiesa della Misericordia, built in the 14th century and restored in the 16th. The latter edifice contains the **Museo della Misericordia**, which displays works by Simone Martini, Taddeo Gaddi, Ugolino di Neri, and other masters.

Leaving San Casciano on the SS 2, you can continue on to **Tavarnelle Val di Pesa** (10 mi/15 km), which was a postal station on the old consular road even in Roman times. From here, you might consider detouring to **Badia di Passignano**.

Above: Coats-of-arms adorn the town halls – this one in Certaldo. Right: Fifteen of San Gimignano's towers have survived.

Turn off to the left and drive toward Sambuca until you see, amidst vineyards, wheat fields and forests, the turreted towers of the abbey, founded by Vallombrosian monks in the 11th century.

Only a few miles past Tavernelle is Barberino Val d'Elsa, with its remnants of medieval fortresses and the Palazzo of the Barberini. Just beyond that, you bear right on one of the several roads leading to Certaldo. One route that can be recommended leads through Bagnano, where you can visit the octagonal chapel of **S. Michele**. Its cupola is a replica of that atop Florence's Cathedral, scaled down at a ratio of 1:8.

The picturesque old town of **Certaldo** is situated on a hill above the modern city and is built entirely of red brick. The author of the *Decameron*, Giovanni Boccaccio, once lived here. His home now houses a center for Boccaccio studies and a library of his works. The red brick main street ends at the **Palazzo Pretorio** or **dei Vicari**. Its facade is adorned with a wealth of armorial bearings in terra-cotta and stone. The church of **SS Michael and Jacob** contains the grave of Boccaccio, as well as the remains of Beata Giulia. Legend has it that she had herself entombed alive for thirty years in a cell next to the church.

The SS 429 leads from Certaldo through the Elsa Valley to Siena. Around Poggibonsi and Colle Val d'Elsa, a number of roads from various directions converge to intersect, ultimately, at S. Gimignano. The shortest and fastest way to S. Gimignano is certainly the one through Poggibonsi, but the smaller roads are much more attractive.

SAN GIMIGNANO

The skyline of San Gimignano is probably the most-photographed image in all of Tuscany. Correspondingly, the tourist traffic in the city and its immediate surroundings is intense, particularly on wee-

kends and holidays, when even Italians swarm up the hill like locusts. One bit of advice: rather than spend hours in traffic trying to make your way up to the over-crowded parking lots by the city walls, it's vastly preferable to park your car lower down and take a beautiful walk across the fields toward the towers, which will serve as guideposts so that you can't lose your way.

San Gimignano is the medieval town *par excellence*; its 13th- and 14th-century structures remain practically unchanged. In the 10th century, this former Etruscan settlement took on the name of the ca-nonized Bishop of Modena, San Gimig-nano, who was supposed to have saved it from a barbarian invasion. In 1199 the town became a *libero commune*, a city with its own independent government. As a free republic, it fought against other nearby cities, Volterra in particular. Inner power struggles divided the population into two camps, who followed either the Guelph Ardinghelli or the Ghibellinese Salvucci. However, such contests were

effectively ended by the devastating plague of 1348, which weakened the city to such an extent that in 1354 it suc-cumbed to Florence once and for all.

San Gimignano had developed into a trade center along the old Frankish Road, which was used by pilgrims on their way to Rome as early as the 8th century. The cultivation of saffron, which was used to color valuable silks, ensured the city's considerable wealth. Most of the most important public buildings were con-structed during the period of the republic, as were the residential towers of the town's leading families, which served, in effect, as miniature fortresses. In the 14th century, there were 72 such residential towers; 15 of these are left today. Import-ant artists from Florence, Pisa, Lucca, and Siena were commissioned to dec-orate churches and homes with their works. In the 13th century, a double ring of city walls was erected to protect the fortified town center and the districts of San Matteo and San Giovanni. Much of it still exists today.

San Gimignano (pop. 8,000) has not grown much since the Middle Ages, and can easily be explored in a day. At the center of town is the **Piazza della Cisterna** with a magnificent fountain built in 1273, and Cathedral Square with the **Cathedral** (*Duomo*) and **Palazzo del Podestà**, both built in the 12th century. Arnolfo di Cambio is thought to be responsible for the **Palazzo del Popolo**, decorated with armorial bearings, at the south end of the square. Completed in 1288, it now houses the municipal administration. The tallest tower is that of City Hall, the *Torre Grossa* – after it was built, no one was allowed to construct anything taller. Most of the private family towers which have survived stand around these two squares. Worth seeing is the interior of the Romanesque Cathedral (remodeled and expanded by Guiliano da Maiano in the 15th century) with

Above: Fresco by Benozzo Fozzoli in San Gimignano's Cathedral. Right: View over the Piazza della Cisterna, San Gimignano.

works by Benozzo Gozzoli, Taddeo di Bartolo, Jacopo della Quercia and Barna da Siena. There are also two frescoes by Ghirlandaio in the chapel of Saint Fina.

The **Via S. Matteo** leads from Cathedral Square to the Porta S. Matteo. It's here and on the **Via S. Giovanni**, which connects the Piazza della Cisterna with the Porta S. Giovanni, that you'll encounter the main stream of tourist traffic, and souvenir shops and restaurants catering to tourists line these two streets.

If you don't care for these supermarkets of "typical Tuscan products" and seek more meaningful, impressions, you need only go a few steps further to experience the real, living San Gimignano, which actually does still exist, even today. And at night, when the busloads of tourists have left, quiet returns to the town. If then you stand on the city walls or on the ruins of the old fortress and take a look at the breathtakingly beautiful landscape around, you'll agree that this town has earned its reputation as one of the most beautiful sites in all of Tuscany.

VOLTERRA

About 20 miles (30 km) south of San Gimignano, you'll come to Volterra (16,000 residents), perched atop a bare hill between the Cecina and the Era Valleys. Here is a starker landscape, planted not with vineyards or olive groves, but divided up into wheat fields or sheep pastures. Volterra's hill consists of clay and sandstone from the Pliocene period (5-2 million years ago), which is subject to severe erosion. Landslides and mudslides are responsible for the phenomenon of the "Balze," deep crevasses which have already swallowed up entire Etruscan necropolises. The ancient settlement of Badia, located a bit outside of town, is also in danger of sliding into the depths.

The first settlements on this hill date back to the early Stone Age. After the Villanova period, these settlements united into a town that became one of the twelve members of the Etruscan League. Remnants of the wall enclosure, the Porta all'Arco adorned with mysterious heads (4th century BC), as well as the **Acropolis**, testify to the former importance of the one-time settlement of *Velathris*.

In the 3rd century BC, the Etruscan city was incorporated into the Roman Empire. Its residents assumed the Christian faith early on, and by the time the Roman Empire fell, Volterra already had a Bishop and was a substantial diocese. From the 12th century on, the city was a free commune with its own independent government and laws, until it came under Florentine rule in the year 1472.

Today, Volterra is a quiet, contemplative town that has maintained much of its medieval character. One of this town's hallmarks is the craft of alabaster processing, continuing a local tradition that reaches back to the days of the Etruscans.

The historic old town is entirely medieval in character. At its center is the **Piazza dei Priori**, considered to be one of the best-preserved medieval squares in

all of Italy. The monumental **Palazzo dei Priori** proudly shows off the armorial bearings of its Florentine governors. Construction on this building began in 1208, making this the oldest City Hall in Tuscany. On the other side of the plaza stands the 13th-century **Palazzo Pretorio** with its signature *Torre del Porcellino*, or Pigs' Tower. The medieval **tower houses**, such as those of the families Buonparenti and Bonaguidi on the Via Buonparenti, west of the Piazza dei Priori, contribute to the city's architecturally homogeneous appearance, a medieval flair which managed to withstand even the architectural improvements and additions of the Renaissance. The **Palazzo Minucci-Solaini** (northwest of the Piazza), for example, fits harmoniously between the medieval tower residences.

The Romanesque **Cathedral** and **Baptistery** are situated on the Piazza S. Giovanni, just a few steps further on. Far more interesting than the exterior of the cathedral are the art works inside, such as the marble ciborium on the altar; the

angels supporting the candelabra at either side of the high altar, by Mino da Fiesole; the Romanesque pulpit; and a 13th-century wooden sculpture showing Christ being taken off the cross. A fresco by Benozzo Gozzoli in the Cappella dell'Addolorata depicts the Adoration of the Magi. The green-and-white striped Baptistery is presently closed for restoration.

In Volterra, you can also see Roman ruins, such as the remains of the **Roman Theater** or the **Roman Baths**. At the highest point of the city stands the mighty **citadel**, the so-called *Maschio*, which Lorenzo the Magnificent had built for defense purposes. Today, this gigantic Renaissance building serves as a prison and can only be viewed from a distance. From the lovely park in front of the castle, however, you can take in the full effect of this impressive edifice.

In Volterra, don't miss the Etruscan **Museum Guarnacci**, which has grown

Above: Even in the days of the Etruscans, craftsmen tooled alabaster in Volterra.

out of the substantial private collection which Mario Guarnacci, a local prelate and scholar, donated to the city in 1761. The museum displays several of the most significant Etruscan artifacts found in the Volterra region. And don't omit to visit one or two of the **alabaster workshops** clustered in the Via Porta all'Arco to watch the modern techniques of this originally Etruscan craft. Of course, much of what's produced today out of this half-transparent gypsum is tourist-oriented kitsch, but you can occasionally find a pretty piece that makes a nice souvenir.

From Volterra, return to San Gimignano and then continue on to **Colle di Val d'Elsa** with its pretty medieval Upper City. From here, it's only 7 miles (10 km) to **Monteriggioni**; this town's well-preserved fortification wall crowns a ridge of hills. But Monteriggioni is far more charming seen from without than from within: the town has totally succumbed to tourism. From here, you can travel the last few miles to Siena along the Superstrada.

CHIANTI
Accommodations

GREVE: *MODERATE:* **Albergo del Chianti**, Piazza Mateotti, 86, tel: 055-853763. **Verrazzano**, Piazza Mateotti, 28, tel: 055-853189.

PANZANO: *LUXURY:* **Villa le Barone**, Via S. Leolino, 19, tel: 055-852215. south of Panzano, Renaissance villa in a dream location.

RADDA: *LUXURY:* **Relais Fattoria Vignale**, Via Pianigiani, 15, tel: 0577-738300. Elegant 18th-century manor house with a renowned winery. Often completely booked out. *MODERATE:* **Residence San Sano**, Loc. San Sano, Lecchi in Chianti, tel: 0577-746130. Old fortress, tastefully redecorated. **Podere Tirreno**, tel: 0577-738212. Warm atmosphere, friendly; good restaurant.

CASTELLINA IN CHIANTI: *LUXURY:* **Tenuta di Ricavo**, Loc. Ricavo, tel: 0577-740221. Quiet location, gorgeous surroundings. **Villa Casafrassi**, about 8 km south of Castellina toward Siena, tel: 0577-740621. Restored estate with large garden. *MODERATE:* **Hotel Salivolpi**, on the road to San Donato, tel: 0577-740484. Friendly and comfortable, reasonably-priced. **Belvedere di San Leonino**, Loc. di San Leonino, tel: 0577-740887. 8 km south of Castellina on the Chiantigiana. Beautiful house in wonderful setting, with swimming pool. Reserve in advance!

S. CASCIANO VAL DI PESA: *AGRITURISMO:* **Azienda Agricola Poggio Borgoni,** Via Borromeo, 134, tel: 055-828089/8228119.

SAN GIMIGNANO: *MODERATE:* **Hotel La Cisterna**, Piazza della Cisterna, 24, tel: 0577-940328. Converted monastery at the center of town, lovely rooms in 18th-century Florentine style. **Hotel Bel Soggiorno**, Via San Giovanni, 91, tel: 0577-940375. Gorgeous 13th-century building with attractive, comfortable rooms and in-house restaruant overlooking the surrounding countryside. **Villa Baciolo**, Loc. San Donato, tel: 0577-942233. 4 km south of S. Gimignano, medieval estate surrounded by vineyards and olive groves. **Le Renaie**, Loc. Pancole, tel: 0577-955044. Simple country hotel with pool and tennis courts.

YOUTH HOSTELS: **Ostello della Gioventù**, Via delle Fongi, 1, tel: 941991. No youth hostel membership necessary; no age limit.

CAMPING: **Il Boschetto**, Loc. S. Lucia, tel: 940352. Lovely location 2 km south of town.

VOLTERRA: *MODERATE:* **Villa Nencini**, Borgo S. Stefano, 55, tel: 0588-86386. **Etruria**, Via G. Matteotti, 32, tel: 0588-87377.

Restaurants

IMPRUNETA: I Cavallacci, Via Aldo Moro, 5. tel: 055-2313863. Lovely country estate with regional specialties, closed lunch and Sundays.

GREVE: Borgo Antico, Via Case Sparse,15, Lucolena. tel: 055-851024. Old Chianti specialties, mainly homemade. Closed Tue. **Casprini**, Via Chiantigiana, 40, Loc. Passo dei Pecorai. tel: 055-850716. Good charcoal-grilled steaks. Closed Wed. **La Novella**, Via Musignano, Loc. Pian del Quarto, San Polo. tel: 055-855195. Family trattoria in an old farmhouse. Reserve in advance; it's worth it!

PANZANO: Trattoria Montagliari, 2 km out of town, tel: 055-852014. A long-standing insider tip, so reserve ahead! Closed Mon.

RADDA: Villa Miranda, on the road to Villa, tel: 0577-738021. Country trattoria. Rustic atmosphere, rustic proprietor, and a little overpriced. Open daily. **La Bottega di Volpaia**, Loc. Volpaia, tel: 0577-738001. Bar-trattoria opposite the Castello, small kitchen, homemade salami. Open daily.

CASTELLINA IN CHIANTI: Albergaccio di Castellina, Via Fiorentina, 35, tel. 0577-741042. Cozy atmosphere, traditional cuisine. Closed Sun. **Pestello,** 7 km toward Poggibonsi, tel: 0577-740215. Very good rustic cooking.

SAN CASCIANO VAL DI PESA: Trattoria Mateuzzi, Via Certaldese, 8, Loc. Ponterotto, tel: 055-828090. Excellent peasant-style food; closed evenings and Tue. **La Tenda Rossa**, Piazza Monumento, 9/14, Cerbaia Val di Pesa, tel: 055-826132. One of Italy's leading restaurants, with corresponding prices. Closed Wed & Thu lunch.

CERTALDO: Osteria del Vicario, Via Rivellino, 3, tel: 0571-668228. Comfortable hotel with restaurant in a former monastery.

SAN GIMIGNANO: Trattoria Franco, Loc. San Donato, 12, tel: 0577-940540. Traditional Tuscan cooking in a former farmhouse. Reasonable prices. Closed Mon. **I Cinque Gigli**, in the **Hotel Pescille**, on the road to Volterra, tel. 0577-940186. In a former castle 4 km outside of S. Gimignano. Simple Tuscan specialties, prepared marvelously. Closed Wed. The hotel has lovely rooms in the moderate price category.

VOLTERRA: Trattoria del Sacco Fiorentino, P.zza XX Sett., 18, tel: 0588-88531. Classic Tuscan specialties in tasteful surroundings. Closed Wed. **La Tavernetta**, Via Guarnacci, 14, tel: 0588-87630. Good food, low prices. Closed Tue.

Museums

Museo etrusco Guarnacci, open daily 9:30 am-1 pm and 3-6:30 pm.

Tourist Information

GREVE: Ufficio del Turismo, tel: 055-853862. **RADDA: Chiantitourist**, tel: 0577-738215. **S. GIMIGNANO: Associazione Pro Loco**, Piazza del Duomo, 1, tel: 0577-940008. **VOLTERRA: A.P.T.**, Via Turazza (to the left of the Palazzo dei Priori), tel: 0588-86150.

PROUD CITIES
RICH ABBEYS
GREAT ART

SIENA
CRETE
VALDICHIANA
CASENTINO

SIENA – CITY OF THE PALIO

Since time immemorial, the Sienese have been known for their collective pride: Dante described them as a "proud people" as early as the 14th century. And they have reason to be proud. Siena has preserved its medieval appearance in a marvelous fashion, keeping up its traditions and barring the damaging inroads of modernity from its city center, which was made a pedestrian zone in 1956. This all helps to keep Siena one of the most fascinating cities in Tuscany, despite the hordes of tourists continually streaming through. Wandering through the narrow streets between the old brick facades, you sense that you're in a living Italian city which, for all of its art treasures, has a vibrant, rather than museum-like, air.

Siena's residents have always set special store by the beauty of their city. And because of this, the city is truly itself a work of art: it was built according to careful plan, following exact regulations and restrictions which had to be strictly upheld. In the 14th century, for example, the city government ruled that all of the windows on the Piazza del Campo had to

Preceding pages: The Crete: landscape of arid beauty. Left: Parade of flag-wavers at the Palio in Siena.

correspond to those of the Town Hall; no one was to be allowed to ruin the city's image by following his own whim. And this, like so many Sienese traditions, has been upheld to the present day.

Little is known of Siena's beginnings. Legend has it that Ascius and Senius, the sons of Rome's founder, Remus, were forced to flee their uncle Romulus and subsequently founded the city on three hills in Etruria. But this story, which dates back to the Renaissance, is merely a charming fiction invented by the Sienese themselves; although it explains why you see the symbol of the Roman she-wolf throughout the city.

The city didn't become truly important until the Middle Ages, when, located on the old trade route of the Frankish Road, it developed into a center of finance and trade. Resources of silver in the surrounding hills helped Siena to wealth and power. In 1472 one of the first great banks, Monte dei Paschi, was founded; it's still going strong.

In the 13th century, the Republic of Siena numbered some 20,000 inhabitants, which made it a major urban center for that period. It continued to flourish until the 16th century, although engaged in constant skirmishes and power struggles with its hated rival, Florence. In 1290, Florence was defeated in the Battle

of Montaperti; but a mere nine years later the Sienese were in turn beaten at Colle Val d'Elsa by Florentine troops. Under the Guelph regime of the "Council of Nine" which followed, important artists were drawn to the city, including Duccio di Buonisegna, Simone Martini, Pietro and Ambrogio Lorenzetti and the sculptor and architect Nicola and Giovanni Pisano. Their work helped shape the appearance of Siena today and made it a true city of the arts.

Decline set in with the Great Plague in 1348; Siena never fully recovered. For some 150 years, the city was shaken by inner unrest, which the efforts of Siena's great, and later canonized, heroes, St. Catherine and St. Bernard, or of Pope Pius II, a scion of the Sienese Piccolomini family, were able to dispel altogether. Finally, Emperor Charles V, an ally of Florence, stepped in, and in 1555 the city

was finally incorporated into the Medici Duchy of Tuscany. Although Siena has been forced into the secondary position of a provincial town ever since, you can still sense traces of its former enmity toward Florence, its onetime rival.

The city's silhouette is visible from afar, crowning the three hills over which Siena has spread in a roughly Y-shaped form, and dominated by the towers of the Town hall and the mighty, black-and-white striped Cathedral. The narrow medieval streets wind crookedly between houses of red-brown brick (artists use a pigment of this shade called "siena"), and lead up hill and down, so that it's hard to keep your sense of direction. At every corner in the Old Town, however, signposts are mounted so that you can always find your way back to the Campo or a number of the town's other major sights.

The Campo

Above: The shell-shaped Piazza del Campo in Siena is held to be one of the loveliest squares in the world.

Center of the city is a piazza which is one of the most beautiful in Italy, if not in

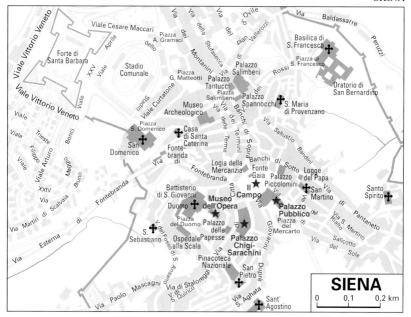

the entire world: the Piazza del Campo. It lies like a great seashell in the hollow between the three hills of the town. Its red brick cobbles divide it into nine clear sections; arranged around this in a semicircle are the lovely, clearly-ordered palaces. In some of the facades, groups of three pointed-arched windows separated by little columns reflect the prescriptions of the medieval building codes. At the upper edge of the piazza, roughly in the middle, splashes the **Fonte Gaia**, or happy fountain. The fountain's original reliefs by Jacopo della Quercia are displayed in the Palazzo Pubblico.

Slightly crooked, the Palazzo Pubblico, or Town Hall, forms the lower edge of the Campo. This gorgeous Gothic building, constructed between 1297 and 1310, perfectly reflects the pride and the unbroken will to freedom which has always characterized the people of Siena. Today, the palace still serves as the headquarters of the city administration.

In front of the palace's left wing is the **Cappella di Piazza**, built in 1352 after the Great Plague. Above it, the Town Hall tower, 288 feet high (88 m; 102 m, if you count its lightning rod), thrusts, brick-red and travertine-white, into the deep blue Sienese sky. This **Torre di Mangia**, named after a sexton whose name was Mangiaguadagni (money-eater), is the work of eight different architects. Lippo Memmi is supposed to have designed the broad travertine platform, which affords a marvelous view of the red rooftops of the city and the hilly countryside around. To the right of the Capella di Piazza, you pass a portrait bust of the money-hungry sexton as you enter the Cortile del Podestà, ornamented with coats of arms. From here, you can climb the 332 steps to the top of the tower – a laborious climb, but not to be missed, nonetheless.

Inside the **Palazzo Pubblico**, a tour of the upper floor (the ground floor belongs to the city administration, and is not open to the public) takes you through a series of marvelously-appointed rooms filled with some remarkable works of art. The

113

Sala del Mappamondo contains two famous frescoes: the Maestà by Simone Martini (executed in 1315, now newly-restored and, since January, 1994, visible in all its former glory), as well as a depiction of the knight Guido Riccio da Fogliano riding to the siege of Montemassi (1328), attributed to the same artist. This fresco is the first known large-scale landscape painting in European art. In the Sala della Pace, you can see the famous allegorical frescoes by Ambrogio Lorenzetti, depicting Just and Unjust Government and the effects of both in the city and the country. These were executed between 1338 and 1340, under the regime of the Council of Nine; it's to them that these marvellous images, which are also interesting depictions of daily life in the 14th century, are dedicated.

The Palazzo's other rooms contain countless other highlights of Sienese art;

Above: Participating in the Palio is an honor for every Sienese. Right: The race itself is a test of endurance for horses and riders.

it would be impossible to list them all here. Take time yourself to stroll through with open eyes and enjoy at your own pace the finer points of works by Sodoma, Taddeo di Bartolo, Jacopo della Quercia, and Sano di Pietro – to name only a few.

The Palio

When you leave the Palazzo Pubblico and come back out onto the broad Piazza del Campo, where a couple of idlers are perhaps loafing around, tired tourists sitting in the sun and resting their feet, or a couple of children splashing each other in the fountain, you may have trouble imagining that, twice a year, thousands of people crowd onto this square and overrun it completely. Every year since the 17th century, July 2 and August 16 have seen the *Palio delle contrade*, a horse race in honor of the Virgin Mary in which the city's 17 historic quarters compete with one another for the trophy. The Palio, or victory trophy, is a flag with the

image of the Virgin, designed anew every year by a different artist.

The Palio is the most fascinating festival in all of Tuscany. It plays an important part in the city's life throughout the year, and the few weeks before it see the preparations for the great event rising to an ever-increasing pitch of intensity.

A Sienese citizen is born into a *contrada*, or city neighborhood, and he remains a member of it his whole life long. A marked self-confidence and interaction according to certain fixed rules are characteristic of the individual contrade, whose members are bound into a fixed social unit. The notably low crime rate in Siena may well be a result of the special sense of community that this system engenders.

Practice races begin in the days leading up to the festival, during which the members of the different contrade start to heat up the competition with mocking songs and insults. By the time the big day rolls around, the tension in the city is palpable everywhere. As the space is too small for

all 17 to run at once, ten contrade participate in each palio: the seven who didn't fit in to the last race, as well as three who are chosen by lot. The horses, too, are chosen by lot; and the jockeys are professionals brought in from outside, who have to complete the breakneck race around the square bareback. Not surprisingly, there are quite often spectacular falls, and because of the hard, trampled-down sand surface, brought in especially for the race, these often result in bad injuries. But before the race begins, the horses and riders are blessed in the churches of whichever contrade they're riding for; the Archbishop of Siena blessed the individual teams, riding by his palace in a blaze of colorful historic costumes; and the Madonna in whose honor all this takes place certainly extends a protecting hand...

After a number of practice runs and a historic, festival parade, the race begins; it lasts hardly more than a minute. Even if you've got to sweat it out for a while on the Campo in the broiling noonday sun in

order to secure a good view of the colorful spectacle, the experience is truly worth the effort. Of course, you can always try to purchase one of the extremely expensive seats on the grandstand, in the windows or on one of the overcrowded balconies around the square; but these plum positions are usually sold out far in advance of the event itself.

After the race, there's a rush of relief which finds expression in cries of joy, enthusiastic embraces, or even tears. The victorious contrada marches through the city in triumph and gives thanks to the Mother of God in the church of the Madonna di Provanzano. And then the celebrations begin in earnest. There's one festive dinner after another, and even the victorious horse takes part, sitting at a place of honor – but unfortunately, all of this is only open to the Sienese.

Above: Alleyway in Siena. Right: The Duomo towers over the city's rooftops.

The Palaces

The gorgeous old palaces of Siena, testimony to the city's past wealth, are easily reached on foot. On the Banchi di Sotto, near the Campo, is the Renaissance **palace of the Piccolomini**, built in 1469, probably after plans by Rossellino. Since 1885, this building has housed the city archives, including certificates and documents designed and executed by famous Sienese artists. Opposite this is the entrance to the university, one of the oldest in Italy, which is documented as early as the year 1240. Today, it's housed in the former monastery of St. Vigilio, dating from the 16th century. A little further on is the **Logge del Papa**, which the Renaissance pope Pius II commissioned from the architect Antonio Federighi for his family.

At the intersection of the Banchi di Sotto with the Banchi di Sopra and the Via del Città is the three-arched **Loggia della Mercanzia**, a 15th-century Renaissance building lightened up with Late

Gothic elements. The Banchi di Sopra leads to the Piazza Salimbeni, where you can see the Gothic palace of the same name. To the right and left of it stand the Renaissance palaces Spanocchi (built in 1470 after designs of Giuliano da Maiano) and Tantucci (1548), respectively. Today, these three palaces house the venerable bank of Monte dei Paschi.

In the Via di Città, you can see the slightly crooked facade and the lovely inner courtyard of the **Palazzo Chigi-Saracini**, today the seat of the Accademia Musicale Chigiana, which was founded in 1923 by Count Guido Saracini. In summer, therefore, the building hosts quite good concerts. Inside, the palace houses a wonderful art gallery, but you can only visit it by special permission. Somewhat further on, at number 126, is another Piccolomini palace, also known as Palazzo delle Papesse because it was commissioned by the sister of Pope Pius II. Built in the style of the Florentine Renaissance, it was constructed between 1460 and 1465.

Siena's Churches

Siena has produced a number of great saints over the years, including the patron saint of Italy, Catarina di Siena. There's a small sanctuary in her honor at Vicolo del Tiratoio 15, a few steps away from the church of **San Domenico**. This powerful Gothic brick building, begun in 1226, is still a Dominican church even today. Inside, a reliquary contains the head of St. Catherine. The chapel dedicated to her also contains two noteworthy frescoes by Sodoma, depicting the Faint and the Ecstasy of St. Catherine. Other art treasures include the ciborium on the main altar and two wonderful marble angels.

Like the Dominicans, the Franciscans and the Augustines built their churches and monasteries at the edge of the city, probably because it gave them more room to construct and expand their large building complexes. On the Piazza di San Francesco is the Gothic **Basilica di San Francesco**, which contains wonderful frescoes by Ambrogio and Pietro Loren-

117

zotti. Its crypt now houses the Law School library.

Below the church, the upper story of the **Oratorio di San Bernardino** (a saint particularly beloved in Italy) shelters paintings by Sodoma. The church of the Augustine order, **Sant'Agostino** on Prato Sant'Agostino, also contains some marvelous works by Perugino, Matteo di Giovanni, Sodoma, and Simone Martini.

The Duomo

Siena's most famous church is at the center of the city, only a few paces from the Campo. The Duomo, or Cathedral, took some 200 years to build, and the mighty edifice you see today is only a portion of the building the ambitious Sienese originally had in mind. It was, in fact, to be merely the transept of a huge new cathedral; but all that was actually realized of this mammoth edifice were the walls that you see to the right of the present Duomo. The devastating plague of 1348, high costs and political developments led to the abandoning of construction. What remained is a masterpiece of Italian Gothic, and certainly impressive enough in its own right.

Giovanni Pisano was the artist responsible for the Duomo's signature green-and-white striped, ornate facade (1284-1296). The originals of his monumental statues and busts are displayed in the cathedral museum. The central bronze portal was executed by the contemporary artist Enrico Manfrini in 1958; the mosaics were completed in the late 18th century. At the right side of the building is the campanile, or bell tower, executed in the same colors of contrasting marble. The windows grow increasingly larger from bottom (one) to top (six).

Inside, the church is veiled in a mystical twilight, with echoes of an oriental

Right: Duccio di Buoninsegna's famous "Maestà" in the cathedral museum in Siena.

mosque in the 26 two-colored columns, the blue ceiling with its gold stars, and the multicolored walls. The ornate floor, which occupied 40 artists for two centuries, is executed in a number of different techniques, from mosaics through sgraffito to marble inlay. The most valuable sections are protected by a wooden floor, and unveiled only between August 15 and September 15. Looking down from a moulding over the columns are the busts of Christ, 172 Popes, and, under them, 36 Emperors from the 15th and 16th centuries. The stoup by the main entrance is the work of Antonio Federighi.

The Duomo's most important work of art, however, is the famous octagonal marble pulpit by Nicola Pisano and his son Giovanni (with some collaboration from such other artists as Arnolfo di Cambio and Donato). A coin automat operates the light, providing 60 seconds of illumination on the masterfully executed reliefs of Biblical scenes. The expressive sculpted figures are full of life, their faces carved with individuality – you can see their descendants on the streets of modern-day Siena.

Other noteworthy art works include the main altar by Baldassarre Peruzzi, the bronze statue of John the Baptist by Donatello (on the left side of the transept, in the Cappella di Giovanni Battista), the Piccolomini Tomb in the right side aisle by the entrance to the campanile, and, above all, the Libreria Piccolomini (left side aisle) with its decorative frescoes by Pinturicchio (1505-1507) depicting scenes from the life of Pope Pius II.

The Baptistery lies below the apse of the cathedral, where the "Sabatelli Steps" (1451) lead down to the Piazza S. Giovanni. The upper part of this baptismal church was never completed; its clearly-organized facade includes parts of the cathedral's apse. Mighty columns, which also carry the weight of the cathedral choir, support the frescoed ceiling. The font is a 15th-century masterpiece, sport-

ing reliefs by Jacopo della Quercia, Donatello, and Ghiberti, among others.

Within a portion of the walls of the never-completed "New Duomo," the **Museo dell'Opera del Duomo** makes its home. This is also the entrance to the unfinished Duomo facade, which commands a wonderful view of Siena and the surrounding countryside. On the museum's ground floor, you can see the originals of Pisano's sculptures for the cathedral; but the showpiece is on the upper floor: the Maestà by Duccio di Buoninsegna. Painted on both front and back, this altarpiece, executed between 1308 and 1311, was honored after its completion with three days of festivities, and adorned the cathedral's main altar for the next 200 years. It represents, in fact, the first masterpiece of the great age of Sienese painting in the 14th century. While the main image is still locked in the conventions of tradition, depicting a rigid figure of an enthroned Madonna against a background of gold and strictly symmetrical figures of saints, the smaller side panels depict scenes from the life of Christ with minute exactitude.

On the top floor of the museum you'll find the painting of the *Madonna with the Big Eyes* (first half of the 13th century). The Sienese swore a vow before this image before marching into the Battle of Montaperti.

Back on the Piazza del Duomo, you can see, to the left of the Duomo, the neo-Gothic, 18th-century Archbishop's Palace. Opposite it is the facade of the hospital Spedale di Santa Maria delle Scale, which was constructed as a hospice for pilgrims in the days of the Frankish Road, perhaps as early as the 9th century. This building contains a wealth of art treasures, which are unfortunately falling more and more into disrepair.

In addition to the particularly important buildings discussed here, Siena contains a wealth of other churches, palazzi, and museums. There's plenty to discover here, and anyone who comes prepared to spend a little more time will soon discover that the city, which may appear

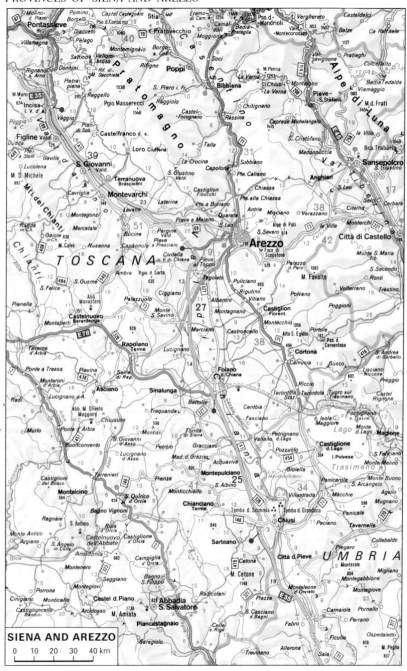

SIENA AND AREZZO

0   10   20   30   40 km

strict and a little forbidding at first glance, only begins to unfold its charms to someone who spends a few hours wandering around. Furthermore, the shopping here is good, whether you're in the market for handicrafts or culinary specialties such as wild boar salami, wine, olive oil or the famous Sienese panforte, a kind of hard fruitcake with almonds, all of which make excellent gifts as well as souvenirs. If you'd like to sample these delicacies yourself, seek out the Piazza del Mercato below the Campo, where every morning, except Sundays and Mondays, there's a produce market.

THE CRETE

South of Siena, the landscape changes its character. The fertile, wooded hills of Chianti give way to barren, arid mounds stretching like the waves of a frozen sea all the way to the horizon. Crete Senesi is the name of this region, a land of heavy, clayey, and often eroded earth that can only be used for growing grain or grazing sheep. A naked, bitter country, but marvelous for its breadth, for the way you can see for miles without obstacle into the distance. Lone farmhouses atop a hill, a few solitary cypresses or pines set as if to underline the junction of two roads or mark the summit of a rise of land: these select, Spartan visual elements help make this land a veritable El Dorado for photographers with a good eye.

The Crete has a different face for every season, determined by the rhythm of sowing and harvesting. In spring, the broad wheat fields are a tender green; in summer, a rich yellow gold; and in autumn, when the fields are shorn by harvesters and plowed anew, a spectrum of earth tones ranging from rust-red through every shade of brown into a tired gray. Interspersed with these are lush fields covered with spring flowers or thinly scattered with a covering of grass, providing fodder for herds of grazing sheep.

Long ago, small, fortified towns developed in this landscape, visible from afar across the hills. The best-known of these are described below; but note that voyages of exploration, particularly along roads highlighted in green, promising particularly lovely landscapes, are, in this region, generally rewarding.

Truffles and Monastic Spirits

The first tour starts in **Asciano**, some 17 miles (25 km) south of Siena, reachable on the scenic road SS 438. At the center of this picturesque medieval village high above the Ombrone Valley, there's an interesting museum with works by Duccio, Matteo di Giovanni, and Ambrogio Lorenzetti. There's a little anecdote about Asciano which Dante mentions in his Inferno: a certain Caccia d'Asciano ran through his vast fortune in a very short time due to his predilection for having his meals decorated with gold coins, which he then spit out as if they were olive pits. While Asciano's inhabitants today have less eccentric eating habits, there is one very special, and almost equally costly, specialty that dominates their menus: truffles, which we'll discuss in more depth later.

From Asciano, go on to **Chiusure**, a small fortified town of red brick, with a magnificent view over the hills and the nearby monastery complex of Monte Oliveto Maggiore. As you proceed toward the monastery, you'll have opportunity to notice the small landslides, triggered by erosion, which are typical of the Crete and which are particularly prevalent around Monte Oliveto.

Surrounded by a grove of cypresses centuries old, the Benedictine monastery of **Monte Oliveto Maggiore** was founded in 1319 by the Sienese lawyer Giovanni Tolomei, who at the age of 40 withdrew from the world and retired to his estate south of Siena in order to live out the rest of his life in prayer and atone-

ment. Following the rules of the Benedictine order, the monks here busied themselves with farming the surrounding lands while at the same time elevating their monastery into a center of religious, scientific and artistic study. Famous scholars were trained here, major artists encouraged. As a result, the walls of the main cloister bear frescoes by Luca Signorelli and Sodoma depicting scenes from the life of St. Benedict.

The abbey is rich in other art treasures, as well: the choir pews with inlays by Fra Giovanni da Verona, richly illuminated music books, a huge old library, and everywhere paintings and frescoes. In one room by the exit from the cloister, the monks sell their own products from the monastery, including olive oil, honey, herbal liquors, posters, books, and ceramics. The former stables are now a hotel with more than 50 beds. If you enter

Above: Wonderful fresco in the cloister of Monte Oliveto Maggiore. Right: In Murlo's Etruscan Museum.

the abbey across the drawbridge of the turreted tower, the first thing you'll see is a relief of the Madonna from the school of Della Robbia; when you leave the lovely Renaissance complex, you'll be sent on your way with a blessing from a relief of St. Benedict, also by Della Robbia.

Not far from Monte Oliveto Maggiore is the village of **S. Giovanni D'Asso**, which is famous for its truffles. Every year on the third Sunday in November there's a sales exposition of these rare white fungi, and every year the community donates a particularly fine specimen to someone who's made notable efforts toward world peace in the year before.

From Monte Oliveto Maggiore, it's about 6 miles (9 km) to **Buonconvento**, which lies at the point where the Arbia flows into the Ombrone. The village's medieval center is well-preserved, and a person strolling through its narrow streets could well imagine he'd been transported back in time into the Middle Ages.

The Etruscans of Murlo

If you follow the Via Cassia about 8 miles (12 km) back toward Siena, you'll come, at Lucignano d'Arbia, to a small road leading off to the left toward the old Etruscan settlement of **Murlo**. It's said of this tiny, beautifully-restored village that its residents have a remarkable resemblance to their Etruscan forbears; and DNA tests on bones unearthed at nearby excavation sites are supposed to have proved that the genetic makeup of this long-vanished people has been amazingly well preserved through the millennia in the people of Murlo. The media, of course, wasn't going to overlook this sensation; and it is true that, if you place photographs of the pizzeria owner, his mother, and other villagers next to portrait heads of Etruscan statues and frescoes, you can't deny that there is a certain similarity. More interesting, on the whole, is the very informative, well-laid-out, and justifiably renowned museum. Not only does it display finds from the excavations on the surrounding hills; it also explores and presents antique techniques of tool or jewelry manufacture.

In the land of fine wine

From Murlo, an unpaved dirt road leads for some 17 miles (25 km) through wonderful oak, beech and chestnut woods and past fine views to **Montalcino**. You can also reach this village by following the less spectacular route of taking the SS 2 and turning off, shortly after Buonconvento, onto the SP 45, which leads up to the village perched on a hilltop 1831 feet (560 m) high, surrounded by vineyards. Here's where the famous – and expensive – wine Brunello di Montalcino is produced; you can sample the product to your heart's content in the restored fortress of the town. But the village isn't only worth visiting for the wine. There's also, for example, the Palazzo dei Priori, a remarkably narrow 13th-century building with an exaggeratedly high tower; or the Diocesan Museum with its 14th-century wooden sculptures; or the lovely frescoes in the church of S. Agostino. It's also lovely just to stroll through the medieval alleyways, past stores selling wine, oil, honey, or ceramics, and take in the marvelous view out over the countryside. In the summer (second half of July), a theater festival takes place here; in October, there's the *Sagra del Tordo* with archery competitions and parades in historic costumes.

To the south of Montalcino rises the Amiata Massif. Driving toward this elevation, after about 7 miles (10 km), you come to one of the loveliest Romanesque monastery churches in all of Tuscany. Standing on a spacious meadow near Castelnuovo dell'Abate, tucked away in

the hilly countryside, is **Sant'Antimo**, a beautiful church built on simple, strong lines out of travertine and alabaster, with a mighty campanile echoed by a nearby cypress in a most photogenic manner. Inside, this three-nave church from the 12th century is light and airy. Pillars and rafters bear the weight of the vaulted ceiling, and their capitals are adorned with remarkable representations of animal heads, plants, and geometric figures. Especially in autumn, when the stark noonday sun angles in through the side windows, the room is enveloped in a feeling of mystic warmth.

Lunchtime in **Castelnuovo dell'Abate** means a stop at the bar and trattoria del Bassomondo, where you can buy homemade cheese, sausage, and homegrown Rosso di Montalcino to take with you, or simply dine on the spot.

From here, a winding road leads on to Ansidónia, where you can choose whether you'd prefer to continue your trip south into the Amiata region or return to Siena by way of the Cassia. In the

heat of summer, the best bet is to detour into the cooler mountain air. Here, you can spend a night or two in the villages Abbadia di S. Salvadore, Pian Castagnaio, S. Fiora, or Arcidosso, all of which lie on the road that curves around the Amiata, and all of which are worth a visit (see the chapter on Grosseto for details). Center of the area is the 5,683-foot (1,738 m) extinct volcano, which has countless springs that deliver water all the way to Siena and Grosseto; around it, particularly to the northeast, the region is rich in minerals and large geothermic fields which are increasingly being used for technical purposes. In places, stinking drilling rigs and steam springs interfere with the lovely landscape, but overall the mountains still have plenty of beautiful spots to offer, where you can hike for hours through an intact natural landscape.

Above: S. Antimo is one of the most beautiful monastery churches in Tuscany. Right: A holiday mood.

Another result of the area's literally volcanic roots is evident in **Bagni S. Filippo**, where warm, sulphurous water flows over a kind of frozen waterfall of calcium into shallow, natural pools. It's a marvellous feeling to sit in one of theses and get a natural massage from the powerful streams of water. There's also an old-fashioned hotel in the village with a thermal swimming pool, but the strong and unmitigated smell of sulphur may not be to everyone's taste.

There's another thermal bath to the north, near Via Cassia and shortly before you get to S. Quircio d'Orcia. A large stone pool filled with spring water at a temperature of 125F (52C) takes the place of the more usual piazza at the center of **Bagno Vignoni**. It's said that the Romans were in the habit of taking the waters here – an inscription states that they dedicated the healing sulphurous waters to the nymphs. The strange, almost other-worldly atmosphere created by the juxtaposition of the still water and the old houses that surround it led the

Russian film director Tarkowski to film parts of his classic movie *Nostalghia* in this town. Today, however, swimming in the old stone pool is forbidden. Those suffering from rheumatism, arthritis, or nerve infections can try to alleviate their pains by paying the admission fee to enter the thermal pool in the Hotel Posta.

S. Quircio d'Orcia, a pretty little town over the river valleys of the Orcia and Asso, contains the Romanesque Collegiata with a beautiful portal attributed to Giovanni Pisano. Other noteworthy sights here include the Chigi and Pretorio palaces.

At this point, the SS 146 branches off in an easterly direction. After nearly 7 miles (10 km) you come to **Pienza**, named for Pope Pius II Piccolomini, who was born at the beginning of the 15th century in the town then known as Corsignano. With an in-depth humanistic education and a broad range of interests, the Pope wanted to transform the place of his birth into an ideal city in the Renaissance sense, according to plans by the architect Rossellino. Unfortunately, he died before his plan could be completely realized; yet one can still describe the central Piazza Pio II with the cathedral, the Palazzi Piccolomini and Vescovile, and the Palazzo Communale with its open loggia as a successful, and unified, work of art. Clever building in a trapezoidal form leads the little piazza to appear much larger than it is. The apse of the Cathedral S. Maria Assunta was built out over the slope; its supports were replaced during the present century, but still haven't proven to be as stable as one would wish.

The Casa dei Canonici, to the left of the church, houses the Museo della Cattedrale, which displays a good collection of liturgical objects.

A true masterpiece is the Piccolomini Palace, modeled on the Palazzo Rucellai in Florence. The square interior courtyard is surrounded by a portico; while the Hanging Gardens on the palace's south side command a marvellous view out over the Orcia valley. Another, more

pieces they've written and staged themselves, generally with a touch of social criticism, in the second half of July.

Like nearly every city in this area, **Montepulciano** was long a bone of contention between Siena and Florence until it finally went over to Florence in 1390. If you approach the city from the west, the first thing you'll see, in a lonely field at the foot of the hill of Montepulciano, at the end of an avenue of cypress trees, is the Renaissance church of S. Biagio. The temple-like travertine building, built in the form of a Greek cross topped with a dome, was the greatest work of Antonio da Sangallo the Elder (1455-1531).

From there, it's uphill all the way to the medieval village, where the greatest buildings demonstrate the style of the Florentine Renaissance. The best place to see this is on the broad, red-paved Piazza Grande at the highest point of the city, surrounded by lovely old palaces. Built in the second half of the 14th century, the turreted Town Hall, its facade allegedly designed by Michelozzo in 1424, is reminiscent of the Palazzo Vecchio in Florence. Its tower commands a breathtaking panoramic view of the whole area. To the left of the Town Hall, some steps lead up to the Duomo which was built in the 17th century on the site of the former parish church. Most notable elements here are the triptych over the high altar, painted around 1403 by Taddeo di Bartolo, depicting the Ascension of the Virgin, and the reclining figures on the tomb of Bartolomeo Aragazzi, secretary to Pope Martin V, which have been ascribed to Michelozzo, as well.

modest palace in Pienza was commissioned by Cardinal Ammanati at the behest of his friend, Pope Pius himself.

By an unfortunate coincidence, Pius II and his architect died in the same year, 1464; after this date, the *città ideale* gradually lapsed back into the sleepy insignificance of a small country town. But visitors may want to take note of the Club delle Fattorie, a kind of mail-order service for the very best things in Italian culinary delicacies (located in the Via del Cancellino 6, tel. 748419). Pienza, in fact, is generally a shopper's paradise for any one looking to buy local products such as oil, wine, herbs, or goat cheese.

Halfway along the road to Montepulciano is **Monticchiello**, a small village that's almost too perfectly renovated. This town has become known for its *Teatro Povera* (Poor Theater); since 1967, the village residents have presented

Opposite the Town Hall, Sangallo the Elder built the Palazzo Contucci, although the building's top floor was completed by Baldassarre Peruzzi. The palace stands atop the oldest wine cellar vaults in the city, which are open to the public. The vats of the famous *Vino Nobile di Montepulciano* were once reserved solely for the city's richest families of ar-

Above: Partial view of the "ideal city" of Pienza. Right: Montepulciano in winter – an unusual view of the city.

istocrats, who were evidently able to afford to employ the most important architects of their time. The Tarugi family, for instance, commissioned Sangallo the Elder with the building of their travertine palace; and the elegant fountain in front of it, with the two griffons and two lions holding the Medici coat-of-arms, is also the work of this master. Other families also commissioned marvelous Renaissance palaces, including the Avignonesi, Cervini, Neri, Orselli (whose former home is today the Museo Civico of the town), and others. In addition to these palaces, there are a number of interesting churches, such as Sant'Agnese, built on the site of a church which was constructed by the saint herself in 1306; the 14th-century Santa Maria dei Servi, with a Gothic facade and Baroque interior by Andrea Pozzo; and Sant'Agostino, with a facade and a group of terra-cotta sculptures by Michelozzo.

The house at Via Poliziano 5 was the birthplace of the Renaissance poet and thinker Poliziano. But the Poliziani is also what the town's inhabitants call themselves, derived from the original, early medieval name of the city, Mons Politianus. And the Poliziani like a good celebration. Like Siena, Montepulciano also has contrade, and these vie with each other in the *Bravio delle Botti* on the last Sunday in August, which involves rolling heavy wine-vats up the steep streets of the town. August 15th sees a costume festival called the *Bruscello*. Since 1976, furthermore, the German composer Hans Werner Henze has organized a summer music festival here, the Cantiere Internazionale dell'Arte (July/August).

From Montepulciano, it's not far to **Chianciano Terme**, one of Tuscany's largest thermal baths, supposed to be particularly effective for liver complaints. The selection of hotels here is impressive; since 1915, they've all been under the same private management. Research labs, clinics, bathing facilities – the town has everything a spa guest could desire, but little to offer the average sight-seeing visitor. However, a museum

127

is under construction which will display Etruscan artifacts from the area.

A similar museum is the main attraction in **Chiusi**, which is situated on a hill past the Chiana valley, a few miles from the Autostrada del Sole. Chiusi was a member of the Etruscan twelve-city alliance; numerous artifacts from this period are preserved in the archaeological museums of Tuscany. One of the most famous of these is the Museo Archeologico Nazionale in Chiusi; it exhibits Etruscan art objects and tools, as well as some Greek vases. This establishment is currently being reorganized and modernized. A great many Etruscan graves have been found in the area around Chiusi – the best-known of these are the Tomba della Scimmia, della Pellegrina and del Granduca – and the museum offers guided tours of the sites. Not far from the Tomba del Granduca is the

Above: Valdechiana cows spend all of their brief lives in their stalls. Right: The extensive Convento delle Celle in Cortona.

Lago di Chiusi, where you can opt to take a more or less refreshing swim.

THE VALDICHIANA

As it was in the days of the Etruscans, the Chiana valley remains the grain center of Tuscany. It's this area which produces the white Chianina cattle with their marvelous meat, which is used for the renowned *bistecca fiorentina*. At Arezzo, the Chiana valley branches off from the Arno valley to the south. The valley itself is fairly densely populated and traversed by the Autostrada del Sole, the Milan-Rome railway line, and a whole network of roads. But clinging to the hillsides on either side of the valley, which has in the course of the centuries undergone everything from repeated floods to malaria epidemics, are old villages which are definitely worth exploring.

The SS 71 leads along the east side of the Chiana valley from Chiusi to Arezzo, which takes you on a brief detour through Umbria and then leads you, at Casti-

glione del Lago, along the banks of the lake of Trasimeno. The lake is lovely to look upon, but a swim here isn't likely to yield much in the way of refreshment, as it's fairly shallow and warm.

Cortona

Some 17 miles (25 km) from Castiglione del Lago is the town of Cortona (population 22,000), which perches on a ledge of rock high over the Chiana valley. The road leads steeply up the olive-grown slopes of Monte Sant'Egidio, ending in a parking lot just below the city itself, where you have to leave your car. From here, it's a bit of a trek to the medieval city center, but the effort is amply rewarded by a fabulous view out over the valley extending all the way to the Amiata massif.

The medieval city of Cortona was built upon the ancient Etruscan settlement Curtuns, to which the old city walls still bear witness. In 1538, the town was incorporated into the duchy of Tuscany.

Cortona is a provincial town full of atmosphere; the best way to get a flavor of it is simply to wander aimlessly through its narrow streets. Center of town is the **Piazza della Repubblica**, from which a huge outdoor staircase leads up to the **Palazzo Communale** (13th century) – an ideal place from which to observe the activity on the piazza itself. Things are all uphill and downhill in Cortona, through old alleyways dating back to the days of the Etruscans; the only level street is the short Via Nazionale, which leads to the Piazza Garibaldi with its broad observation terrace.

To the right of the Palazzo Communale is the Piazza Signorelli with the 13th-century Palazzo Pretoria, which today houses the **Museo dell'Accademia Etrusca**, a collection of Roman, Etruscan and Egyptian artifacts. Particularly notable here is the 16-armed bronze candelabra dating from the 5th century BC. A few steps further on, on the piazza in front of the cathedral, the small but noteworthy diocesan museum displays mas-

terpieces by Fra Angelica, Pietro Lorenzetti, Luca Signorelli and Sassetta.

The city's most important building, however, is about 2 miles (3 km) to the southeast, at the edge of town: the Renaissance church of the Madonna dei Calicinaio (15th/16th centuries).

Somewhat off the main road is the Capuchin monastery delle Celle, which St. Francis himself founded between 1211 and 1221. Dating from somewhere between the 4th and 1st centuries is the *Tanella di Pitagora* or Grave of Pythagoras, the best-known of the many Etruscan graves that have been found in the area.

Cortona was the home town of painters Luca Signorelli and Pietro da Cortona.

AREZZO

Only some 27 miles (40 km) separate Cortona from Arezzo. Traveling between

them, you pass **Castiglion Fiorentino**, a fortified town of Roman origin. Its town hall (16th century) houses a museum with paintings from the 13th-16th centuries, as well as valuable objects of gold.

Because it lay conveniently situated on main transportation routes, at the confluence of the Arno and Chiana valleys and near the Arno valley, **Arezzo** was already an important center of trade in the days of the Etruscans and the Romans, famous for the excellence of its artisans and craftsmen.

At first a free city-state, Arezzo was sold to Florence in 1384 for the sum of 40,000 gold florins. This ushered in a period of decline, brought about in part by the increasing swampiness of the Chiana valley. Since the 19th century, the city has seen a second flowering as an economic center; because of its internationally-known clothing and gold industries, it doesn't rely on tourism to the same extent as its neighbors.

Today, Arezzo (pop. 92,000) is a lively and pleasant little city. In particular, it

Above: The Corso Italia is one of Arezzo's busiest shopping streets. Right: Arezzo is a treasure-trove for lovers of antiques.

draws admirers of the painter Piero della Francesca, whose cycle of frescoes in the church of S. Francesco is indubitably among the high points of Renaissance painting. But the city has many other sights which make it worth a visit. In addition, it's a perfect point of departure for trips through the upper Arno valley (Casetino) and the upper Tiber valley.

The **Duomo S. Donato**, started in the late 13th century and completed in the 15th, stands at the highest point of a city that snakes around the hill in a great semicircle. Notable here are the 16th-century stained-glass windows by Guillaume de Marillat as well as the painting of Mary Magdalene by Piero della Francesca. In front of the cathedral there's a large area of green park, called the Prato, with lovely views out over the countryside; behind this is the Medici fortress which was commissioned by Cosimo I in the 16th century. A little below the Duomo, in the Via dell'Orto 28, is the house where Petrarch is supposed to have been born on July 20, 1304. The house, however, dates from the 16th century; today, it houses the Accademia Petrarca di Lettere, Arti e Scienze.

If you walk down the Corso Italia, the 13th-century Palazzo Pretorio, its facade adorned with armorial bearings, is on your right; today it's home to the city library. Diagonally across from it is the oldest church in Arezzo, the Romanesque **Pieve di Santa Maria**. Its unusual facade is divided into three rows of blind arches, while its mighty campanile with 80 windows in its three stories is locally known as the "Tower of 100 Holes." Inside, the church is simple, even severe. Behind the high altar is a polyptych by Pietro Lorenzetti. The church's apse gives onto the Piazza Grande, the city's asymmetric, sloping main square, surrounded by beautifully restored medieval houses. At one end, the square is bounded by Vasari's Palazzo delle Logge; while adjacent to the Pieve's choir is the Palazzo del Tribu-

nale with its tapering open-air staircase. Next to it is the Palazzo della Fraternità dei Laici. On the south side of the square there are a number of antique shops; Arezzo is a veritable Mecca for anyone interested in old furniture or gadgets. On the first weekend of every month, the city hosts one of the most important antiques markets in Italy; its stands spread throughout the entire Old City.

Below the Piazza Grande, the Via Mazzini and the Via Cavour will bring you to the Piazza **S. Francesco** with the famous church of the same name. Started in 1290, this building with the red brick facade has been continually expanded and renovated until into the present century. Its spacious interior, however, is pure Gothic, so that there's nothing to distract the eye from the wonderful frescoes. Most impressive of these are those of Piero della Francesca with the cycle of the legend of the cross, but you'll have to take this on faith: the work is currently being restored, and can only be seen in the form of small-scale reproductions.

Other monuments which attest to the city's cultural significance through the ages include the church of S. Domenico with a painting by Cimabue; Santa Maria delle Grazie with its Renaissance portico; a number of palaces; and the old city gates. The town's most important artists are represented in the Museum for the Middle Ages and Modernity. The former monastery of S. Bernardo, built on the remains of a Roman amphitheater, now houses the Archaeological Museum, displaying prehistoric finds as well as Etruscan and Roman artifacts. Here, too, you can see the famous "Aretin Vases," which were already highly esteemed in the days of the Roman Emperors. Incidentally, the Roman art patron Gaius Maecenas, a great friend of the Emperor Augustus whose name has entered many European languages as a synonym for "patron," was born in what was then

Above: The "Giostra del Saracino," a 14th-century equestrian tournament. Right: Piero della Francesca's "Pregnant Madonna."

known as Arretium. He and Petrarch aren't the only famous local sons: other Aretines include the musician Guido Monaco, who invented musical notation (11th century); the painter, architect and art historian Giorgio Vasari (16th century); and the writer and satirist Pietro Aretino (16th century). The city is also among the oldest university towns in Europe: its university was founded as early as the 13th century.

Another piece of the city's heritage is the **Giostra dei Saracino**, a festive tournament that's been staged since the 14th century and probably dates back to the time of the Crusades. Two representatives of each of the four city neighborhoods lower their lances and ride against the figure of a "Saracen"; the point is to hit it as exactly as possible. When they're hit, the Saracens spin around and hurl beer and leather balls at the riders. The team which collects the most points wins the Golden Lance. The pageant is held on the first Sunday in September on the Piazza Grande.

THE CASENTINO

The Casentino region belongs to the "other," less well-known Tuscany. This mountainous, forested region extends north of Arezzo along the upper Arno valley. Anyone who likes solitude, nature, and tranquil little mountain villages along with his art and culture has come to the right place. Because it's off the beaten travel and access routes, this area has always been a region of preference, first for hermits, but also for wealthy families who built summer residences here; and this solitude has also allowed it to preserve its unspoiled nature and simple lifestyles. Locals still craft wood and ceramics according to traditional methods, and till their fields in accordance with the rhythm of the seasons.

From Arezzo, take the SS 73 to the east. By the town Le Ville, a side road leads off to the little village of **Monterchi**, which is known for the unusual Madonna del Parto by Piero della Francesca. This fresco, which just ended a course of renovations in 1993, is today found in a little museum at the edge of town. The extremely pregnant Madonna, flanked by an angel at either side, challenge the viewer with an inimitable Piero gaze, today shielded by a pane of protective glass. The work remains impressive, even in these modest surroundings.

From Monterchi, the road leads past the medieval city of Anghiari to **Sansepolcro** (Holy Sepulchre), which gets its name from relics of Christ's tomb which were preserved here. Originally, the town was under the administration of the Camaldolian order, which founded a monastery here. After being a free commune for a time in the mid-13th century, it came under a succession of different rulers, until Pope Eugene IV finally sold it to Florence for 25,000 ducats.

Sansepolcro is a peaceful little place, but filled nonetheless with fascinating art treasures. The main attraction is the Pina-

coteca Communale, which contains some of Piero della Francesca's most famous works, including the *Resurrection*, *Madonna della Misericordia*, and others. The reason is simple; the artist was born here. Among the town's other sights are the Palazzo delle Laude (late 16th/early 17th centuries), today the Town Hall; the Palazzo Pretorio; and the Duomo, which contains a few valuable works of art itself. Along the central Via Mateotti, residential towers from the 14th and 15th centuries convey a flavor of the Middle Ages – an appropriate background for the Palio della Balestra, a crossbow archery competition held on the second Sunday in September.

From Sansepolcro, the SS 3 leads through the Upper Tiber Valley to Pieve S. Stefano (10 miles/15 km away). Here, the winding and marvelously scenic SS 208 leads off to Bibbiena. A few kilometers behind Pieve S. Stefano, a little road leads off the 7 miles (10 km) to the mountain village of Caprese Michelangelo, where Michelangelo Buonarotti

was born on March 6, 1475, the son of the town's Mayor. A small museum in the Casa Communale houses objects relating to the artist, including copies and photographs of some of his works.

A small road runs from here to meet up, after 9 miles (13 km), with the SS 208 at Chiusi della Verna. Here, the Franciscan monastery of **La Verna** perches atop Monte Penna at an altitude of 3,695 feet (1,130 m). Parts of this monastery complex, in which St. Francis is supposed to have received his stigmata, date as far back as the 13th century. In the church, visited by countless pilgrims, there are terra-cotta reliefs by, among others, Andrea della Robbia, the most important ceramicists of the 15th century.

The mountain road S 208 leads on to **Bibbiena** in the Arno valley, the most important center of industry and trade in the Casentino. Probably of Etruscan

Above and right: The Franciscan monastery of La Verna attracts pilgrims from all over the world.

origin under the name Vipena, the city was hotly contested in the Middle Ages because of its strategic location. Its notable sights include the Palazzo Dovizi (early 16th century) and the church of S. Lorenzo with its adjacent Renaissance monastery. From Bibbiena, you can proceed south along the Arno valley back to Arezzo (23 miles/33 km), or continue northward along the scenic SS 70 to Pontassieve and Florence.

If you choose the latter route, you'll come, after a few kilometers, to the medieval town of **Poppi**, which sits high atop a solitary hill in the Casentino Valley. The castle of Count Guidi, begun in the 12th century and later known as the Palazzo Pretorio, is one of the most significant medieval buildings in all of Tuscany. Dante, it's said, wrote Canto XXIII of the *Inferno* here. There are plenty of unhappy legends told about this castle. The square in front of the fortress, today a pretty garden, was said once to have been the site of bloody duels; the losers were thrown into a dungeon under the

lawn. And in the so-called "Devil's Tower," the lascivious widow of a Guidi was locked up and left to starve to death – by the villagers, irate at her habit of luring young men to the palace and, after having her pleasure with them, mercilessly and cruelly killing them. Even the little 17th-century church of Madonna del Morbo has a bloody history, so to speak; it was designed during a plague epidemic by Francesco Folli da Poppi, inventor of the blood transfusion.

From Poppi, you can detour over to the famous **Hermit's Monastery of Camaldoli** (9 miles/13 km away), whence the order of the Camaldolians got its name. Founded in 1012 by St. Romuald, standing in the middle of a thick forest at an altitude of 3,597 feet (1,100 m), the monastery's distinctive feature are its cells, today 50 in number, which sit like a row of little huts, each at exactly the same distance from the other. Women were once forbidden to set foot on the grounds; today, this is a popular spot for day-trips, yet has managed to preserve its mystical air. A guesthouse is available for visitors who want to brush up on their meditation skills; while the monks sell their own products, such as tea, honey, and cosmetics, in the old monastery apothecary.

On the way to Florence, you pass another famous monastery: the **Abbey of Vallombrosa**, perched 3,142 feet (961 m) up in the wooded mountains of Pratomagno which form the Casentino's western border. This monastery was founded in the early 11th century by Florentine nobleman Giovanni Gualberto Visdomini, who retreated into the forest to lead the simple life of a hermit. Together with a few other like-minded souls, he founded the Vallombrosa order, which still exists today as a chapter of the Benedictines, spread throughout Italy. So powerful was the monastery in the Middle Ages that its abbots bore the title of Conte or even Marchese. The complex's present appearance is the result of 17th-century renovations and reconstruction; highlights include the refectory and the mighty open fireplace in the kitchen.

PROVINCE OF SIENA
Accommodations

SIENA: LUXURY: **Certosa di Maggiano**, Via di Certosa, 82, tel: 0577-288189. **Park Hotel**, Via Marciano,16, tel: 0577-44803. **Villa Patrizia**, Via Fiorentina, 58 tel: 0577-50431.

MODERATE: **Hotel S. Caterina**, Via Piccolomini, 7, tel: 0577-221105. **Antica Torre**, Via Fieravecchia, 7, tel: 0577-222255. **Duomo**, Via Stalloreggi, 34, tel: 0577-289088. **Residence Fattoria di Catignano**, Loc. Catignano, tel: 0577-356744.

BUDGET: **Piccolo Hotel Il Palio**, Piazza del Sale, 19, tel: 0577-281131. **Bernini**, Via della Sapienza, 15, tel: 0577-289047.

YOUTH HOSTELS: **Guidoriccio**, Via Fiorentina, Loc. Stellino, tel: 0577-52212. **Casa del Pellegrino**, Convento, Via Camporegio, 31, tel: 0577-44177. *CAMPING:* **Colleverde**, Strada die Scacciapensieri, 47, tel: 0577-280044.

ASCIANO: MODERATE: **Il Bersagliere**, Via Roma, 39/41, tel: 0577-718629.

MURLO: MODERATE: **L'Albergo di Murlo**, Via Martiri di Rigo Secco, Vescovado, tel: 0577-814033. **Mirella**, Casa Chiavistrelli, Loc. Casciano, tel: 0577-817667.

MONTALCINO: MODERATE: **Al Brunello**, Loc. Bellaria, Traversa Osticcio, tel: 0577-849304. **Il Giglio**, Via Soccorso Saloni, 49, tel: 0577-848167.

BAGNI S. FILIPPO: BUDGET: **Terme S. Filippo**, tel: 0577-872982.

BAGNO VIGNONI: LUXURY: **La Posta**, tel: 0577-887112. **Le Terme**, tel: 0577-887150.

SAN QUIRICO D'ORCIA: MODERATE: **Palazzuolo**, Via Santa Caterina, 43, tel: 0577-897080. *AGRITURISMO:* **Il Rigo**, Loc. Casabianca, tel: 0577-897575/897291.

PIENZA: MODERATE: **Albergo Corsignano**, tel: 0578-74850. **Hotel Il Chiostro**, tel: 0578-748400.

MONTEPULCIANO: MODERATE: **La Terrazza**, Via di Voltaia nel Corso, 84, tel: 0578-757440.

BUDGET: **Duomo**, Via S. Donato, 14, tel: 0578-757473.

CHIANCIANO TERME: LUXURY: **Ambasciatori**, Viale della Libertà, 512, tel: 0578-64171. **Grand Hotel**, Piazza Italia, 80, tel: 0578-63333. **Grand Hotel Terme**, Piazza Italia, 8, tel: 0578-632254.

MODERATE: **Astoria**, Via G. Roncacci, 15, tel: 0578-64044. **Conte**, Via Ugo Foscolo, 26, tel: 0578-60205. **Firenze**, Via della Valle, 52, tel: 0578-63706.

CHIUSI: MODERATE: **Centrale**, Piazza Dante,

3, Loc. Chiusi Scalo, tel: 0578-20118. **Il Patriarca**, SS 146, Loc. Querce al Pino, tel: 0578-274407. *BUDGET:* **La Sfinge**, Via Marconi, 2, tel: 0578-29157.

Restaurants

SIENA: Antica Trattoria Bottega Nuova, Strada Chiantigiana toward Gaiole, 29, tel: 0577-254230. Classic Tuscan cuisine from local products, reasonably-priced. Closed Sun. **Mariotti da Mugolone**, Via dei Pellegrini, 8/12, tel: 0577-283235. In the city center, good Sienese specialties – try local pastries for dessert. Closed Thu. **Al Marsili**, Via del Castoro, 3, tel: 0577-47154. Also in the old city; closed Mon. **La Torre**, Via Salicotti, 7, tel: 0577-287548. Simple, low-priced trattoria. Closed Thu.

MONTE OLIVETO MAGGIORE: La Torre, by the entrance to the monastery complex. Simple food, pleasant atmosphere.

BAGNO VIGNONI: Osteria del Leone, tel: 0577-887300. Good and inventive cooking; but there may be long lines for a table. Closed Monday. Restaurant in the **Hotel Terme**, quite good food.

MONTALCINO: Al Brunello di Montalcino, Loc. Bellaria, tel: 0577-849304. Regional specialties, with an emphasis on game. Closed Thu. **Il Moro**, Via Mazzini, tel: 0577-849384. Simple regional cuisine, closed Thu. **Giardino da Alberto**, Piazza Cavour, 1, tel: 0577-849076. Good food at reasonable prices. Closed Wed. **La Cucina di Edgardo**, Via S. Saloni, 21, tel: 0577-848232. Very personal service; menus with a number of different courses, and reasonable prices. Closed Wed.

CASTELNUOVO DELL'ABATE: Bassomondo, tel: 0577-835619. Tasty snacks, homemade salami and cheese. Closed Mon.

MONTEFOLLONICA: La Chiusa, Via della Madonnina, 88, tel: 0577-669668. Montefollonica is on the N 327, which leads off between Pienza and Montepulciano to Torrita di Siena. The town has become famous for its restaurant, said to be one of the best in Tuscany. The food is excellent, the atmosphere only so-so. The prices refelct the quality of the food. Closed Tue.

CHIUSI: Ristorante Zaira, Via Arunte, 12, tel: 0578-20260. Excellent food, closed Mon.

Museums

SIENA: Palazzo Comunale, Piazza Del Campo, Opening hours: Jan 1-March 14 and Nov 16-Dec 24, 9:30 am-1:45 pm; March 15-Nov 15, 9:30 am-7:45 pm; Sun and holidays 9:30 am-1:45 pm; closed Christmas and Easter. **Town Hall Tower**: open in summer 10 am-6 pm. Pinacoteca Nazionale: Palazzo Buonsignori, Via S. Pietro 29. Opening hours: 8:30 am-2 pm (winter); Tue/Sat 8:30 am-7 pm, Mon 8:30 am-2 pm (summer), Sun and holidays: 8:30 am-1 pm. Closed Jan 1-May 1 and Christmas. Cathedral:

open daily in summer 9 am-7 pm, closed for lunch in winter. **Libreria Piccolomini** (in the cathedral): summer: 9 am-7 pm, closed midday in winter. **Cathedral Museum**: summer: 9 am-7:30 pm, Oct. 9 am-6:30 pm. Nov./Dec. 9 am-1:30 pm.

ASCIANO: Museo di Arte Sacra, P.zza F.lli Bandiera, for info call 0577-718207. **Museo archeologico**: Corso Matteotti, 46. Opening hours: summer 10 am-12:30/4:30-6:30 pm, mornings only in winter. Closed Mon.

MURLO: Museum in the Castello: Tue-Fri 9:30 am-12.30/2:30-5:30 pm; Sat, Sun, holidays: 3-6 pm. Closed Mon.

PIENZA: Cathedral Museum: Piazza Pio II, tel. 0578-748072. Open: April-Oct. 9 am-noon/4-6 pm, closed Tue.

MONTEPULCIANO: Museo Civico, Via Ricci, 11, open 9 am-1 /3-6 pm, closed Mon & Tue.

CHIUSI: Museo Nazionale Etrusco, Via Porsenna, 17, tel. 0578-20177. Open 9 am-1:40 and 3-7 pm. The museum also contains information about the Etruscan graves.

Sights

Monastery Monte Oliveto Maggiore, open 9 am-12:30 and 3-5:30 pm.

The Fortezza in Montalcino is open daily 9 am-1 pm/2-6 pm (winter), July-September until 8 pm. In winter, it's closed Mondays.

The abbey church of **Sant'Antimo** is open 10:30 am-12:30 and 3-6 pm (summer), 11 am-12:30 and 3-5 pm (winter).

Baths of S. Filippo. The chalk basins and pools are a very impressive sight. At the moment, however, you can't actually swim there, since there's a risk that the stone might break off.

The Horti Leonini in S. Quirico d'Orcia (16th-century) are one of the earliest examples of Italian landscape gardening.

The Palazzo Piccolomini in Pienza is open June-Sept. 10 am-12:30/4-7 pm and Oct.-May 10 am-12:30/3-5 pm.

You can climb the **tower** of the **Town Hall** in **Montepulciano** from 8 am-1:30 pm.

Tourist Information

SIENA: Piazza del Campo, 56, tel: 0577-280551.

PROVINCE OF AREZZO
Accommodations

CORTONA: *MODERATE:* **Albergo S. Michele**, Via Guelfa, 15, tel: 0575-604348. **San Luca**, Piazza Garibaldi, 2, tel: 0575-603787. **Sabrina**, Via Roma 37, tel: 0575-604188. *YOUTH HOSTEL:* **Ostello S. Marco**, Via Maffei, 57, tel: 0575-601392.

AREZZO: *LUXURY:* **Etrusco**, Via Fleming, 39, tel: 0575-984066. *MODERATE:* **Continentale**, P.zza Guido Monaco, 7, tel: 0575-20251. **Europa,** Via Spinello, 43, tel: 0575-357701. *BUDGET:* **Astoria**, Via Guido Monaco, 54, tel: 0575-24361. Cecco, Corso Italia, 215, tel: 0575-20968.

CAPRESE MICHELANGELO: *MODERATE:* **Fonte della Galletta**, Loc. Alpe della Faggeta, tel: 0575-793925.

BIBBIENA: *MODERATE:* **Borgo Antico**, Via B. Dovizi, 18, tel: 0575-536445.

POPPI: *MODERATE:* **Parc Hotel**, Via Roma, 214, tel: 0575-529994. *BUDGET:* **Casentino**, P.zza Repubblica, 6, tel: 0575-529090.

SANSEPOLCRO: *MODERATE:* **Borgo**, Via Senese Aretina, 80, tel: 0575-736050. **Fiorentino**, Via L. Pacioli, 60, tel: 0575-740350.

Restaurants

CORTONA: Cacciatore, Via Roma, 11, tel: 0575-603252. Closed Wed. **Trattoria dell'Amico**, Via Dardano, 12, tel: 0575-604192. Typ. trattoria atmosphere. Closed Mon. **Trattoria Dardano**, Via Dardano, 24, tel: 0575-601944. Closed Tue.

AREZZO: Il Cantuccio, Via Madonna del Prato, 76, tel: 0575-26830. Good, traditional Tuscan specialties; prices are acceptable. Closed Tue.

ANGHIARI: Locanda al Castello di Sorci, 3 km south of Anghiari, tel: 0575-789066. Very rustic, and crowded. Closed Mon.

SANSEPOLCRO: L'Oroscopo, Via P. Togliatti, 66/68, Loc. Pieve Vecchia, tel: 0575-734875. Fixed menu, must be ordered in advance. Hotel and pizzeria in same building. Closed Tue, open for dinner only.

Museums and Sights

CORTONA: Museo dell'Accademia Etrusca (in the Palazzo Casali), opening hours: 9 am-1 pm/3-5 pm (winter); 10 am-1 pm/ 4-7 pm (summer). The museum is closed Mondays. **Diocesan Museum**: 9 am-1 pm/3-5 pm (winter); 9 am-1 pm/3-6:30 pm (summer). Closed Mon. **Etruscan grave Tanella di Pitagora**, open in summer 10 am-1 pm/4-7 pm, in winter 9 am-1 pm/3-5 pm.

AREZZO: Archaeolog. Museum, Via Margaritone, 10, open 9 am-7 pm. **Cathedral Museum**: Thu, Fri & Sat 9 am-7 pm, closed Sun and holidays. **Basilica S. Francesco**: Closed for lunch; only in summer on Sun & holidays is it open all day. **Casa Petrarca**, Via dell'Orto, weekdays 10 am-12/3-5 pm.

SAN SEPOLCRO: Pinacoteca Comunale, open daily 9:30 am-1 pm/2:30-6 pm.

POPPI: Castello di Poppi, Sat & Sun 9:30 am-12:30/2:30-5:30 pm.

Tourist Information

A.P.T. Cortona, Via Nazionale, 70, tel: 0575630352. **A.P.T. Arezzo**, Piazza della Republica, 28, tel: 0575-377678.

RUINS, BATHS, THE SEA

MAREMMA / AMIATA
GROSSETO / GREEN HILLS
SILVER COAST
ETRUSCAN TOUR
COLLINE METALLIFERE
PROVINCE OF LIVORNO

The Province of Grosseto

With the mighty Amiata Plateau to the east, the gentle hills of its interior, and the long stretch of coast bordering the Tyrrhenian Sea, the province of Grosseto is a region that's been blessed both by nature and by history. The Etruscans were the first to "discover" it; they arrived in the 8th century B.C., and stayed because of the area's wealth of natural resources. They were also the first to drain the swampy coastal region of the Maremma. Some 500 years later, they had to yield pride of place to the Romans, who proceeded to build their settlements atop the Etruscan ruins.

Christianity followed in the 5th century. The old Etruscan centers Populonia, Sovana and Roselle were early bishoprics. After a brief hiatus under the Lombards and the Franks – both of whom were also interested in the region's minerals – the Aldobrandeschi family took control of the area in the 8th century. A process of *castellamento* set in and by the 12th century, nearly every hilltop was crowned with a castle. Small wonder that the Aldobrandeschi's pride led to their

Preceding pages: In S. Maria in Sovana. Left: Social life is often played out on the street.

downfall. Dante Alighieri had Umberto atone for his family's sins in the *Divine Comedy*, where he appears with his neck bent under a heavy stone.

The rest of the story is quickly told. In the 14th century, the Republic of Siena took control of the region. Yet in spite of the ample supply of fortifications, they had to yield the coastal regions to the Spanish, who left the Maremma to its own devices, which meant, in effect, to malaria. It wasn't until the Congress of Vienna in 1815 that the region was made part of the Grand Duchy of Tuscany.

The Hapsburgs, and after them the Italian government under the "Duce," Mussolini, drained the "bitter Maremma," as it's called in one song. After it had thus been freed from malaria, the region became a source of grain. Its mineral resources have long since been exhausted; today, the province's wealth lies mainly in its varied landscape and its rich past.

THE MAREMMA

Gateway to the Maremma – as the entire region is often called today – is a bridge on the road SS 223 which leads over an inaccessible valley by Bagno di Petriolo, about halfway between Siena and Grosseto (the rising stench of sulphur betrays the presence of a hot springs in

141

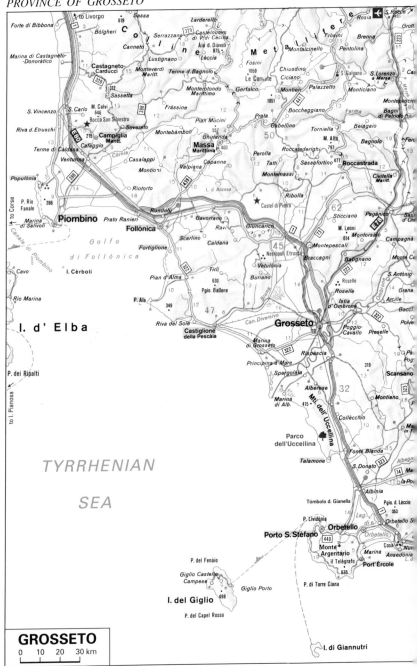

GROSSETO

0   10   20   30 km

the area). About 7 miles (10 km) further on, you encounter the first testimony to the area's medieval past: the **Abbey of San Lorenzo**, built around 1200 by the Ardenghesca family. What's left today are the entrance gate and the Late Romanesque church with a facade rivalling that of the abbey church of Sant'Antimo.

At Civitella Marittima, which grew out of a 12th-century Ardenghesca castle, the road branches off toward **Roccastrada**, the largest town in the northwest Maremma. It lies 1,553 feet (475 m) up on a plateau of volcanic rock, from which you have a view out over the Grosseto plain and the sea, all the way to Corsica.

In the Middle Ages, Roccastrada was a center for silver and copper mining; testimony to these period are the remains of the old city walls. From Roccastrada, you can reach Grosseto and the sea along the SS 73, passing old mountain villages such as Sticciano and Montepescali, the "balcony of the Maremma," commanding a view of the entire Grosseto coast. It's here that the Greco-Roman hero Herakles (or Hercules) is supposed to have descended to the underworld.

If you follow the main road on to Grosseto, you'll reach **Paganico** about 5 miles (7 km) south of the turnoff to Roccastrada. Surrounding the little medieval town center here is an impressive rectangular city wall dating from the 14th century. This is a good point of departure for a tour around the nearby Amiata Massif.

Around the Amiata

The extinct Amiata volcano (5,683 feet/1,738 m), together with the mountains Labbro (3,901 feet/1,193 m), Buceto (3,767 feet/1,152 m), Civitella (3,620 feet/1,107 m) and Poggio Zoccolino (3,384 feet/1,035 m) form the largely visible border between the provinces of Siena and Grosseto. Inhabitants of the eleven communities in this region, however, swear allegiance only to "their

An excursion through the Amiata massif is also a tour through some 3,000 years of history. The towns here all developed from medieval fortifications. Since the days of the Lombards, foreign powers have been interested in this border region between the Empire and the Papal States. Nearby, moreover, was the pilgrim route *Via Francigena*, which linked the Frankish Empire with Rome. Powerful families in the Late Middle Ages and Renaissance hearkened back to the Etruscan mining tradition and stripped the area of natural resources. In modern times, this rather rough area has escaped widespread notice – which has enabled it to preserve its natural beauty.

From Paganico, the SP 26 leads past Montenero and Montegiovi to **Arcidosso**, some 20 miles (30 km) away. The town is perched on a mountain saddle between Monte Amiata and Monte Labbro, at an altitude of 2,220 feet (679 m). From far away, you can see the Rocca with its turreted tower, a monument from around the year 1000 that signals the village's medieval origins. In the 9th century, Arcidosso belonged to the abbey of San Salvatore, then to the Aldobrandeschi family, and finally to the city of Siena.

Amiata," and see themselves as islanders, rather than Grossetans.

The mountains are covered with thick chestnut and beech forests, and crisscrossed with brooks and streams. At a height of between about 2,000 and 2,600 feet (600-800 m), springs form a kind of ring around the massif, and there were settlements around these even in prehistoric times. The Etruscans mined red mercury sulphide in these mountains; and inhabitants continued to live from mercury mines, agriculture and sheep-herding all the way up to the 1970s. Since the closing of the mines, all that's left to them now is the timber industry; and the region is placing considerable hopes on tourism, staking out nature parks and clearing hiking trails. As a result of attempts to create jobs after the mines' closing, therefore, the landscape here is lovingly and actively tended.

Over the centuries, a little city grew up within the fortress and outside the city walls; for a long time, its economy centered around the mineral resources of the surrounding mountains. To reach the picturesque old city with its little, winding alleyways, take the Corso Toscana through an old city gate with a clock tower, a reconstruction of a 19th-century original. A side street leads off the Corso Toscana to the Porto del Castello, a second city gate, adorned with the coats-of-arms of the Medici and Arcidosso families.

North of Arcidosso is the village of **Castel del Piano**, which once belonged, like Arcidosso, to the Benedictine abbey of San Salvatore, but which was nonetheless administered by the inhabitants

Above: Surprising "brief encounter" in the forests around Amiata. Right: Forested hills around Monte Amiata.

themselves. In 1214, the Aldobrandeschi put an end to such autonomy, only to be ousted themselves in 1331 by the ubiquitous Sienese.

Castel del Piano has a medieval city center surrounded by a ring of Renaissance buildings, and a more modern exterior. The town's five towers and circular city plan are reminiscent of Siena. Along the Corso Nasini, the houses are built atop the former city wall, and thus form the border of the oldest part of town. In front of this, on the Piazza della Madonna, is the largest church in the Amiata, the Chiesa dell'Opera.

Some 5 miles (7 km) north of Castel del Piano, **Seggiano** lies on a gentle rise of land. Streams form a natural border around this former castle, which is numbered one of the oldest in the region. At the entrance to the city, shaded by olive trees, is the Baroque Tempio della Madonna della Carità, built by the survivors of a plague epidemic in 1603. The town itself has preserved little of its medieval character; but its little churches do con-

tain a few 14th- and 15th-century masterpieces. Signs point the way to the ruins of the Castello del Potentino (c. 1040) and the ruins of the monastery of Colombaio, where St. Bernardino of Siena once stayed.

From Castel del Piano, a road leads east to the peak of the Amiata. On the other side, it leads down again to **Abbadia S. Salvatore**, a mere 2,655 feet (812 m) high. This town derives its name from the nearby Abbey, the oldest power center of the Monte Amiata. Legend has it that St. Salvatore met the Lombard king Rachis here – reason enough to found Tuscany's first-ever abbey on the spot in 762 A.D. A more probable factual reason was the Lombard interest in this border area between the Frankish Empire and the Papal State. The abbey belonged, in turn, to the Benedictines, the Camaldolians, and the Cistercians. In the 18th century, the monastery was dissolved and turned into residential apartments; but monks returned to inhabit parts of the old buildings in 1939.

Next to the abbey is a fortress which developed into a flourishing mining center during the Middle Ages. The wealth of mineral resources in the area meant that the most powerful families in the region – the Aldobrandeschi, Sforza, and Piccolomini – were constantly struggling with the Republic of Siena for control. Until the middle of the 20th century, the town and surrounding communities lived from mercury mining. The local Mining Museum documents the history of this industry in the area.

Also worth a visit is the Romanesque abbey church, consecrated in 1036, although it suffered a rather unfortunate course of restorations around 1930. Noteworthy here are the T-shaped ground plan, the oldest such in Tuscany; the two-towered facade; the crypt with its 36 slender, tall columns, each decorated with a different capital; a 12th-century wooden

Above: Patience for a granddaughter. Right: The water of Santa Flora issues from taps 70 miles away.

cross; and Francesco Nasini's fresco of the Martyrdom of St. Bartolomeo.

South of Abbadia San Salvatore, amid a chestnut wood with views of the Paglia plain, at an altitude of 2,524 feet (772 m) is **Piancastagnaio**. This town, too, was once an Aldobrandeschi castle which fell into Sienese hands in the 15th century. Witnesses to its past include the 13th-century defensive fortress at the entrance to the Old City; the church of Santa Maria Assunta (1279); the Palazzo Communale (14th century); and the 13th-century Palazzo del Podestà on the former Piazza del Commune, as well as the Palazzo Bourbon del Monte (1611) on the Piazza Belvedere. Outside the city walls is the Convent of San Bartolomeo with frescoes dating from the 13th and 14th centuries. From Piancastagnaio, the SP 18 leads directly to Santa Fiora, another former mining center on Monte Amiata.

If you'd like to extend your Amiata tour, follow the signs to **Castell'Azzara**, the "Fortress of Gambling." This name originates with the story that two brothers of the Sforza family are said to have thrown dice to determine who should have the medieval castle. The dice appear in the castle's coat-of-arms. Comprised of gray stone houses, the town lies on a steep slope which looks out all the way to Latium. To the west, Monte Civitella blocks the view. The lodes of red mercury sulphide here drew the Umbers, and later Etruscan settlers.

About 14 miles (20 km) separate Castell'Azzara and **Santa Fiora**. This picturesque village with its pretty old city is popular with vacationers and winter sports enthusiasts. A winding road leads through well-tended woodlands to the town; on the way, individual signs indicate geothermic drilling holes. The state electric company Enel is trying to make use of the underground warmth which is present throughout the area.

From the south, a bridge leads into the village, which is divided into three parts.

First building here was the castle, protected by a natural rocky trench and rough cliffs. On the Piazza Garibaldi, you can see what's left of the fortress, a clock tower, and the Renaissance Sforza palace. To the southwest is the old city Borgo with the Poor Clares convent; the parish church of S. Flora and Lucia, which contains some terra-cotta works by Della Robbia; and the Jewish ghetto. Outside the city walls is the quarter of Montecatino, where an old basin, the Peschiera, catches the waters of the Fiora.

The monumental cemetery is the last resting place of David Lazzeretti. Called the "Christ of poor people," he was hunted by the authorities and shot in 1878. His crime: preaching the doctrine of equality and communal property in this impoverished area. In 1872, he founded a Christian brotherhood of peasants, shepherds, and artisans, called the *Giurisdavidici*, and built a church on the peak of Monte Labbro. You can still see the ruins today; and his ideas of social renewal have also survived among the inhabitants of this inhospitable region. There's access to the one-time cult spot at Bagnore; also located there is the turnoff to the **Parco Faunistico**, where wolves and stags again roam the woods.

A winding, lovely road leads to the west, back to Paganico. After about 7 miles (10 km), you can see the holiday town of Monticello Amiata, perched 2,400 feet (734 m) on top of a mountain. This town, too, grew out of a *castrum*. A tower rises from it like a raised index finger, signalling, perhaps, a warning.

There are lovely views to be seen from the SP 7 as it leads rapidly downhill. Cinigiano, a friendly little city with old city walls, is already some 1,300 feet (400 m) lower than Monticello Amiata; its main sources of income are agriculture and cattle-breeding. The road leads on past Sasso d'Ombrone, where a bridge leads over the river Ombrone (with its source in Umbria, and named for the original Umber people), and soon you're back at Paganico and on the expressway between Siena and Grosseto.

SOUTH OF THE AMIATA

As you go farther south, you come to other villages which saw their true flowerings in the Middle Ages, including **Campagnatico**, one of the oldest holdings of the virtually omnipresent Aldobrandeschis. In the Late Middle Ages, the city's history was one of destruction, epidemics, decline, and finally oblivion. It was the Tuscan Grand Duke Leopold II who called the little town back to life in the 19th century by establishing a small industrial plant. In the town quarter of the Via Casacce, however, some of the town's original medieval character is preserved. Beneath the castle ruins, on the Piazza Garibaldi, you can still see the former pilgrims' hospice **Ospedale di Sant'Antonio**, which was administered by the order of Knights Templar.

To the right of the SS 223 are the little mountain settlements of Batignano and

Above: Grosseto's Cathedral is adorned with colored marble.

Montorsaio. The castle of Batignano owed its importance in the Middle Ages to its proximity to silver and lead mines. Before the Republic of Siena stepped in to take things over in the 14th century, vassals of the Aldobrandeschi held sway here. At the edge of town, the convent of Santa Croce is worth a visit. In summer, it hosts a festival called "Musica nel Chiostro," or music in the convent (mid-July to mid-August): for the last few years, the Britisher Adam Pollock has staged little-known, rarely performed operas here. In Batignano's town center is the church of San Martino; its oldest sections stem from a church in Roselle dating from the 8th century.

The archaeological excavations of **Roselle** are on a rise of land some 5 miles (7 km) from Grosseto. Protected on the west by Lagus Prilius, a lagoon which has since been drained, and by the hill Poggio Moscona to the south, Roselle, founded in the 7th century BC, had a strategically advantageous position which enabled it to become one of the twelve most powerful cities of the Etruscans. Its inhabitants supported themselves by agriculture, and supplied the Romans with grain. Rusellae, as it was originally known, long resisted alliance with the new super-power. When the Romans finally gained control of the city in 294 B.C., they fitted it out with the standard facilities: forum, amphitheater, and thermal baths.

It was in Roselle that the Aldobrandeschis built their first castle in 862. Under the Lombards, the city became the seat of a bishopric, but had to yield pride of place to Grosseto in 1138, as much of its population had departed due to the fact that the land was becoming increasingly swampy, bringing disease and other problems in its wake. The last residents left the city in the 16th century, and abandoned it to its fate.

Today, you can see the 9,810-foot (3,000 m) cyclopean city wall, dating from the days of the Etruscans, which is up to 23 feet (7 m) high in places. Other remains include cisterns, water pipes, and parts of the Roman additions, such as the amphitheater. The necropolis indicates that people were already living here during the Iron Age. Some of the artifacts found here are displayed in the Archaeological Museum in Grosseto. The site is open all day long in summer.

GROSSETO

The lively main city of the province, Grosseto (population 65,000) probably developed from an old Etruscan settlement. Today, the plains extend to the sea; in Roman times, however, there was a lagoon here. Etruscans, Romans, and, in the Middle Ages, monks kept struggling with the attempt to drain the swampy, malaria-ridden area.

First documented in the year 803, the castle was originally the property of the Aldobrandeschis; and it was during their dominion that it became a bishopric in 1138. In 1336, it was conquered by

Siena, and incorporated into the Duchy of Tuscany in 1569. The Medici had the hexagonal ring wall enclosing the historic center and the fortress built between 1565 and 1593; it is still well preserved today. Around 1835, Leopold II (whose monument stands on the Piazza Dante) had the ring transformed into an area of parks and streets, removing the star-shaped defensive moats which had once surrounded the city.

Leopold II also joined his predecessors in the fight to drain the Maremma and thus check the constant threat of malaria. Armed with more modern technology, he was more successful, and therefore rang in a new period of prosperity for the city.

The **cathedral of San Lorenzo**, with its striped marble facade, dates from the 13th century (the facade was renovated in 1840-1845), as does the simple church of **San Francesco**. The painted wooden cross on the main altar here is from the hand of Duccio di Buoninsegna (1289). Displayed in the **Museum of Archaeology** are prehistoric, Etruscan, and Roman artifacts from Roselle, Vetulonia, Pitigliano and the whole Fiora valley.

THE GREEN HILLS OF THE MAREMMA

A good place to start an excursion through the forested hills in the southeastern part of the province is Istia d'Ombrone, 5.5 miles (8 km) from the province's capital. As late as the 1920s, fear of malaria drove the well-heeled Grossetans to withdraw from the plains, taking children and possessions, and set up shop every summer in this former fortress of the Bishops of Roselle. The medieval city wall with the 13th-century Porta Grossetana, and the fact that there was a market held here as early as 1032, shows that people were able to appreciate this village's excellent location very early on.

Past Arcille, Baccinello and Cana, the road eastward leads to **Roccalbegna** in

the upper Albegna valley, a distance of some 24 miles (35 km). Rising behind the town is a steep cliff topped by a fortress; the houses crowd together at its foot. "If the cliff should ever shake, then *addio*, Roccalbegna," residents joke. Around 1250, Roccalbegna, too, was under the thumb of the Aldobrandeschi; today, only ruins remain of their once-proud fortress. Narrow little streets have helped the town, however, preserve its medieval character. One church worth a look is the Romanesque-Gothic SS Pietro e Paolo, which contains a triptych by Ambrogio Lorenzetti. Other religious treasures are exhibited in the Museum of Sacral Art.

4 miles (6 km) from town, 2,515 feet (769 m) up, is the castle **Triana**, or Piccolomini. This imposing, well-preserved fortress is first mentioned in 776. Today, the complex belongs to a religious society and is not open to the public.

Above: Shaded avenue of pines in the Parco dell'Uccellina. Right: Maremma cows with their distinctive, sweeping horns.

Back, then, to Roccalbegna, and farther southeast along the SS 323, toward the sea. Halfway there is the village of **Scansano**, with medieval origins similar to other Aldobrandeschi fortress towns. In the 19th century, this town was official summer headquarters for the Grosseto city officials, who fled from the malaria in the hot summer months. Today, Scansano is a modern small city with an agriculturally based economy. It has a medieval town center as well as a museum.

Continuing toward the coast, you pass **Pereta**, built atop a mountain like a fortress. Ranged one against the other, the houses themselves form the city wall; in the middle of town is a high tower from the 12th century. A turreted city gate, restored in 1546, leads into the medieval town center. Pereta was the last place of refuge for Nello della Pietra and Marghereta Aldobrandeschi, an aristocratic couple who lived bigamously and finally had to be separated by armed force.

From here, it's downhill all the way. The thick woods begin to thin out, and

agriculture kicks in again by the time you reach **Magliano**. Here, once upon a time, was the old city of **Heba**, an Etruscan settlement which later went over to the Romans. All that's left of it today are the name and the necropolis, buried in the volcanic limestone of the surrounding hills. You can get more information at **Pro Loco** in Magliano.

With its 1,000-year-old Aldobrandeschi castle as a focal point, Magliano itself lies on a hilltop 419 feet (128 m) above sea level, surrounded by a wood of venerable olive trees which reach all the way up to the fortified city walls. Near the church Annunziata is the huge "Witches' Tree," said to be the oldest olive tree in Europe. You enter the town's Old City through the Porta Nuova, then turn left. On the Piazza del Popolo is the turreted city gate of San Martino, near which stands the Romanesque church of the same name, which was completely restored after World War II. On the Piazza Libertà, the Palazzo dei Priori rises up in a blend of the Gothic and Sienese styles;

it dates from 1430, and is ornamented with coats-of-arms of the *Podestà* from the 15th and 16th centuries.

Corso Garibaldi leads to the church of San Giovanni with its Romanesque ground plan, which is nonetheless a typical specimen of Renaissance architecture in the Maremma. A short footpath to the south brings you through the olive groves to the white ruins of the 11th-century church of San Bruzio. You can still see the apse, its capitals ornate with allegorical figures. A pagan temple supposedly once stood on this site, linked to the town by an underground tunnel.

If you're in a hurry, drive straight on to the sea along the SS 323. The road is lined with eucalyptus trees which were supposed to clear the air of the germs of malaria. Perhaps, however, you'll have time to detour to the **Parco dell'Uccellina**, a nature reserve between the fishing village of Talamone and the mouth of the Ombrone river. The park was set up in 1975 and is one of the few oases in the Maremma where the Mediterranean flora

151

have been preserved in their original state. Roaming around here are wild pigs and porcupines, badgers, otters, fallow deer, rare birds, and the white Maremma cattle with their sweeping horns, tended by the shepherds of the Maremma, the butteri. This region, furthermore, is a rich lode for archaeologists. The oldest finds here have been stone tools from the days of Neanderthal Man.

You can enter the park, and buy tickets, at Albarese. Bring along sturdy shoes so you can enjoy the nature trails, which are set up around the life cycles of the various indigenous animals. From June 15-September 30, you can only visit the park as part of a group tour.

THE SILVER COAST

The "Silver Coast" is a region of long sand beaches and pine woods. To explore

Above: Evening on the Argentario. Right: The old mill of Orbetello.

it, start out at the fishing village of **Talamone**, sitting on a protrusion of rock at the southern end of the Parco dell'Uccellina. Badly damaged in World War II, the village had to be totally reconstructed. This wasn't its first entry into military history, however. In 225 BC, the Romans beat the Gauls on Campo Regio, while in 1860 Garibaldi's 1,000 loyal followers stocked up here with provisions before setting out to conquer the mainland.

In Antiquity, it was the Argonauts who were said to have founded Talamone – or so, at least, runs the legend. The Etruscans found this to be a good base for their merchant marine, and proceeded to establish a harbor. Sole testimony to a turbulent and colorful history are the ruins of a medieval fortress. The remains of the town's Etruscan temple are on display in the archaeological museum in Florence.

From Talamone, it's about 3 miles (4 km) to the Via Aurelia Etrusca (SS 1), which leads in the direction of Rome to **Monte Argentario**. The rocky Argentario promontory has given its name to the

entire surrounding coastline: once an island in the long-distant past, it is linked to
the mainland by two narrow tongues of
land, or *tomboli*. A shallow lagoon has
formed between the sand dunes; thrusting
into it from the mainland like the prow of
a ship is the spit of land on which rests
Orbetello. An artificial dam from 1842
also links the city with the Argentario.

The old Etruscan harbor was conquered first by the Romans, then by Siena
in the Middle Ages, and finally by the
Spanish, who made Orbetello their main
naval base. In 1555, Philip II made the
city the capital of the so-called Stato dei
Presidi, a federation which included the
Argentario, Talamone and Porto Azzurro. Later, in 1815, the city was incorporated into the Duchy of Tuscany.

All of these various rulers left their
various marks. The city's cyclopean wall,
dating from the 4th century BC, is Etruscan; the Cathedral (1376) is Sienese Gothic; and the city wall (1557) is Spanish.

Today, Orbetello is a particularly
popular destination with ecologically

minded tourists. The lagoon contains
both a World Wildlife Fund nature
reserve and an observation station of the
Italian League of Bird Protection. But
don't forget the mosquito repellent.

Within the pine woods of the *Tombolo
della Giannella*, to the north, are vacation
communities. At Santa Liberata, where
you can still see the remains of a Roman
villa, you're already in the Argentario,
with its dense growth of maquis and the
rocky, inaccessible cliffs of its coast. To
the north is the charming little city of
Porto Santo Stefano, which has been an
active harbor since the days of the Etruscans. Today, there are more yachts than
fishing boats in its slips, and the lively
bay is well suited for more urbane living.
A picturesque frame is provided by the
old city with its 17th-century Spanish
fortress and the holiday villas scattered
around. From Porto Nuovo, there's regular ferry service to the islands of Giglio
and Giannutri.

On the southern side of the Argentario
is the luxurious vacation town of **Porto**

153

Ercole. Hercules, *Ercole*, is supposed to have founded this port city; and it is at least proven that its Romanesque monastery Tre Fontane was a gift of Charlemagne. After it was conquered by the Spanish in 1557, the town became a naval base; relic of this period is the Spanish Fort Filippo to the left of the harbor, as well as the castle opposite.

In the 17th century, these were joined by Fort Stella in the south of town. On the Cala Galera, where the southern spit of land known as *Feniglia* begins, the painter Michelangelo Merisi, better known as Caravaggio, died of malaria.

This tour of the Silver Coast ends at the Lago di Burano. If you're coming from Orbetello, leave the Via Aurelia Etrusca at Ansedonia, a community which is little more than a collection of holiday cottages. From here, there's a splendid view of the sun setting behind the Argentario.

Above: Porto S. Stefano. Right: The "Empress" in Niki de Saint-Phalle's sculpture park in Capalbio.

A bumpy road leads to the excavations at **Cosa**, on a ledge of rock at an altitude of 370 feet (113 m). Cosa, dating from 273 BC, was the first Roman settlement on the Etruscan coast. But the city was abandoned by the 1st century BC; and the Visigoths dealt it the *coup de grâce*. Today, you can see an impressive field of ruins with a small museum (open only in the morning). Below this promontory is the harbor of Cosa. In the 15th-century Torre della Tagliata here, Giacomo Puccini worked on his opera *Tosca*.

At the front edge of the cliff is the *Tagliata etrusca*, an artificial canal which is supposed to guarantee that the sea water can flow freely in and out, preventing the silting up of the harbor. A similar channel is the *Bagno della Regina*, a natural cut in the rock 850 feet (260 m) long and up to 20 feet (6 m) wide, which has been artificially enlarged. For safety's sake, there's also an artificial drainage canal between the lake of Burano and the sea. All of this was created more than 2,000 years ago, and continues to fulfill its function. The

World Wildlife Fund has declared the swamp area around the **Lago di Burano** to be a protected nature preserve; entry, therefore, is forbidden in the summer.

AN ETRUSCAN TOUR

If you want to pay a visit on the ancient Etruscans, you have to be prepared to work for it, since these people preferred to live in high places, at a safe distance from the swamps or their enemies. Spreading from the coastal cities of Vetulonia and Populonia and the early inland settlements of Volterra and Chiusi, they extended all the way into Umbria and Latium. They founded cities and settlements, drained the Maremma with a clever drainage system, and mined ore and minerals from the wooded Colline Metallifere.

Start about 7 miles (10 km) inland from the Lago di Burano, at **Capalbio**. You can walk around this well-restored village, now a favorite summer residence of Roman television personalities, along

its intact medieval city walls. Within the labyrinth of alleyways there's a 12th-century Romanesque church with Sienese-school frescoes next to a medieval tower. Nearby, the artist Nikki de Saint-Phalle has set up an irreverent sculpture garden, which has been open to the public since the summer of 1994 (open in July and August from 3 to 8 pm).

Capalbio is surrounded by thick woods; in the 19th century, the outlaw Domenico Tiburzi found these a very effective hiding place. Today, it's only wild pigs who perform their evil deeds there – or hunters, who find chasing the pigs an entertaining pastime.

From Capalbio, a road leads northwest to Marsiliana (9.5 miles/14 km). This region is predominantly agricultural. At the junction with the SS 74, at the end of an avenue of cypresses, you can see the former **Castrum Marsiliani**, which today belongs to the Orsini princes. Hidden in the undergrowth along the Camarrone are Villanova period and Etruscan graves. The Greek and Phoenician grave

offerings excavated here have been brought to the museum in Grosseto.

The Maremmana SS 74, which links the Via Aurelia with the lake of Bolsena, is the fastest way to get to the excavations of the Etruscan sites at Pitigliano and Sovana. Between fields and forests, the road wends its way up to the 1,452-foot-high (444 m) town of **Manciano**.

Because of its strategically advantageous location, this medieval fortress attracted the Aldobrandeschi, the Orsini, and finally the Sienese. It was the latter who left the 15th-century castle within the old city walls, which still commands a breathtaking view. Visitors here should stroll through the old city and look in at the Prehistoric Museum, which displays finds from throughout the Fiora valley.

A mere 12.5 miles (18 km) lie between this town and Pitigliano. In the virtually inaccessible thickets of the Poggio Buco,

Above: Grown out of the rock – Pitigliano.
Right: Social hour on the piazza.

just before the bridge over the Fiora, there are Etruscan graves and remains of archaic walls. The forms of the graves indicate that this must have been one of the very early settlements (around the 8th century BC).

Soon, the landscape changes, as the thickly forested valleys give way to a barren plateau. Pitigliano appears without warning after a bend in the road, high above a gorge and looking as if it's grown out of the yellowy-red volcanic rock, an impression furthered by the fact that the houses are constructed of the same porous stone as the surface on which they rest.

From the west, Pitigliano can only be reached by a high aqueduct, built in 1545. At the entrance to the old city, guarded by a stone lion, rises the mighty, turreted silhouette of the 15th-century **Palazzo Orsini**. The Orsini family took over this fortified town from the Aldobrandeschi in the year 1293. Today, the palace contains the Archaeological Museum, with some 1,500 artifacts from

prehistoric and Etruscan times. The medieval city center is a warren of tiny streets linked by narrow flights of stairs, which sometimes end in front of a house wall or at the city wall, from which you can look out over the surrounding countryside. The Baroque church doesn't seem to fit in very well with the overall image. In the Middle Ages, Pitigliano was a refuge for Spanish Jews fleeing the Inquisition; testimony to this is the Jewish cemetery at the entrance to the village. Today, the residents seem to be predominantly old people.

From Pitigliano, you can go on to the cliff town of **Sorano**. As you approach your view of the city is blocked by new buildings; past them, you can see that the town is built of and on the same volcanic limestone as Pitigliano. Columbari, characteristic cliff caves which are today used to store wine, are testimony to the site's Etruscan origins. One noteworthy sight is the broad 16th-century Orsini fortress in the south of the city. Farther on are the church of San Nicola, completely reno-

vated in the 17th century; the Palace of the Orsini Counts (1551); and the Sasso Leopoldino with its clock tower (18th century).

Unfortunately, Sorano, like so many other out-of-the-way villages in Tuscany, is slowly dying out. More and more people are leaving the village, some of them driven away by the frequent landslides. The beautiful old city center is decaying; there's no money for renovations, and the village is being left to its fate.

In nearby San Quirico, signs indicate the way to the ruined castle **Vitozza**. Only the remains of walls and a few subterranean apartments remain of this 12th-century Aldobrandeschi complex, which was inhabited until the 18th century.

A gorge between rock walls of porous stone leads to the medieval **Sovana**, which was a flourishing Etruscan community in the 7th century BC. Here, too, time seems to have stood still. A handful of buildings of the yellow-red volcanic limestone along the cobblestone streets attest to the town's glorious past: the

157

ruins of the Aldobrandeschi fortress, the 12th-century Romanesque church of S. Maria and its coeval Cathedral of SS. Peter and Paul, which turns its back, or apse, on the village. Unusual is its octagonal dome, which betrays the influence of the Lombards. Sovana was the birthplace of Pope Gregory VII (1073-1085), who forced the Emperor Henry to undertake the now-axiomatic Journey to Canossa to petition for his forgiveness.

Around Sovana, Etruscan graves lie concealed by the Mediterranean undergrowth of maquis; they convey an impression of the wide variety of the grave architecture of the period. A small footpath off of the San Martino road leads to the **Grave of the Siren** (3rd-2nd century BC); its name derives from a relief over the rubble of the grave chamber, which depicts a somewhat weather-worn mermaid. Nearby is the **Tomba Ildebranda**

Above: The pleasures of a warm bath in the sulphurous water of Saturnia. Right: Shepherd in the coastal regions of the Maremma.

(3rd century BC), a luxury grave in the form of a temple with a row of columns, which you can only observe from the outside. Behind the burial mound is a cavone, an Etruscan passageway hewn into the rock, which is so narrow that hardly any light penetrates it.

The provincial road leads to another Etruscan center, Saturnia, which you'll smell before you can see: the strong odor of sulphur rises from these thermal springs, where first the Etruscans, then the Romans cured their bodily aches and pains. Set above the springs is the white town, built of bleached travertine rock. Saturnia is said to be the oldest city on the peninsula, dedicated to Saturn, god of fertility and dissemination. The town's recorded history begins around 800 BC. Within the old city walls, probably begun even before the Etruscans arrived, is the medieval center with a castle and well-tended piazzas surrounded by little stone houses. A walk along the cobblestone Via Clodia leads you through the old Porta Romana in the walls.

Scattered around the countryside north of the city are funerary urns from the Villanova period and stone Etruscan grave sites. Many of the graves have vanished over the years; it's said that local residents were happy to make use of these blocks of travertine lying around the countryside in building their own houses.

The thermal baths in the outrageously expensive hotel Terme di Saturnia below the city make the sulphurous waters available to wealthy hotel residents. If you follow the drainage canal, you'll come to an abandoned mill where the water forms natural pools and where you can, winter and summer, enjoy the healing waters free of charge. This is particularly fun on romantic moonlit nights.

On the way back to the coast, you'll come, about 5 miles (7 km) further on, to the picturesque mountain village of **Montemerano**. This town has a tower that's as crooked as the one in Pisa, just not as famous. Its 13th-century church S. Giorgio contains valuable frescoes and panel paintings, including a lovely polyptych by Sano di Pietro. There's an unusual story behind the *Madonna della Gattaiola*, from the school of Sassetta, that hangs here; for centuries, it was used as the door to a grain silo, with a little door cut in it for cats, before it was rescued and returned to its proper function.

The northern Etruscan settlements

For further excursions into Etruscan territory, the best point of departure is **Castiglione della Pescaia**. This pleasant holiday town is set among broad pine forests: on one side is the sea; on the other, the mountain Petruccio with its medieval fortifications. The Pisans built this castle, as well as the doughty city walls, with three gates and eleven towers. Here, where the lagoon of Lagus Prilius flowed into the sea, archaeologists have excavated a Roman bath facility.

In the modern part of town, which has spread into the foothills of the castle mountain, there's a harbor for sailors and fishermen as well as a lovely little sand

beach which gets wider as you go north, around the holiday complexes Riva del Sole, Roccamare and Le Rocchette. It's the pine woods behind this beach, incidentally, that form the setting for the novel *The Secret of the Pineta* by the successful authors Fruttero and Lucentini.

Continuing north, you'll see settlements atop nearly every hill, medieval fortresses to which people could retreat in the event of Saracen attack. One such is Buriano, a possession of Lamberto Aldobrandeschi around 900. Just next to it, **Vetulonia** sits atop a hill at a height of 1,125 feet (344 m). For years, the Etruscan settlement of *Vetluna* was believed lost. Not until 1850 did experts agree that the city must have been located here, atop the hills of Colonna di Buriano. Further evidence are coins embossed with the city's emblem, a trident and two dolphins, discovered in the burial sites.

Above: An especially notable set of horns. Right: The beauty of daily life in provincial Tuscany.

After Populonia, Vetulonia was the oldest Etruscan settlement, one of the powerful Alliance of Twelve Cities. It saw its greatest flowering in the 7th and 6th centuries BC due to the reserves of silver and ore in the nearby Colline Metallifere. Its subsequent decline was a result of the silting up of the lagoon on whose banks it lay, as well as continued attacks from the hostile Saracens.

A little ways down from the town are the funerary complexes with chamber graves and stone circle graves. Most architecturally interesting are the **Tomba della Petriera**, where a 72 foot (22 m) grave gives onto a rectangular, two-story burial chamber, and the **Tomba del Diavolino**, under a hill of earth 261 feet (80 m) in diameter. Excavations have also brought the remains of Roman streets to light. Part of the wealth of artifacts from this site, some dating from the Villanova period, are displayed in the Antiquarium at the entrance to Vetulonia; the rest have been taken to the archaeological museum in Florence. The medieval village was built upon, and with, the ruins of the older city, which can be seen from the remains of the fortification walls.

Somewhat farther north is the village of Giuncarico, a fortified Aldobrandeschi possession which came over to Siena in the 13th century. To the west, you can see the hill with the thermal bath of **Caldana**, which is first mentioned in the year 940. To reach the old city within the rectangular walls of the 16th-century castle, you go through a medieval city gate; at the end of the Via Montanara is the 12th-century church of San Biagio.

Another hill, another castle: **Gavorrano** sits in thick woods at an altitude of 893 feet (273 m). A baptismal church is supposed to have stood here as early as 1188. Notable is the elliptical form of the castle walls; also worth a look is the marble 13th-century Madonna and Child by Giovanni d'Agostino in the parish church. The statue was illegally sold at the beginning of this century, and returned by a Roman antiques dealer. Until recently, Gavorrano was a center for pyrite mining.

Like an eagle's aerie, **Scarlino** perches atop a hill 749 feet (229 m) high, looking down over the surrounding countryside. Its name derives from the Gothic word *Scheril*, or torch, for this town served as a kind of lighthouse. Its 12th-century fortifications belonged, in turn, to Roselle, Pisa, and Piombino. Excavations in the castle courtyard have shown that this spot has been inhabited since the Bronze Age. The Renaissance palace houses the archives of the city's history.

On the left side of the Gulf of Follonica road are the ruins of the Romanesque collegiate church San Michele. A little further on, on the same side, a path leads to the overgrown ruins of the monastery **Monte di Muro**, home to the heretical Dolcino monks for one chapter of its long history. It was destroyed by the Turks in the 16th century, and abandoned once and for all in the 18th.

By Portiglione are the quarries for pyrite from Gavorrano. Just next to these is a nature preserve with a sand beach, Cala Violina, which you can only reach on foot or by bus. Things are certainly more comfortable in the elegant town **Punta Ala** (from the SS 322, turn left at Pian d'Alma, and go 6 miles/9 km). Privately owned until quite recently, the town has a small harbor, lovely sand beaches, pine woods, and luxurious holiday and recreation facilities. The place itself, however, has very little in the way of atmosphere or charm.

COLLINE METALLIFERE

Etruscans, Romans, Lombards, Sienese, Florentines: all flocked to the area bordered by the Ombrone to the south and the Cecina to the north, lured by natural resources of copper, silver and iron. Possessing the Colline Metallifere meant, simply, wealth and power.

In the 15th century, however, the territory emptied out. The mines closed, and

there was a constant threat of malaria because of the coastal swamps. People didn't trickle back until the 19th century.

Follonica was founded in the year 1832, when the Grand Duke Leopold founded the first iron and steel foundries. These are still dominant features in what has become the most densely-populated community of the Colline Metallifere.

This city on the sea is a prime example of how the industrial age, pared with complete disregard for thought-out city planning, can utterly destroy a picturesque little town and all of the natural beauty that surrounds it. At best, the only sights this locale has to offer are such artifacts of industrial archaeology as the abandoned steel foundries, as well as a couple of public monuments such as the church of San Leopoldo (1836) designed by Carlo Reishammer, one of the first steel buildings in Tuscany.

Above: The cathedral of Massa Marittima.
Right: 11th-century relief by an unknown master on the cathedral of S. Cerbone.

A mere 10 miles (15 km) further on, however, you find yourself, mercifully, returned to the past at the excavation site of **Lago dell'Accesa**. Almost perfectly round, this glass-clear body of water swallowed up, or so the story goes, an entire village, simply because the inhabitants insisted on working on St. Anna's Day rather than resting. Nearby, the remains of an Etruscan settlement have been steadily coming to light since excavations began in 1980. The settlement was a kind of satellite of Vetulonia; finds from the site are displayed in the museum at Massa Marittima.

Massa Marittima

Originally a Roman estate (*Massa*) in a coastal region (*Marittima*), this former seat of a bishopric developed, in its heyday, into one of the true gems of medieval Tuscany. Massa Marittima is enchanting for its location alone. Some 16 miles (23 km) from Follonica, 1,243 feet (380 m) high, it looks out over the fertile plain toward the sea. This site was settled even in prehistoric times, and Etruscans, Romans, and, later, various medieval powers stayed because of the metal resources. In 1310, the world's oldest code of mining laws was passed here.

The town's recorded history begins when the Bishop of Populonia sought refuge in Castello Monte Regio after pirates had destroyed his own city. Massa experienced its true heyday in the Middle Ages. By 1300, there were already 10,000 people living within its walls. The copper and silver mining industries brought prosperity, while its protected located in a natural fortification of hills allowed this independent city-state to preserve a measure of independence for a considerable period, even after it was taken over by Siena in 1335. Later, however, as malaria continued to spread, its population dropped to a mere 500. The city remained uninhabited into the 19th century, which meant that its historic center has been preserved almost intact.

The lower, older section of the city is the Romanesque **Città Vecchia** (11th-13th centuries), while to the west is the mainly Gothic **Città Nuova** (13th century and after), which contains the ruins of the Castello Monte Regio and the Sienese fortress. Unusual is the fact that the newer part of the city is at a higher altitude than the older.

Another notable feature is the asymmetric division of the Piazza Garibaldi in the center of the lower city. In the midst of a rather severe ensemble of city palaces is, as if on a pedestal, the loveliest church in the Maremma, the **Cathedral of San Cerbone**. Begun in the 13th century in the Pisan Romanesque style, it gradually evolved into Lucchese Gothic. Flooded with light, the interior contains such treasures as an ornate baptismal font from 1267 (in the Baptistery, to the right) or the altarpiece of the *Madonna della Grazie* by the school of Duccio from 1316 (in the left transept). Also gorgeous

are the early Christian reliefs on the inner side of the facade, of unknown provenance. The crypt preserves relics of St. Cerbonius; stone reliefs on the casket narrate the story of this saint's life. Opposite the cathedral, the Palazzo Pretorio now houses an archaeological museum.

If you go on toward the SS 441, which links Massa Marittima and Siena, you'll catch sight among the chestnut trees of **Montieri**, 2,302 feet (704 m) up, which is thought to stand atop the ruins of an Etruscan settlement. Around the year 1000, the town was a bone of contention between Volterra and Siena, who both wanted control of its silver mines to use for minting their coins. Emperor Frederick II also helped himself from this source in the second half of the 12th century. When the pits had been mined dry, however, the town began to decline. Today, only the many buildings dating from the 13th and 14th centuries attest to its former wealth. Look in at the Romanesque parish church of SS Michele e Paolo, which was renovated in 1540.

163

Shortly before the SS 441 intersects with the SS 73, which leads from Grosseto to Siena via Roccastrada, you can detour off to the **Abbey of S. Galgano**, a little ways from the road. Some people may recognize this, one of Tuscany's most impressive ruins, from Tarkowski's film *Nostalghia*. In the Middle Ages this monastery church, of which only the walls, facade, apse and columns remain standing today, was one of the most important Cistercian abbeys around. Decline set in, however, in the 16th century, and the facility was dissolved altogether in 1783 by the Grand Duke of Tuscany. Try to visit this site at sunset, which illuminates this broad space, its floor overgrown with grass and open above to the heavens, with a special kind of light.

A little above these ruins is the burial church of St. Galgano. The round building is reminiscent of an Etruscan tumulus grave; in the chapel, a later addition, are frescoes by Ambrogio Lorenzetti.

If you drive back toward Massa along the SS 441, you'll pass through Boccheggiano, which was an important mining center in the Middle Ages, and then, a little over a mile (2 km) further on, come to a road leading off left toward **Montemassi**. This medieval Borgo, with the twice-fortified castle in the middle, was once the Aldobrandeschi's most important fortress. The Sienese battle for the city has been immortalized and preserved in a mural by Simone Martini on a wall of Siena's Palazzo Communale.

On the way back to the Via Aurelia, a little road just past Ribolla leads off to **Castel di Pietra**. It was here that Nino Pannocchieschi imprisoned his first wife, Pia dei Tolomei, because he wanted to marry Margherita Aldobrandeschi.

THE PROVINCE OF LIVORNO

The Etruscan Maremma extends over the border of the province and into Li-

Above: In the ruins of the abbey of S. Galgano. Right: Etruscan graves in Populonia.

vorno, as the name *Riviera degli Etruschi*, Etruscan Coast, indicates.

Populonia was the only Etruscan city that lay directly on the sea. Today, you get there by following the Via Aurelia and turning off at Venturina onto the road to **Piombino**, which lies at the southern end of the maquis-covered peninsula of Massoncello. In 809, refugees from Populonia founded the town on the spot where the Roman harbor of Falesia had once been located. At that point, the area belonged to the Gheradesca, who turned it over to Pisa in 1013. In 1399, Gherado D'Appiano created the independent principality of Piombino, which also included the islands of Elba, Pianosa and Montecristo. They were far from tranquil times, for many people wanted to control the harbor and mines of Elba, including Alfonso d'Aragona, Cesare Borgia, Cosimo del Medici and even Napoleon Bonaparte. Since the principality was turned over to the Duchy of Tuscany in 1815, things have been a good deal quieter in this city, which today as then bases its economy on iron processing. This industry is reflected in the skyline, dominated by factory chimneys.

Still pretty, however, are the old city with the 15th-century Palazzo Communale and the church of Sant'Antimo from 1377, which contains a marble baptismal font by Andrea Guardi. From the terrace of the Piazza Bovia, which juts out into the sea, you can see the islands of Elba and Capraia. Ferries run from Piombino to Elba several times a day.

Populonia, called *Pupluna* by the Etruscans, is 7 miles (10 km) away on the road toward San Vincenzo. Its history is closely linked with that of iron ore mining on Elba and in the Colline Metallifere. The city's heyday was in the 7th century BC, although excavations have shown that copper and bronze were processed here during the Villanova period. In the early Middle Ages, Populonia became the seat of a bishopric, an honor transferred to Massa Marittima in 835. After 1339, the town was incorporated into the principality of Piombino, and the

castle and the walls were built; parts of the walls are still standing. The museum displays Etruscan artifacts from the necropolis on the Gulf of Baratti. Where today umbrella pines cast shade was the site of a 4th-century industrial center devoted to processing iron ore from Elba. The graves came to light at the beginning of the 20th century, when people were making attempts at putting to use some of the debris from the old mines that were lying around the area.

Near the coastal road is the necropolis of **San Cerbone**, which includes the *Tomba del Bronzetto di Offerente*, a grave shaped like an ancient house (6th-5th centuries BC) and the *Tomba dei Carri* (7th/6th centuries), a chamber grave under a hill with a number of burial sites at the end of a corridor. Many of the graves have been plundered in the course of the years; everything that was left was

brought to be displayed in the museum in Florence.

By the vacation town of San Vincenzo, tucked away amid the pines, is the turnoff to Campiglia Marittima. Leading off on the left, by a gravel pit, is a track that narrows down to a footpath leading to Rocca San Silvestro. The ruins of this fortress of the Gheradesca (c. 1050) were abandoned around 1400 because the mines had been exhausted. Below the Rocca is an excavation site where finds have been uncovered demonstrating how the Etruscans processed iron; the path leading to it is well-signposted.

Campiglia Marittima is a gorgeous little medieval city dominated by the ruins of a 12th-century castle. On a clear day, you can see from here all the way to Elba. The city doesn't have any particularly notable art works to show for itself, but its winding narrow streets, old houses, and stone arches made it well worth visiting. Especially attractive are the 15th-century Palazzo Pretorio and the church of San Lorenzo (13th century).

Above: Village life in Campiglia Marittima.
Right: Geothermic power plant in Lardarello.

Not far away, between vineyards and olive groves, is **Suvereto**, which probably gets it name from the cork oak woods (*sughero*) which once covered the hills of this region. Here, in 1313, the corpse of Emperor Henry VII was cremated; the ashes were then taken to Pisa, there to be interred in the cathedral.

Following the Via Moncini, you'll pass through the 14th-century Porta alle Sicili and enter the Upper City. When the Sienese took over the city in 1335, they built a fortress around the Castello Monte Region. Just behind the gate is the Torre del Candeliere, build by the free citizens of Massa in 1228. Here, in the Upper City, is the church of Sant'Agostino (1313) and the former convent of Santa Chiara. In 1380, a son was born here to the Albizeschi family; he was later to become the Franciscan saint Bernard.

14 miles (20 km) north of Massa Marittima on the SS 439, sulphurous water bubbles up in the **Baths of Bagnolo** near Monterotondo Marittimo.

And in Larderello, about 10 miles (15 km) further north on the SS 439, there's also a penetrating smell of sulphur hanging in the air. Furthermore, there's all kinds of bubbling and steaming going on from various crevices in the earth: a diabolical impression that has little to do with the usual Tuscany cliches. In 1777, the German chemist Franz Höfer discovered boric acid in the steaming pools of water, heated to temperatures of up to 446F (230C) by volcanic lava just under the earth's crust. Not long after, in 1818, the Frenchman François Larderel started using this hot steam for industrial purposes. The town that grew up near the industrial site still bears his name today.

Since 1905, the steam has also been used to produce electricity. Like thick silver snakes, a tangle of steel pipes winds its way through the countryside, bypassing or connecting with cooling towers and an electric plant. Together with four other geothermic power plants in the

Amiata region, so much electricity is produced here in the Valle del Diavolo (Devil's Valley) that the needs of a major city like Florence can easily be covered.

The Palazzina Larderel (1818) houses a technical museum where you can learn more about the development of geothermic production of electricity.

Going back in the direction of Massa Marittima, a road 4 miles (6 km) behind Monterotondo Marittimo leads left into the area whence springs the river Cecina. There, on a small, winding road at an altitude of 2,531 feet (774 m) is **Gerfalco**, which was a fortress of the counts of Pannocchieschi in the 13th century, and was destroyed by an earthquake in 1502. A few walls, or fragments of walls, remain. It's in these mountains that the red marble is quarried used to adorn the cathedral of Siena.

Towering over the town is the mountain of Le Cornate, the highest elevation in the Colline Metallifere at 3,466 feet (1,060 m). Local legend has it that this was the site of the Witches' Sabbath.

PROVINCE OF GROSSETO

Accommodations

GROSSETO: *LUXURY:* **Bastiani Grand Hotel**, Via Gioberti, 64, tel: 0564-20047. **Lorena**, Via Trieste, 3, tel: 0564-25501.
MODERATE: **Maremma**, Via Fulceri de Calboli, tel: 0564-22293. **Nuova Grosseto**, P.zza Marconi, 26, tel: 0564-414105. **San Lorenzo**, via Piave, 22, tel: 0546-27918.
BUDGET: **Quattro Strade**, V. Aurelia Sud, 1, tel: 0564-25581. **La Pace**, Via della Pace, 10, tel: 0564-456280.

ARCIDOSSO: *MODERATE:* **Aiole**, Loc. Aiole, tel: 0564-967300. **Faggio Rosso**, Loc. Aiole, tel: 0564-967274. **Toscana**, Via D. Lazzaretti, 39, tel: 0564-967488.

CAPALBIO: *MODERATE:* **Il Bargello**, Via Circonvallazione, 24, tel: 0564-896020.
BUDGET: **La Mimosa**, Via Torino, tel: 0564-890220. **La Palma**, Via della Stazione, 5, tel: 0564-890341.

CASTEL DEL PIANO: *MODERATE:* **Impero**, Via Roma, 7, tel: 0564-955337.
BUDGET: **Da Venerio**, P.zza G. Carducci, 18, tel: 0564-955244. **Amiata**, Via D. Alighieri, 10, tel: 0564-955407.

CASTIGLIONE DELLA PESCAIA: *LUXURY:* **L'Approdo**, Via Ponte Giorgini, 29, tel: 0564-933466. **Riva del Sole**, Loc. Riva del Sole, tel: 0564-933625.
MODERATE: **Lucerna**, Via IV Novembre, 27, tel: 0564-933620. **Roma**, Via C. Colombo, 14, tel: 0564-933542.
BUDGET: **Aurora**, Via F.lli Bandiera, 19, tel: 0564-933718. **Il Gambero**, Via Ansedonia, 29, tel: 0564-937110.
CAMPING: **Baia delle Rocchette**, Loc. Rocchette, tel: 0564-941092. **Rocchette**, Loc. Rocchette, tel: 0564-941123. **Santapomata**, Via delle Rocchette, tel: 0564-941037.

FOLLONICA: *MODERATE:* **Golfo del Sole**, Via Italia, 301, tel: 0566-60218. **Lampada di Aladino**, Via Firenze, 10, tel: 0566-53535. **Piccolo Mondo**, Via Carducci, 2, tel: 0566-40361.

MANCIANO: *LUXURY:* **Terme di Saturnia**, Saturnia, Via della Follonata, tel: 0564-601061.
MODERATE: **Il Boscaccio**, Via P. Pascucci, 9, tel: 0564-620283. **Villa Acquaviva**, Loc. Acquaviva, tel: 0564-602890.
BUDGET: **Rossi**, Via A. Gramsci, 3, tel: 0546-629248.

MASSA MARITTIMA: *MODERATE:* **Il Sole**, Corso della Libertà, 43, tel: 0566-901971.
BUDGET: **Duca del Mare**, Via D. Alighieri, 1/2, tel: 0566-902284.

MONTE ARGENTARIO: *LUXURY:* **Baia d'Argento**, Porto S. Stefano, Loc. Pozzarello, tel: 0564-812643. **Il Pellicano**, Porto Ercole, Loc. Sbarcatello, tel: 0564-833801. **Villa Portuso**, Porto Ercole, Poggio Portuso, tel: 0564-834181.
MODERATE: **Marina**, P. Ercole, Lungomare A. Doria, 30, tel: 0564-833123. **Belvedere**, Porto S. Stefano, Via Fortino, 51, tel: 0564-812634.

ORBETELLO: *LUXURY:* **Telamonio**, Talamone, Via Garibaldi, 4, tel: 0564-887008.
MODERATE: **I Presidi**, Via Mura di Levante, 34, tel: 0564-867601/2. **Sole**, Via Colombo, 2 tel: 0564-860410.

PITIGLIANO: *BUDGET:* **Corano**, Loc. Corano, SS Maremmana, tel: 0564-616112. **Guastini**, Via Petruccioli, 4, tel: 0564-616065.

PUNTA ALA: *LUXURY:* **Cala del Porto**, Via del Porto, tel: 0564-922455. **Gallia Palace Hotel**, Via delle Sughere, tel: 0564-922022. **Golf Hotel**, Via del Gualdo, tel: 0564-922026.

ROCCASTRADA: *MODERATE:* **Caolino d'Italia**, Loc. I Piloni, tel: 0564-575466.

SANTA FIORA: *BUDGET:* **Eden**, Via Roma, 1 tel: 0564-977033. **Fiora**, Via Roma, 8, tel: 0564-977043.

SOVANA: *MODERATE:* **Taverna Etrusca**, Via Pretorio, 16, tel: 0564-616183.

Restaurants

GROSSETO: Enoteca Ombrone, Viale G. Matteotti, 63, tel: 0564-22585. Good food at good prices. Closed Sat eve and Sun.
Canapone, Piazza Dante, tel: 0546-24546. Traditional middle-class fare, closed Sun.
La Buca San Lorenzo, Viale Manetti, 1, tel: 0564-25142. Good fish dishes, inventive presentation, relatively expensive. Closed Mon.
Il Terzo Cerchio, Istia d'Ombrone, P.zza Castello, 2, tel: 0564-409235. Whatever menu the proprietor recommends is likely to be great; and the prices are completely acceptable. Closed Mon.
Osteria del Ponte Rotto, Istia d'Ombrone, Via Scansanese, 36, tel: 0564-409373. Traditional Maremma cuisine, good soups. Closed Wed.
Il Pescatore da Pizzica, Via Orcagna, 61, tel: 0546-49135. Comfortable family-owned trattoria in a former farmhouse. Closed Mon.
CAPALBIO: Da Maria, Via Comunale,3, tel: 0564-896014. Good, simple specialties of the Maremma, with especially tasty soups. Closed Tuesdays.
La Vallerana, Loc. Vallerana, tel: 0564-896050. Simple family business near Capalbio with good, traditional Maremma specialties. Closed Wed.
CASTIGLIONE DELLA PESCAIA: Corallo, Via Sauro, 1, tel: 0564-933668. Marvelous fish

dishes in a small pension. Reserve in advance. Closed Tue.

La Portaccia, Via San Benedetto Po, 13, tel: 0564-935318. Fresh fish specialties at moderate prices. Closed Mon.

Pizzeria Napoletana, Via Roma, 5, tel: 0564-935059. Lovely setting with a view of the harbor.

FOLLONICA: Leonardo Cappelli, Piazza XXV Aprile, 32, tel: 0566-44637. Elegant ambience, fine cooking at fairly high prices, marvelous wines. Closed Mon.

MAGLIANO IN TOSCANA: Aurora, Chiasso Lavagnini, 12/14, tel: 0564-592030. Typical old city restaurant with traditional specialties. Closed Wednesdays.

Sandra, Via Garibaldi, 20,tel: 0564-592196. Good food at reasonable prices and in nice surroundings. Closed Mon.

MONTEMERANO: Caino, Via Canonica, 3, tel: 0564-602817. Good food based on homemade dishes (pasta, etc.). Closed Wednesday in winter.

ORBETELLO: Il Nocchino, Vie dei Mille, 64, tel: 0564-860329. Good vegetable and fish dishes at reasonable prices. Closed Mon.

PORTO SANTO STEFANO: Orlando, Via Breschi, 3, tel: 0564-812788. Speciality: fish soup. Reasonable prices. Closed Thu.

Siro, Corso Umberto, 1, tel: 0564-812538. Great location with sea view and seafood. Closed Mon.

PORTO ERCOLE: Grotta del Pescatore, Via delle Fonti, 9, tel: 0564-833970. Good food, moderate prices. Closed Wed.

SATURNIA: Il Capriccio, Via del Poggio, 113, tel: 0564-607711. Traditional cooking, but with inventive touches such as snails or frogs' legs. Open dinner only Monday to Friday, lunch and dinner on weekends.

SOVANA: Scilla, Via di Sotto, 3, tel: 0564-656131. Traditional cooking with homemade pasta. Closed Tue.

Museums

GROSSETO: Museo Archeologico e d'Arte della Maremma, Pizza Baccarini, closed Wed.

Archaeological excavation site at Roselle, open from sunrise to sunset, tel: 0564-402403.

FOLLONICA: Museo del Ferro (iron museum), closed Sun and holidays.

MASSA MARITTIMA: Museo della Miniera (Mining Museum), Via Corridori. Guided tours: in winter 10 am-noon/3-4 pm, in summer 10 am-12:30/3:30-7 pm. Closed Mon.

Museo di Arte e Storia delle Miniere (Museum of Mining and Mining History): April 1-July 15 and September: 10-11 am/3-5 pm. March-October by arrangement. Closed Mon.

Museo Comunale in the Palazzo del Podestà, permanent exhibits of paintings and archaeological finds, open 10 am-12:30 pm and 3:30 pm-7 pm; October to March 9 am-1 pm and 3 pm-5 pm. Closed Mondays.

LARDERELLO: Geothermic Museum, open daily except New Year's, Easter and Christmas. Guided tours: tel: 0588-67724.

Nature preserves and parks

Parco faunistico del Monte Amiata, Arcidosso, tel: 0564-966867. The park is open daily except Mondays from sunrise to sunset. The best hiking seasons are in early summer (when there's a wealth of wildflowers) and autumn (middle of October to middle of November). There are plenty of well-marked trails.

Parco Naturale della Maremma, (Parco dell'Uccellina) Entrance in Alberese. In summer (June 15-Sept 30) admission to the park is only possible as part of a guided tour: Wednesday, Saturday and Sunday at 7 am and 4 pm. At other times of year you can move freely through the park on Wednesday, Saturday, Sunday and holidays, or take guided tours on other days. For further information, call: tel: 0546-407098.

Sights

Baths in **Saturnia**, below the hotel.

Tourist Information

A.P.T. Grosseto, Viale Monterosa, 206, tel: 0564-454510/343427.

Tourist office: Via Cavour, 5, tel: 0564-484111.

PROVINCE OF LIVORNO

Accommodations

PIOMBINO: *MODERATE:* **Ariston**, Via Ferrer, 7, tel: 0565-224390.

Collodi, Via Collodi, 7, tel: 0565-224272.

Esperia, Lungomare Marconi, 27, tel: 0565-42284.

CAMPIGLIA MARITTIMA: *BUDGET:* **Rossi**, Via Indipendenza, 190, tel: 0565-851256.

I Cinque Lecci, Via della Stazione, 30, tel: 0565-851021.

Sights

Necropolis of S. Cerbone, Populonia, open year-round from sunrise to sunset. Guided tours, tel: 0565-29545/29339.

Tourist Information

A.P.T. Livorno, Piazza Cavour, 6, tel. 0586-898111/899798/899112.

TUSCAN ARCHIPELAGO

**ELBA
GIGLIO
GIANNUTRI**

The Tuscan Archipelago, consisting of the islands Elba, Capraia, Gorgona, Pianosa, Montecristo and, farther south, Giglio and Giannutri, was once connected to the mainland. These "islands of pirates and saints," rich in history and legends, were inhabited as early as 50,000 BC. Today, one thing visitors can count on is fabulous swimming. Some of the islands are completely uninhabited; others are closed to visitors. Montecristo is a protected bird sanctuary; Gorgona and Pianosa, by contrast, house prisons.

ELBA

The largest of the islands, Elba, has an area of 80 sq. miles (223 sq. km) and lies about 6 miles (10 km) from the mainland. To the west, the countryside is almost Alpine in character, with a kind of stark, intense beauty. Contrasting with this is the agricultural character of the hilly plains in central Elba and the terraced countryside in the east, built up over the years by the residue left by the iron mines. Because of its mild climate and beautiful bathing coves, the island is a popular holiday destination.

Preceding pages: In Giglio Castello on the Isola del Giglio. Left: Making oyster-baskets on Elba.

Because of its natural resources of iron ore, Elba (from Latin *ilva*, iron) has been the object of contention from earliest history. At first, the Etruscans shipped the metalliferous rock over to the mainland, where there were more trees to fire their kilns and keep them burning. The Romans were not happy with the Etruscans' monopoly in the iron trade; the island was, therefore, one of the first objectives in the Roman conquest of Etruria.

Time and again, Elba was a bone of contention in conflicts between Barbarians from the north and pirates from the south. Not until the 11th century, under the Pisans, did things let up. In 1392, the island was incorporated into the Principality of Piombino, and its troubles began all over again. Elba has gone down in the history books as the site of Napoleon Bonaparte's exile in 1814, from which he set off for Waterloo 10 months later. Shortly thereafter, in 1815, Elba was awarded to the grand duchy of Tuscany. The island's blast furnaces were destroyed in World War II, and Elba's main industry has been tourism ever since.

Coming from Piombino or Livorno (Leghorn), you'll land at the island's capital, **Portoferraio**. Construction of this city on a rocky promontory in the north of the island began in 1548 under Cosimo di Medici. It became a master-

173

LIGURIAN SEA

Isola d' Elba

TYRRHENIAN SEA

I. Pianosa

I. del Giglio

TUSCAN ARCHIPELAGO

0 10 20 30 40 50 km

to I. del Giglio, I. di Giannutri

to I. di Giannutri

piece of military architecture with a circular wall starting at the old port; an octagonal watchtower; the star-shaped Forta Stella; and the Forta Falcone higher up.

The Porta a Mare or Medicea is the gate to the old city. Following Via Garibaldi past the city hall, where you can find a granite Roman sacrificial altar in the courtyard, you'll come to the Villa dei Mullini (Mill Villa), Napoleon's city residence, today a museum. The disenfranchised emperor spent part of his time in his country house, Villa San Martino, located on the road to Procchio. The Neo-Classical facade was later added by Prince Demidoff, who also assembled the Napoleon collection. If you feel in need of a little refreshment after visiting the museum, you'll find one of the most beautiful sand beaches on the north coast of Elba at the Gulf of Biodola, some 4 miles (7 km) away. The town of Forno takes its name from the remnants of Etruscan smelting furnaces found here.

Right: Fishing boats in Portofino harbor.

Continuing along the winding road, you'll come to **Procchio**, a busy holiday resort with a white sand beach. From here, you can take a short trip up to the Etruscan mountain settlement of **Monte Castello**. Charred remains of houses were hidden under piles of Roman cobblestones, a sign that the village was not abandoned in a wholly peaceful manner.

After another 4 miles (7 km), you come to **Marciana Marina**; the town's 12th-century Saracen tower dominates the landscape for miles around. Marciana Marina's quaint old city quarter and its lively seaside promenade are popular vacation spots. In the past this was the harbor for the old mountain town of Marciana, from where the Appiani ruled their principality of Piombino between 1399 and 1634. The Casa degli Appiani (15th century) and the mint, where the princes coined their gold and silver pieces, are testimony to this period.

Situated amidst terraced vineyards and dense forests, the town can only be visited on foot due to its narrow, stepped

174

streets. A small archaeological museum displays finds from the area. Near the 15th-century fortress by the city gates is the start of a well-marked path leading to the oldest pilgrimage chapel on the island, Madonna del Monte, with its miraculous picture of the Madonna. A cable car runs from Marciana up to the summit of Monte Capanne (3,329 feet / 1,018 m), the highest point on the island.

Not far from Marciana is the terraced spa town of **Poggio Terme**, known for the curative mineral waters issuing from its spring, Fonte Napoleone. Churchill, di Chirico and Delacroix are among the many who have vacationed here. The town is a good point of departure for hikes up Monte Capanne or visits to the hermitage of San Cerbone, where the Bishop of Populonia retreated when he was fleeing from the Lombards in 572. The path leading there starts at the cemetery of Poggio Terme.

From here, a road leads inland through chestnut and pine forests to Monte Perone (2,060 feet / 630 m), whose flat

peak affords a good view out over the entire island. From Marciana, the coastal road winds along the steep slopes of Monte Giove. The holiday resorts of Zanca and Sant' Andrea have tiny sand beaches, and there's excellent diving off the coast. Roman and Greek artifacts from ancient shipwrecks have been salvaged all along this coast, a reminder of how treacherous the sea here can be.

It is difficult to reach the coast from the road. There is, however, a path leading to the lighthouse Faro di Punta near Patresi Mare. The Punta Nera, the westernmost point of the island, is shortly before Chiessi. Besides a few wall fragments in some maquis thickets, nothing remains of the erstwhile settlement of Pomonte. But hikers can certainly set out from here to explore the interior of the island.

After the long stretch of rocky coast, the white sand beaches of the resorts Fetovaia, Seccheto and Cavoli are a welcome, and enticing, relief. A little over a mile (2 km) past Cavoli, a road on the left leads to **San Piero in Campo**, a moun-

175

tain village above the Gulf of Marina di Campo. Here, there's a 12th-century Romanesque church, San Nicolò, with frescoes dating from the 14th and 15th centuries. It stands on the site of a Roman temple to Glauco, the god of the sea, built during the reign of the emperor Octavian.

Marina di Campo has everything a tourist's heart desires: a seaside promenade, a sand beach, shops, harbor, even a surfing and sailing school. Main attraction of the neighboring town of Lacona is Spiaggia Grande, a wide, sandy beach.

Passing Golfo Stella and its small beaches and coves, you'll come to the **Calamita peninsula**, the part of the island richest in natural mineral resources. The magnetite ore within Monte Calamita is said to affect the compass needles of passing ships. Surface iron ore mining gradually transformed the hills here into a terraced countryside of vineyards and olive groves. A winding road

Above: Discussing the latest gossip in Giglio Castello.

leads to **Capoliveri**, a picturesque hilltop town surrounded by vineyards; its crooked alleyways converge at the town square. *Caput Liberum*, mountain of liberty, was a place of refuge for Roman citizens in trouble with the law. Not far off is the 16th-century pilgrimage church Madonna delle Grazie. At the end of the peninsula are small bathing beaches and the nature reserve *Costa dei Gabbiani*.

At about the same latitude as Capoliveri, but on the east coast of the island, is the Spanish Forte Focardo (1678). Across the bay is the holiday port of **Porto Azzuro**. Built by the Spanish in the 17th century, this fort has been used as a prison since the 19th century. The Spanish were also responsible for the nearby pilgrimage church, with a replica of the black Madonna di Monserrat.

The northern part of east Elba is known for its rare minerals; and experts and laypeople alike will find plenty of interest in the collections in **Rio Marina**. The history of this town has been linked to iron ore mining for 2,500 years. At the beginning it was a loading port, and the octagonal watchtower (1534) served as protection. Built of stone which, because of its high iron content, rusts, the residential houses here were constructed around 1800 when the administration of the ore mines was moved here from Rio nell'Elba. With the closing of the mines in 1982, the fate of the town was sealed. Remains of Roman and Etruscan smelting ovens have been found nearby.

The neighboring town of **Cavo**, popular even with the Romans as a summer residence, is where the mine directors lived. From here, the road passes through lush greenery and then barren country on the way south to Rio nell'Elba. Every building here is like a small fortress. The inhabitants had to keep defending themselves against pirate attacks or enemy siege. Today, the small houses where the miners once lived are summer cottages. From here, an unpaved road leads to the

Bay of Nisportino with its small, sandy beach and the tourist center of Nisporto.

On the way back to Portoferraio, a road shortly after Bagnaia branches off to a ruin called Volterraio. This site, an island landmark, was built by the Pisans in the 13th century, supposedly upon the ruins of an Etruscan settlement. For a long time, this fortress, which commands a view of the Bay of Portoferraio, was the safest point on the whole island. Unfortunately, it has been left to decay. Because of the danger of falling, only experienced hikers should attempt a visit. Shortly before the capital of the island and near the San Giovanni thermal baths lies the Roman country house delle Grotte.

GIGLIO AND GIANNUTRI

Giglio, 8 square miles (21 sq. km) in area, is the Tuscan Archipelago's second-largest island. Ferries run the 8.5 miles (14 km) from Porto Santo Stefano out to the island several times a day. The inaccessible coast is popular with divers; there are few beaches. The locals live mainly from farming and tourism.

This rocky island is overgrown with maquis and has three main towns. Giglio Porto is the port on the east coast; Giglio Castell is a charming little inland town with narrow winding streets, a 13th-century fortress, and an ivory sculpture of Christ by Giambologna in the parish church; and Campese, on the west coast, sports the picturesque Torre del Campese, which the Giglio citizens' army used as a defense against the attacks of pirates from the south.

Giannutri (1 sq. mile/2.6 sq. km), the southernmost of Tuscany's islands, is inhabited only in summer. Upon it are the ruins of a Roman villa from the 1st century BC. Cistercian monks arrived around 1000, and at the end of the 19th century Captain Gualtiero Adami voluntarily lived here for 40 years as a kind of modern-day Robinson Crusoe.

ELBA
(Telephone area code: 0565)
Accommodations
PORTOFERRAIO: *MODERATE:* **Airone Hotel**, Loc. San Giovanni, tel: 929111. **Biodola**, Loc. Biodola, tel: 936811. **Hermitage**, Loc. Biodola, tel: 936911. *BUDGET:* **Grotte del Paradiso**, Loc. Le Grotte, tel: 933057. **Punta Pina**, Loc. Bagnaia, tel: 961077.
CAMPO NELL'ELBA: *MODERATE:* **Montecristo**, Via Nomellini, 11, tel: 976861. **Select**, Via Mascagni, 2 tel: 077702. **Hotel dei Coralli**, Viale degli Etruschi, 81, tel: 976336.
CAPOLIVERI: *MODERATE:* **Elba International,** Loc. Nargno, tel: 968611. **Antares**, Loc. Lido, tel: 940131. *BUDGET:* **La Voce del Mare**, Loc. Naregno, tel: 968455. **Villa Miramare**, Loc. Pareti, tel: 968673.
MARCIANA: *LUXURY:* **Desirée**, Loc. Spartaia, tel: 907311. **La Perla**, Loc Procchio, tel: 907371. *MODERATE:* **Corallo**, Loc. Pomonte, tel: 906042. **Delfino**, Loc. Procchio, tel: 907455.
MARCIANA MARINA: *LUXURY:* **Gabbiano Azzurro II**, Viale Amedeo, tel: 997035. *MODERATE:* **La Conchiglia**, Via XX Sett., 43, tel: 99016. **Marinella**, Viale Margherita, 38, tel: 99018.
PORTO AZZURRO: *MODERATE:* **Belmare**, Banch. IV Nov., 21, tel: 95012. **Cala di Mola**, Loc. Mola, tel: 95225.
RIO MARINA: *LUXURY:* **Ortano Mare**, Loc. Ortano, tel: 939159. *MODERATE:* **Cristallo**, Loc. Cavo, tel: 949898. **Maristella,** Loc. Cavo, tel: 949859. **Rio**, Via Palestro, 31, tel: 962722.
Restaurants
Il Chiasso, Via Sauro, 9, Capoliveri, tel: 968709. Fish dishes, fairly expensive. **Olga**, Via dell'Amore, 54, Portoferraio, tel: 971446. Lovely setting, good food, moderate prices.
Museums
Napoleon Museums: *Villa dei Mulini* in Portoferraio and *Residenza Estiva*, Loc. S. Martino, both open 9 am-5 pm, Sun 9 am-12:30 pm.
Tourist Information
A.P.T. Portoferraio, Calata Italia, 26, tel: 914671.

GIGLIO
Accommodations
PORTO: *MODERATE:* **Arenella**, Via Arenella, 5, 0564-809340. **Castello Monticello**, Via Provinciale, tel: 809252.
CAMPESE: *MODERATE:* **Campese**, Via della Torre, 18, tel: 0564-804003.
Tourist Information
A.P.T. Grosseto, Via Monterosa, 206, tel: 0564-454510/454527

ALONG THE COAST TO THE NORTH

RIVIERA DEGLI ETRUSCHI
LIVORNO
PISA / PROVINCE OF PISA
LUCCA

RIVIERA DEGLI ETRUSCHI

Steep or gentle and sandy, lined with pine forests, the Etruscan shoreline or Riva degli Etruschi, which reaches from Piombino up to Livorno, has something for everyone. Along the coast are tempting opportunities for a swim; in the hilly hinterland, you can visit small fortified towns that grew up around monasteries and *castelli* in the Middle Ages; and there's plenty to occupy lovers of nature.

Following the SS 1 northward, you'll come, 5 miles (8 km) past the resort of San Vincenzo, to a road leading right to **Castagneto Carducci**. This town was named for author and Nobel Prize winner Giosuè Carducci, who spent his youth here and in neighboring Bólgheri. By the year 1000, the aristocratic Lombard family of the Gherardesca had already taken possession of the *castello* outside the city gates. Now as then, this family also owns the ruined castle in Donoratico, as well as the castello in **Bólgheri**, a town linked to the SS 1 by a famous three-and-a-half-mile (5 km) cypress avenue.

Near La California, a road leads up into the hills and to the picturesque town

Preceding pages: Evening in Marina di Pisa. Left: An unusual view of Pisa's Cathedral and Baptistery.

of **Guardistallo**. The town's 11th-century castle was destroyed by an earthquake in 1846, but the medieval town center with its narrow, winding streets has remained intact. From here, you can look down to the sea and the plains around Cecina by the mouth of the river of the same name; its source is in the hills around Volterra. In 1818 there was only one man living here, but now the town has become a popular holiday destination for Italian families. Displays in the museum next to the town hall demonstrate that the area was inhabited even in prehistoric times. Another archaeological museum with Etruscan finds from the Cecina valley is located in the neighboring town of **Rosignano Marittimo**.

LIVORNO (LEGHORN)

The foundation stone of today's Livorno was laid on March 28, 1577, at the behest of Cosimo I di Medici. The reason for reestablishing the old town of Liberna at the defensive tower Matilda (1103) was to replace the former Roman naval base of Portus Pisanus, which became Pisa's harbor in the Middle Ages, but which had since become unusable. The architect Buontalenti drew up a new city plan, with the Fortezza Nuova and the cathedral contained within pentagonal city

walls. A Fortezza Vecchia, designed by Antonio di Sangallo, had already been completed in 1534. Livorno quickly flourished. In the 18th century it became the second-largest city in Tuscany, a position it still holds today.

From an art-historical perspective, the modern, busy city has little to offer, since many of the Old City's buildings were destroyed in World War II. Still worth a visit, certainly, are the Medici monuments; the old fishermen's quarter Quartiere Venezia, crisscrossed with canals; and the City Aquarium on the Terrazza Mascagni at the end of Viale Italia. Everything else in Livorno revolves around the harbor, the largest commercial and passenger port in Tuscany.

At the beginning of this century, painters Amadeo Modigliani and Giovanni Fattori, whose works hang in the Museo Civico Giovanni Fattori, helped the city to a degree of fame. The former

Above: Three and a half miles (5 km) of cypress forest line the road to Bólgheri.

Villa Fabricotti on Piazza Matteotti, by contrast, houses a city museum with the usual collection of archaeological finds.

Halfway between Livorno and Pisa begins the nature preserve and park of Migliarino, where wild boar and fallow deer romp about amidst the oaks and pines. On the southern edge rises the magnificent Romanesque basilica San Pietro a Grado, which was built in the 11th century on the remains of a previous Lombard construction (6th century). The church's frescoes depict scenes from the life of St. Peter and portraits of the popes.

PISA

In Antiquity, the Arno River flowed into a lagoon off the sea, which silted up during the Middle Ages. On the south bank of this lagoon, on the site of present-day Livorno, the emperor Augustus founded the naval base of Portus Pisanus. On the opposite bank, a settlement developed which had already existed in the days of the Etruscans: Pisa. After the fall of the Western Roman Empire in 476, all Tuscany suffered under the attacks of plundering invaders: cities and country alike became destitute and depopulated. Only the seaport Pisa, now 7.5 miles (12 km) inland, and the Lombard town of Lucca escaped this fate. Pisa even expanded its marine supremacy; its fleet successfully defended itself against the Saracens, and in 1063 defeated the Arabs at Palermo. After this, Pisa was undisputed ruler of the Mediterranean, and developed trade connections and increased its wealth unchecked. This led to a significant upswing of art and culture between the 11th and 13th centuries; the Pisan Romanesque style soon influenced architecture throughout the Mediterranean.

On land, Pisa's enemies were the cities of Lucca and Florence, which wanted free access to the sea. At sea, the city's main competitors were Amalfi and Genoa; the latter finally dealt Pisa a devastating defeat in 1284. The powerful maritime republic of Pisa never recovered from this blow. Not until the 16th century did Pisa experience a revival, after Medici patronage had led to the building of houses, bridges, and a connecting canal to the sea, as well as the expansion of the university.

Entering the old city through the west gate of the medieval city walls, you'll find the overwhelming piazza **Campo dei Miracoli** spreading out to your left. The cathedral, baptistery, famous leaning bell tower, or campanile, and monumental cemetery are richly decorated with white Carrara marble, blind arches on the ground floor, and elevated walkways with arches and pillars.

Construction of the cathedral began in 1064, financed by the spoils of the battle in Palermo. In order to give himself room to play with, the architect Buscheto, whose background was Byzantine, chose a building site on the edge of town. Popular wisdom had it that one motivation for this choice was to make the neighboring

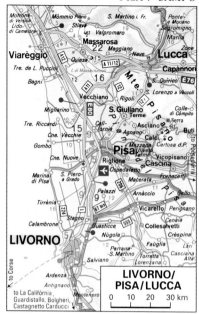

Lucchese jealous. Certainly, it rapidly became clear, even in the course of construction, that the swampy alluvial land was not an ideal surface on which to build. Solid proof of this fact is the city's hallmark, the Leaning Tower.

The **cathedral** consists of a five-aisled nave, extended by Rainaldus in the 12th century; a three-aisled transept; and a presbytery rounded off by an apse. The cruciform church was crowned with a unique oval dome. You enter through bronze doors dating from around 1180, with reliefs depicting scenes from the lives of the Virgin and Christ. The two-tone pointed arches lining the nave echo the architecture of Islamic mosques; the mosaic of the apse, part of which was executed by the painter Cimabue (1302), also betrays the Byzantine influence. The pulpit, by Giovanni Pisano (1302-1311), is decorated with dramatic reliefs depicting scenes from the New Testament; this masterpiece, however, broke off in 1559, and the restoration that was carried out in 1929 was not quite true to the original. In

the right transept is the tomb of Henry VII, Holy Roman Emperor and patron of the city, who died at Buonconvento in 1313. Further treasures are displayed in the Museo dell'Opera del Duomo.

In planning the artistic decoration of the **Baptistery** (1153), architect Diotisalvi stayed true to the plan of the cathedral's facade, with blind arches and a columned gallery; Gothic stylistic elements were added a century later by Nicola and Giovanni Pisano. Not until 1358 was the baptistery finished off with its vaulted roof and topped with the figure of Christ you see today. Inside, the baptismal font is by Guido Bigarelli (1246); while the showpiece, the hexagonal pulpit by Nicola Pisano, is the first example of Gothic sculpture in Italy. Its reliefs also depict scenes from the New Testament.

The 180-foot (55 m) **Campanile**, the famous leaning tower with its 180 col-

Above: Relief sculpture on the Baptistery door in Pisa. Right: S. Maria della Spina on the bank of the Arno.

umns, was begun in 1173 according to designs by Diotisalvi or Bonanno, but wasn't completed until a century later, because the alluvial sand kept giving way during construction. Attempts to compensating for the tilt by actually bending the tower in the other direction proved unsuccessful. At present, the tower is 13 feet (4 m) from the vertical, and leaning a bit more every year. Because of the danger of falling, the tower has been closed to visitors since 1990.

The cemetery **Campo Santo Monumentale**, begun in 1277, completes the ensemble of the "Square of Miracles." A colonnade surrounds the elongated courtyard of this rectangular, walled site, filled with soil supposedly brought from the Holy Land. Gravestones are set into the ground, while on the wall you can make out remains of the frescoes that were almost completely destroyed in World War II. From sketches of the frescoes in the **Museo delle Sinopie**, on the opposite side of the Campo, you can see just how much was lost.

Because of the overwhelming impression of the Campo dei Miracoli, it's easy to lose sight of the fact that the city has other things to offer. Furthermore, there doesn't seem to be much interest in trying to acquaint visitors with other parts of the city; signposts are few and far between. If you want to get to know Pisa, therefore, arm yourself with a good city map and a discoverer's curiosity.

There is, for instance, the Benedictine church **S. Zeno** (10th/11th centuries) located at the east gate of the old city. Even the Pisans themselves didn't discover this until 1972, when the stucco had been removed. Restoration brought a facade of yellow volcanic limestone, adorned with Roman capitals, to the light of day. Also unusual is the vestibule, which resembles a portico. On the nearby Piazza Martiri di Libertà is the 13th-century Dominican church **S. Caterina**, with a Romanesque marble facade with blind arches and a rose window; the sculpture on the main altar is by Nino Pisano. From the opposite side of this square, the Via San Lorenzo leads to the **Piazza dei Cavalieri**, the center of the maritime republic of Pisa. In the 16th century, the order of the Knights of St. Stephen commissioned Giorgio Vasari to redesign the square. Accordingly, the palace of the Anziani family became the Palazzo dei Cavalieri with a painted facade (today, it houses the renowned Scuola Normale Superiore), and two medieval towers were turned into the Palazzo dell' Orologio. In the so-called Hunger Tower, Count Ugolino della Gherardesca, held responsible for the city's defeat by the Genoese in 1284, was sentenced to starve to death. Vasari also built a church on this square.

By following the arcaded shopping street of Via Oberdan, you'll come to the banks of the Arno. The **Museo Nazionale San Matteo** at Lungarno Mediceo, housed in a former Benedictine convent, displays Tuscan, specifically Pisan sculpture and painting, featuring painted wooden crosses (12th/13th centuries) and original architectural models of the Baptistery. You can cross the Arno on the

185

single-arched **Ponte di Mezzo**, site every June of the historic festival Gioco del Ponte. On the bank of the river is the church Santa Maria della Spina, basically an outsized stone reliquary for a small thorn from Jesus' crown. This small church with ornate Gothic gables, the only 14th-century religious building that's survived, had to be moved in 1871, as the Arno was proving too much of a threat. Heading downriver in a westerly direction, you'll come to the monastery church of the Vallombrosan order, **S. Paolo a Ripa d'Arno**, with a two-tone marble facade and the same architectural elements as the cathedral. This jewel of 12th-century Pisan Romanesque architecture includes the octagonal chapel of Sant'Agata with its pyramidal dome.

PROVINCE OF PISA

The country around Pisa also profited from the fortunes of the maritime republic. Around the year 1000, this territory began to fill up with people: settlements were founded; fortresses and churches built. Development was furthered by the steady stream of travelers along the trade route of the Frankish Road.

Extending between Pisa and Lucca is the hilly region of Monte Pisano, foothills of the Apuan Alps. The largest community is a former Roman spa, **San Guiliano Terme**. Until well into the 19th century, this resort was popular with the aristocracy, who built their summer villas here. A typical example is the 16th-century Villa Roncioni in the district of Pugnano, surrounded by a romantic park.

East of Pisa, in the Valle Graziosa, is a town with a turbulent history: **Calci**. The site has been occupied by Etruscans, Romans, Lombards, Pisans and Florentines, by turns. It is also said to be the place where, in 1375, Saint Catherine persuaded the British plunderer John Hawkwood to place his troops in the service of the church. Noteworthy sights here are the Pisan Romanesque parish church (11th/12th centuries), a gem of sacral architecture, and the nearby **Certosa di Calci**. This monastery was founded in 1399, but didn't receive its present Baroque appearance until the 17th century. Its cloisters and fresco-decorated halls can only be visited with an official guide. A recent arrival here is a new museum of nature and local history.

Difficult of access, the slopes of Monte Verucca (1,919 feet/587 m) behind the Carthusian monastery support the ruins of the abbey San Michele and a fortress which was razed in 1342. There is said to be an underground passageway connecting the fortress with the nearby watchtower of Caprona and even with Pisa; but this passage has yet to be discovered.

From Calci, a winding road goes past Trecolli to the medieval fortress of **Vicopisano**, a possession of the Bishop of Lucca since the 10th century. The 13th-century towers rising above the houses were restored by Brunelleschi after Florence conquered the town in 1407. There are valuable wooden sculptures in the Romanesque parish church.

You can also encounter a living past in the small villages nestled in the mountains south of the Arno, where the people live from their vineyards and olive groves. **Pontedera**, however, is known for a slice of more recent history: it's here that Vespas are produced, the motorbikes which since the '50s have been virtually synonymous with the Italian way of life.

Approximately 10 miles (16 km) south of Pontedera is **Casciana Terme**, where Roman citizens, and later the Countess Mathilde, went to be treated for gout and rheumatism. Passing Lari and the former Pisan castle Ponsacco, from which you can detour to the nearby Medici Villa Camugliano (1533), you'll return to the expressway connecting Pisa to Florence.

Right: View of Lucca from the Torre Guinigi.

LUCCA

Only 12.5 miles (20 km) lie between Pisa and Lucca. But the two cities aren't so much separated by miles, or by Monte Pisano, as by a long history of rivalry which broke out in armed combat through the ages. Halfway between them stands the Nozzano Castle, built in 1126 by Matilde of Canossa to ward off Pisan attacks. In the neighboring town of Ripafratta, Pisa built a defensive castle for exactly the same purpose.

A Roman military base with streets laid out in a chessboard pattern, with a forum and amphitheater, standing on the swampy soil of the Serchio River valley – that was Lucca in year 180 BC (*luk* is Etruscan for marsh). In 568, the Lombards selected this town to be their capital in Tuscia. They left behind a number of Romanesque churches and the pilgrimage road *Francigena*, a route which facilitated the Lucchese's cloth trade. In the 11th century, Lucca's citizens declared their city politically autonomous and ex-

panded their sphere of influence to Versilia and Garfagnana. Aside from short interruptions, Lucca remained independent until 1799, when the French marched in. The city was appointed to the duchy of Parma in 1815, and belonged, after 1847, to the grand duchy of Tuscany.

The impressive fortification wall with its 11 bastions, measuring more than 2.5 miles (4 km) in length, up to 98 feet (30 m) in width, and 117 feet (12 m) high, completely encircles the city. In the days of the Romans the town already boasted a city wall, albeit of far more modest proportions, of which you can still see a few remains. In the late Middle Ages, a second circular wall was built to encompass the suburbs of S. Maria Forisportam in the east and San Frediano in the north.

Today, the center of Lucca is the tree-shaded Piazza Napoleone with its magnificent Ducal Palace, begun in 1578 and continually renovated over the years since. Starting at the piazza is the Via Duomo, on which is located the church of San Giovanni; until the 8th century, this

church was the seat of the bishopric. The present-day construction dates from the 13th century; the rectangular baptistery with its lancet arch cupola was added a hundred years later; and the facade wasn't built until around 1600. Recent excavations in the church's interior have unearthed Roman remains. Just a stone's throw away is the **Cathedral of San Martino**, one of Italy's oldest churches (6th century), which was fundamentally changed at the beginning of the 12th century and fitted out with a campanile in 1233. On the ground floor of the Romanesque facade with its three storeys of blind arches, three columned arcades lead into the vestibule. The stone labyrinth on the right pillar is a symbol of the pilgrimage road *Francigena*. By peering through two hatches in the portals, travelers who had to leave town before sunrise could take one last look at the

face of Jesus on the wooden crucifix known as the *Volto Santo*. This sculpture, which is borne through the city in a ceremonial procession every September, is one of the most famous works of Christianity. Popes and kings came to Lucca just to see it. According to the legend recounted by the frescoes on the inner side of the facade, the wooden crucifix is by one of Jesus' apostles, and miraculously turned up in Lucca in the 11th century.

There is yet another world-famous work of art inside the church: the marble tomb of Ilaria del Carretto by the Sienese sculptor Jacopo della Quercia, commissioned by the ruler Paolo Guinigi in 1406 in memory of his prematurely deceased wife. In the aisle on the right, there's a painting by Tintoretto depicting the disciples of Jesus at the Last Supper (1590).

The Via Arcivescovato begins behind the cathedral and leads to the Palazzo Guinigi. In Lucca, it's said that the most powerful man is he who can see the farthest; and indeed, from the observation platform atop the 230 steps of the Guinigi

Above: The Piazza dell'Anfiteatro echoes the oval of the former Roman amphitheater.
Right: Flower-seller on Piazza S. Michele.

Tower, you can actually see the entire city and surrounding area, and thus have a feeling that things are under control.

The Via Guinigi runs into the Via Mordini, which follows the course of the old Roman wall. Here is where the Roman amphitheater once stood; in the Middle Ages, its walls were incorporated into residential dwellings. This explains the elliptical shape of the Piazza Anfiteatro. Behind this is the church **San Frediano**, with a marvelous 12th-century mosaic on the facade. Both the campanile and the high interior with an open roof truss are typical of the Lucchese Romanesque style. In the first side chapel on the right is a baptismal font dating from the 12th century, and to the left at the rear of the church, in the Trenta Chapel, is a marble altar by Jacopo della Quercia (1422).

Lined with lovely shops, the street Via Fillunga leads back to the center of town. Set into the plain facade of **S. Cristoforo** is an iron cross comprised of two measuring-sticks. This was used, in case of doubt, to determine whether or not a cloth dealer had cheated a customer. If he had, his stand was broken into pieces, or *bancarotta* – hence the word bankrupt. The Via Roma ends at the Piazza San Michele, once the site of the Roman forum. The church of **S. Michele in Foro** has stood here since the 12th century, stone expression of the pride of citizens who erected this in defiance of the bishop's power. Seen from outside, with its blind arches and pillars, the church is reminiscent of the cathedral in Pisa. The ornamental highlight is the ornate facade; its wealth of decoration culminates in a four-story pillared gallery towering over the roof of the church.

From here, it's not far to the birthplace of the opera composer Giacomo Puccini (*Tosca, La Bohème*) on Via Poggio. Also nearby, on Via Galli Tassi, is the city palace of the Mansis (17th century), which houses the state painting collection. But it's in the National Museum in the Villa

Guinigi (1418), on Via della Quarquonia at the eastern edge of the old city, that art lovers will come into their own. As well as Etruscan and Roman sculptures and Lombard jewelry, you can examine medieval wooden crucifixes or peruse examples of the Lucchese weavers' art.

Grandiose villas of the rich city merchants are typical features of the countryside around Lucca. The grounds, in particular, tend to be lavishly decorated with statues, waterworks, flower beds in geometric patterns, and topiary labyrinths. Some especially fine examples are located northeast of the SP 435 in the direction of Pescia, such as the **Villa Mansi** near Segromigno Monte or the **Villa Reale** in Marlia. In the 17th century, the latter had one of the most famous estate gardens around; only part of the classical layout has survived, but it's nonetheless worth a visit. The park of the 16th-century **Villa Torrigiani** near Camigliano, also considered a masterpiece of landscape gardening, was famous in its day for no-holds-barred parties.

RIVIERA DEGLI ETRUSCHI
Accommodations
SAN VINCENZO: *LUXURY:* **Park Hotel**, Via d. Principessa, 116, tel: 0565-704111.
MODERATE: **Il Delfino**, Via Colombo, 15, tel: 0565-701179. **La Vela**, Via V. Emanuele II, 72, tel: 0565-701529. *CAMPING:* **Park Albatros**, Loc. Pineta di Torre Nuova, tel: 0565-701018.
CASTAGNETO CARDUCCI: *MODERATE:* **La Torre di Donoratico**, Loc. La Torre, 42, tel: 0565-775268. **Zi Martino**, Loc. S. Giusto, tel: 0565-766000. **Hotel Bambolo**, Via Bambolo, 31, tel: 0565-775346. *CAMPING:* **Belmare**, Via del Forte, 1, tel: 0565- 744092. **International Etruria,** Via della Pineta, tel: 0565- 744254.
ROSIGNANO MARITTIMO: *LUXURY:* **Villa Parisi**, Via della Torre, 6, tel: 0586-751698.
MODERATE: **Atlantico**, Via D. Martelli, 12, tel: 0586-752440. **Miramare**, Via Marconi, 8,tel: 0586-752435. *CAMPING:* **Campo dei Fiori**, Loc. Campo dei Fiori, tel: 0586-770096. **Tripesce**, Via Cavalleggeri, 88, tel: 0586-788167.
Restaurants
SAN VINCENZO: **Gambero Rosso**, P.zza della Vittoria, 13, tel: 0565-701021. One of Italy's best restaurants. Closed Tue. **Il Bucaniere**, Via Marconi, 8, tel: 0565-703387. In a former bathing facility; same owner as Gambero Rosso, but lower quality and lower prices. Closed Tue.
CASTAGNETO CARDUCCI: **Da Zi' Martino**, Loc. S. Giusto, 262, tel: 0565-763666. Family trattoria on the turnoff to Bolgheri.

LIVORNO
Accommodations
LUXURY: **Palazzo**, V.le Italia, tel: 0586-805371. **Rex**, Loc. Antignano, Via del Litorale, 164, tel: 0586-580400. *MODERATE:* **Gennarino**, Viale Italia, 301, tel: 0586-803109. **Universal**, Loc. Antignano, Viale Antignano, 4, tel: 0586-500327.
Restaurants
La Chiave, Scali delle Cantine, 52, tel: 0586-888609. Good fish dishes, relatively high prices. Closed Wed. **Il Sottomarino**, Via Terrazzini, 48, tel: 0586-887025. Simple traditional meals, Livornese fish dishes. Closed Thu. **Trattoria Antico Moro**, Via E. Bartelloni, 59, tel: 0586-884659. Very Italian, rustic. Closed Wed.
Museums and sights
Museo Civico G. Fattori, Villa Fabricotti. Opening hours: daily except Mon 10 am-1 pm, Thu 4-7 pm. **Acquario Comunale D. Cestoni**, Piazzale Pietro Mascagni: 10:30 am-12:30/3-6 pm (summer), 2-5 pm (winter).
Tourist Information
A.P.T. Livorno, Piazza Cavour, 6, tel: 0586-898111/899798/899112.

PISA
Accommodations
LUXURY: **Hotel dei Cavalieri**, P.zza della Stazione, 2, tel: 050-43290. *MODERATE:* **Grand Hotel Duomo**, Via S. Maria, 94, tel: 050-27141. **Arno**, P.zza della Repubblica, 6, tel: 050-542648. **Villa di Corliano**, Rigoli, 12 km out of town on the N 12 to Lucca, tel: 0505-818193. **Casetta delle Selve**, Pugnano (near Rigoli), tel: 050-850359. Dream location, comfortable ambience.
Restaurants
Sergio, Lungarno Pacinotti, 1, tel: 050-48245. Marvelous food, central location. Closed Sun and Mon lunch. **La Mescita**, Via Cavalca, 2, tel 050-544294. Imaginative cooking, reasonable prices. Closed Sat lunch and Sun. **Da Bruno**, Via L. Bianchi, 12, tel: 050-56818. Traditional cooking, closed Mon eve and Tue.
Museums and sights
Campo Santo and **Baptistery open** 9 am-7 pm, until 5 pm in winter. The cathedral closes for lunch (until 3 pm).
Museo dell'Opera del Duomo, on the Piazza Duomo, open 9 am-12:45 pm and 3-7 pm (until 5 pm in winter).
Museo Nazionale di S. Matteo, open 9:30 am-4 pm (winter) and 9 am-1/3-6 pm (summer); holidays 9 am-1 pm, closed Mon.
Tourist Information
A.P.T. Pisa, Piazza Duomo, tel: 050, 560464 and at the train station, tel: 42291.

LUCCA
Accommodations
MODERATE: **La Luna**, Corte Compagni 12, tel: 0583-493634. **Universo**, Piazza Puccini, 1, tel: 0583-493678. **Villa Casanova**, Balbano (15 km west of Lucca), tel: 0583-548429.
Restaurants
Da Giulio in Pelleria, Via S. Tommaso, 29, tel: 0583-55948. Lucchese cuisine at bargain prices. Closed Sun and Mon. **Canuleia**, Via Canuleia, 14, tel: 0583-47470. Good traditional food. Closed Sat & Sun. **La Mora**, Loc. Ponte a Moriano, tel: 0583-57109. Great Garfagnana specialties, reasonable prices. Closed Wed eve, Thu. **Caffè Di Simo**, Via Fillungo, 58. Historic café.
Museums
Museo dei Costumi in the Palazzo Controni-Pfanner, Via degli Asili. Open: 9 am-1 pm, closed Mon. **Museo Nazionale di Villa Guinigi**, Via della Quarquonia, open 9 am-2 pm, closed Mon. **Pinacoteca Nazionale**, Via Galli Tassi, 43, 9 am-7 pm, Sun 9 am-2 pm, Mon 2-7 pm.
Tourist Information
A.P.T. Lucca, Via Veneto, 40, tel: 0583-493639, and Piazzale Verdi, tel: 0583-53592.

ENDLESS BEACHES, WHITE MARBLE

VERSILIA

CAMAIORE

PIETRASANTA

SERAVEZZA

MASSA

LUNIGIANA

VERSILIA

Versilia – white beach, white light, white marble. If you're taking the expressway from Lucca to this stretch of coast, more than 12 miles (18 km) long and up to 7 miles (10 km) wide, your first view will be of the nature preserve on Lake Massaciuccoli, stretching away to your left. Here, in the largest marshland area in Tuscany, dwell more than 250 species of nesting birds, some of them extremely rare. The swampland used to extend farther north; today, it's been drained, and the coast has been swept by a sea of red roofs among the pines.

After the final draining of the coastal strip, the area was reforested to protect the dried-up swamps from the brackish salt water. To the right of the expressway are wooded hills scattered with little villages. Behind them are the looming forms of the Apuan Alps, where marble is still legally quarried today, although part of the region was declared the Parco Naturale delle Alpi Apuane in 1985. This apparent contradiction continues to be a source of discussion, not to say controversy.

Preceding pages: Ornate facade of S. Martino. Left: Artists from around the world come to work marble in Pietrasanta.

In this mountainous country with its narrow valleys, peaks reaching heights of up to 6,540 feet (2,000 m), broad gullies, chestnut forests, green meadows and rugged cliffs, hikers, mountain climbers and spelunkers can expect to find everything their hearts desire.

A hundred years ago, this coastline boasted only a few scattered fishing villages. Marshes and malaria did an effective job of squelching interest in the area and keeping people away before the region was drained in the 18th century under the direction of the Venetian Bernardino Zendrini. But the real boom didn't begin until 1890, when swimming became fashionable. The well-to-do were the first to arrive, followed by intellectuals and artists eager for a chance to unwind in the mild climate of Versilia and enjoy its broad sand beaches sloping gently into the sea. Even today, this stretch of coast continues to rely on tourism, and its main industries focus on leisure activities.

Viareggio

A trip through Versilia begins in Viareggio. Of course, this coastal city existed well before the 19th century, even if the architecture of the elegant city villas and public baths would tend to con-

193

VERSILIA

0   10   20   30   40 km

was this period which witnessed the opening of the first public baths and luxury hotels, which attracted visitors from home and abroad; including British poets Lord Byron and Percy Bysshe Shelly; the latter drowned here in 1822.

Center of the city is the coastal promenade. Anyone strolling from the Burlamacco Canal at the harbor basin to the casino of Principe de Piemonte (1938) has rows of Art Deco buildings from the 1920s, decorated by artists such as Galileo Chini and Lorenzo Viani, as a marvellous backdrop. Only the Chalet Martini with its exotic, oriental gable, a wooden Liberty construction next to the imposing Caffè Margherita, withstood the devastating fire at the beginning of the 20th century. An additional ornamental Art Deco highlight is the memorial to fallen soldiers erected in 1927 on the Piazza Garibaldi.

Parallel to the seashore promenade on the way into town are two large pine forests, the Pineta di Ponente and the Pineta di Levante. These are particularly inviting on hot summer days, when they give you a chance to rest in the shade.

For more than 100 years, Viareggio has been the capital of the Italian carnival. During carnival season (usually in mid-February) you can see parades with magnificent floats processing along the seashore promenade.

South of the city is the district **Torre del Lago**, which has grown up around the 15th-century watchtower by Paolo Guinigi on the shore of Lake Massaciuccoli. The town has become well-known thanks to the composer Giacomo Puccini, who lived and worked here. His house, the Puccini Villa directly on the lake, was built on the ruins of the Guinigi Tower. Today it is a museum, and hosts an annual "Pucciniano" festival every August.

Directly bordering Viareggio to the north is the town of **Lido di Camaiore**. Although first mentioned in a document as early as 1293, the site was not actually

tradict that impression. As early as 1172, the Lucchese and the Genoese had built a small castle on the site where the watchtower Torre Matilde was later erected in 1544. The original castello, erected to keep an eye on the mutual enemy, Pisa, was named Via Regia, King's Street, as it lay on a road controlled by the emperor Frederick Barbarossa. In 1599, the church San Pietro was added; it was subsequently re-christened Ss. Annunziata after a further extension. Apart from these, all that remain from this period are the dilapidated houses along Via Catena. After the successful drainage in the middle of the 18th century, the area rapidly developed into a popular summer residence for the Lucchese.

Viareggio has Marie Louise, the duchess of Bourbon, to thank for its chessboard layout with tree-lined boulevards, as well as the port of Darsena Europa (1820), where the shipyards today mainly produce large luxury yachts. It

Right: A popular beach in Versilia.

settled until early in the 19th century; before that, the swamps had made any kind of established life here impossible. About a century later, the poet Gabriele d'Annunzio came here on holiday, ushering in an era of illustrious vacationers and bathing guests.

For many years, marble from the quarries of Seravezza was shipped from **Forte dei Marmi** to destinations all over the world. The small fort for which the town was named was commissioned in 1788 by Grand Duke Leopold, who intended it to protect the port and its residents from any nasty surprises from the sea. Since the turn of the century, the town's fabulous location and white beach have attracted visitors from all over the world, including Aldous Huxley, Thomas Mann and the Italian actress Eleonora Duse. Forte dei Marmi has remained an elegant vacation spot ever since. Tradition dictates that you show yourself once a day out on the breakwater that stretches more than 300 yards (300 m) out into the sea.

THE WHITE GOLD

At first glance, it looks as if there were patches of snow on the mountains, shimmering in the sun. On closer inspection, you'll find that these are actually marble. While in other areas you find wine roads marked out for visitors, here, running parallel to the coast from Pietrasanta to the neighboring province of Massa-Carrara, there is a "marble road" through the Apuan Alps. Passing overhead traveling cranes, marble workshops and souvenir shops, the road leads to the quarries, where for more than 2,000 years huge blocks have been cut out of the mountain, to be tooled and carved by stonemasons and artists.

Calcium carbonate: in essence, that's the main ingredient of this valuable white stone . Its history begins some 200 million years ago, when the Apuan Alps were still under water. The bodies of dead sea creatures drifted down to collect on the ocean floor, where they slowly turned to limestone. Then, 30 million

195

years ago, Africa and Europe began moving towards each other, and the soft limestone was pressed together, fused into crystalline marble, and thrust upward to form mountains. The Apuan Alps, with their veins of white treasure, were born.

The process begun by nature was continued, many years later, by man, when people began using chisels to force shape upon the hard substance. The colonial power of Rome was the first to discover the "white gold," which it used from then on to adorn its temples, villas and baths. When the impressive rock came back into the height of fashion in the Renaissance, architects, builders and sculptors traveled from afar to test the shimmering rock for their purposes. Leading the way was Michelangelo Buonarroti, who wanted Apuan marble and nothing else for his David and his Pietà. He personally climbed down into the quarries of Monte

Above: Marble quarries are eating away at the Apuan Alps. Right: Even with modern technology, it's a dangerous place to work.

Altissimo to select his own "statuario," which had to be white as snow, lovely as porcelain, and hard as rock.

The list of fellow-artists from later centuries who came to Versilia for its white rock is long, reaching from such past giants as Donatello, Bernini, and Canova to such 20th-century luminaries as Henry Moore, Giò Pomodoro, Hans Arp and Fernando Botero. Some of their contemporaries have settled in the area, because nowhere else can you find such a collection of talented craftsmen who are able to realize the artists' ideas in marble. Actually, these stonemasons are artists themselves, who learned their craft at the art school in Pietrasanta or in their fathers' workshops. Today, however, people complain that there's a lack of young blood. The trade demands a lengthy period of apprenticeship, and it's often hard to tell whether you really have the talent for this kind of work after several years of training.

Standing in front of a marble sculpture in a museum or a magnificent church fa-

cade, you easily forget that these masterpieces are also made of sweat and tears. In the precipitous mountains of Versilia, however, you can get some idea of just how difficult it was to pound the marble out of the mountain by hand – without the aid of any machinery – and transport it to the coast. The Romans had their slaves do the work. They bored holes in the cliffs, inserted wooden stakes and poured water over them until they expanded enough to pry the blocks from the mountain. After this the blocks, each of which weighed tons, were lowered down the mountain on ropes, inch by inch, a process which cost many stonecutters their lives. In later years, the quarrymen worked with explosives. They tried again and again until they managed to blast out a block of the size they desired; this inexact process meant that tons of valuable rock was wasted. Today, you can still see the debris lying around.

It's only since the last century that blocks have been cut from the mountain with the aid of water and steel cables, which nowadays are studded with diamonds. The huge blocks are transported down to the sea on trucks, along steep, unsafe roads. Statistics show that this is still dangerous work: the quarries claim an average of 13 lives each year.

The marble mining industry has remained Versilia's most important industry. Approximately a million tons of marble are mined yearly, to be shipped, either as building material or in processed form, all over the world. Don't miss out on the chance to see the stonemasons at work, watching them use jackhammers, chisels and years of experience to hew works of art, kitsch and replicas from the rough blocks of marble.

CAMAIORE

Around Camaiore, the capital of Versilia, there are few signs that the bustling marble industry is located anywhere nearby. From the quiet little town of Camaiore it's only a little ways into the "back country," to little villages like Ca-

197

soli or Trescolli which are ideal departure points for long, peaceful hikes.

Camaiore's **Borgo Nuovo** was designed on the drawing board, as it were, at the same time as Pietrasanta, in 1255. Lucca needed it as an outpost to control the Via Aurelia, which here coincided for long stretches with the Frankish Road linking the Frankish Kingdom and southern Italy. Center of town is the **Piazza San Bernardino** with the 13th-century collegiate church of S. Maria Assunta, which contains remarkable art treasures. Next to the church **S. Michele** (10th century) on the Piazza Diaz is a museum of sacral art; among its treasures is a magnificent Flemish tapestry from 1516.

At the cemetery, the abbey church **San Pietro**, restored in 1100, presents a fine example of the simple Lucchese architecture of the 11th/12th centuries: the emphasis is on correct proportions, and decorative elements, of the sort which appear in Pisan architecture of the same period, were omitted altogether.

Another two miles (3 km) further along the road to Lucca, a road branches off to Pieve S. Stefano, which, dating from the 9th century, is one of the oldest parish churches in Versilia. After another 3 miles (5 km), turn right to get to Massarosa, where there are a few ruins from Roman times, including the ruins of a thermal spa complex and a villa from the 2nd century BC.

FROM PIETRASANTA TO SERAVEZZA

Take SS 439 from here to Pietrasanta, at the foot of the "white mountains." If you have the time, you can make a little detour into the hilly countryside: at the cemetery shortly before Pietrasanta is the turnoff down to Valdicastello Carducci,

Right: A sculpture waits patiently to be completed.

the home of the famous poet Giosuè Carducci (1835-1907). The community has converted his birthplace into a museum.

Pietrasanta, named for its founder Guiscardo Pietrasanta, Podestà (or mayor) of Lucca, developed between 1242-1250 below the Lombard fortress of Rocca di Sala, and was expanded between 1316 and 1328 by the Lucchese Grande Castruccio Castracani Antelminelli. As of 1513, this fortified town became Medici property, and it thus later went over to the grand duchy of Tuscany. However, it wasn't until 1824, after Leopold II had the neighboring swamps drained, that the city began to flourish. Because of its abundance of marble, Pietrasanta soon became a Mecca for sculptors. One marble workshop follows upon another, and the entire city seems to be made of the white rock – down to its very curbs and benches.

The Porta a Pisa at the small fortress, Arrighina (1324) is the last intact gate to the old city. From here it is just a few steps to **Cathedral Square**, where the city's most significant monuments are located. The cathedral of **San Martino**, built in 1330 atop a earlier construction from 1255, has a white marble facade with a fabulous Gothic rosette by Riccomanni. The red campanile (16th century) provides a nice contrast. Most notable elements in the interior of this three-aisled church, which was altered in the 17th century, are the marble pulpit by Stagio Stagi (1504) and the beautiful staircase by Andrea Baratto (17th century) catch your eye. The other church on Cathedral Square, Sant'Agostino, is supposed to have been erected at the behest of the obsessive builder Castruccio Castracani. The facade, with its blind arches and rows of marble Gothic columns, gives you the impression that more was supposed to have been built onto it. In the cloister of the adjacent monastery (1500), which is still used for seminars and meetings and boasts and excellent library, are

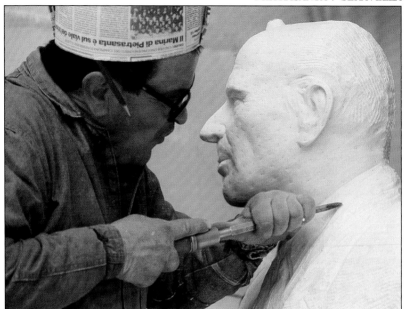

images depicting the life of Saint Augustine. Next to the church and monastery is the beginning of the street leading up to the remains of the fortress, Rocca di Sala.

The small marble-mining center of **Seravezza** is located 3 miles (5 km) farther north. It was in the spectacular quarries of nearby Monte Altissimo (5,196 feet / 1,589 m), where you can still watch how the "white gold" is cut out of the mountain, that Michelangelo went to select the raw materials for his sculptures.

The Romanesque parish church of **La Cappelle**, near Azzana, on the way to the marble quarries, profited from Michelangelo's journey; the artist himself is said to have designed the marble rosette above the portal. It's known, therefore, as "The Eye of Michelangelo."

Seravezza, nestled in a narrow green valley, has a few significant monuments to show for itself. Among them is the Cathedral of San Lorenzo, which developed out of the remains of an ancient temple in 1422 and was enlarged 200 years later. Its splendid decor is a veritable ode to

marble. Another noteworthy building here is the **Palazzo Mediceo** on the bank of the Vezza, which the Medici Prince Cosimo I had built according to plans by Ammannati in 1560. The stone trout on the fountain in the courtyard refers to the legend that Cristina de Medici once caught an enormous trout here.

Seravezza is an ideal departure point for excursions to the nearby mountains, on foot or by car. It's not far from Stazzema, which is one of the most beautiful towns in this part of the Apuan Alps. From here, you drive past marble quarries as you follow the old Via d'Arni deeper into the Garfagnana, which forms the eastern boundary of the Apuan Alps beyond the Cipollaio tunnel.

THE PROVINCE OF MASSA

Stessa spiaggia, stesso mare – the same beach, the same sea. Although the province of Massa also has a stretch of coast with long, sandy beaches and pine forests, tourism takes a back seat to the marble industry in the overall hierarchy of the region's economy. Try, then, to be understanding, rather than annoyed, that there are no signs marking the way to the ruins of Luni (2nd century BC), a Roman town deserted in the 13th century and only recently rediscovered just 1.2 miles (2 km) from the sea. To get there, follow the SS 1 and, at about the latitude of Marina di Carrara, follow signs to the restaurant Chioccia d'Oro. The well-preserved amphitheater is worth the search. More than 2,000 years ago, it was from Luni that the prized marble, which back then was still called Luni marble, was shipped to sites throughout the ancient world. There are additional Roman finds displayed in the adjacent archaeological museum.

The ruins of Castello di Aghinolfi rise out of a thick forest near Montignoso off a small minor road linking Seravezza and Massa. The octagonal tower is sometimes taken as an example of the Lombard style of fortress-building, sometimes ascribed to the Byzantines. From here it is only 2.5 more miles (4 km) to **Massa**. This small provincial capital that developed below the medieval fortress of Malaspina was first mentioned in a document from the year 882. Although the city had a certain importance even in the Middle Ages due to its location on the important north-south axis, the rise and fall of Massa was closely linked to the fortunes of the Malaspina family from Fosdinova, who were princes of the city between 1442 and 1790. As concrete proof of his power, Alberico Cybo Malaspina had a Renaissance palace built next to the fortress, and linked the two buildings by an archway. In 1557, a Cybo Malaspina built another palazzo on the Piazza degli Aranci in the center of town, although the decoration on the building's facade was not completed until 1701. The cathedral

Right: Tendola, a village in the Lunigiana, the northernmost region of Tuscany.

of Massa at the end of Via Dante has a modern marble facing (1936); the structure, however, is from the 15th century. Inside, you'll find, among other things, a fresco by Pinturicchio over the Baroque altar, a triptych by F. Lippi, a 16th-century terra-cotta crèche, and a 13th-century wooden crucifix; here, too, are the tombs of all of the princes and bishops from throughout the city's history.

That **Carrara**'s skyline is also dominated by marble comes as no surprise. Since 1473, when a Malaspina obtained feudal rights to the city, this city's political fortunes have been closely linked to those of Massa. It was 100 years later that a member of the Cybo Malaspina family had the city wall built, as well as the palaces on Piazza Alberica and the princely Renaissance palace (which has served as the Accademia di belle Arti since 1805), next to the medieval watchtower. The Romanesque-Gothic Cathedral of San Andrea (11-14th centuries) with its Pisan facade also received a new marble facing in this period. If you're interested in knowing more about the history of marble, look in at the museum on Via XX Settembre, near the stadium.

Narrow and winding roads lead from Carrara to the mining area, most of them along watercourses white with marble dust. Only about 4 miles (6 km) away are the Fantiscritti quarries, where you can still see the train tracks along which, until 1962, the stone was transported to the port of Marina di Carrara.

The small dusty town of Colonnato (1,740 feet / 532 m) nestled in the mountains was originally a Roman slave colony; later it became a settlement for the quarrymen.

Heading north on SP 446, a gray asphalt strip along the Canale di Gragnana, continue as far as Fosdinovo and on into Lunigiana. In between, there is a side road to the right leading off to the holiday spot of **Campo Cecina** (4,437 feet / 1,357 m). To escape the heat the residents

of Versilia meet here in the summer; instead of lying on overcrowded beaches, they prefer to hike along the marked trails in the quiet mountains, where they can rest in the huts of Belvedere and Carrara.

Fosdinovo, located at an altitude of 1,635 feet (500 m) upon a steep mountain spur, was the place from which the counts of Malaspina controlled the important transportation routes of the area in the Middle Ages. Their 13th-century castle at the end of town was converted into a grand palace during the Renaissance. Also notable is the parish church San Remigio, containing the tomb of Galeotto Malaspina and the Bianchi oratory (1666).

LUNIGIANA

From here it is only a hop, skip and a jump to Lunigiana, which snakes its way into Emilia Romagna. Although this small river valley at the junction of Tuscany, Liguria and Emilia Romagna was once a pivotal spot of Italian history, it is now practically forgotten. Many inhabitants had to leave their old, gray houses to search for work elsewhere. Little-known even to the Tuscans, the Magra river valley enjoyed its heyday in the Middle Ages, when pilgrims, singly or in droves, passed through on their way to Rome. There was a castle atop almost every hill; in all, 160 of them were built to keep an eye on the roads and valleys. Many of them are examples of the building frenzy of the extended family of the counts of Malaspina, who wanted to leave their mark on Lunigiana. Some of these castles still stand intact, while the romantically dilapidated state of others, such as the charming remains of the Comano castle, call to mind the glorious days of troubadours, noblewomen, evil knights and scheming sextons. Legends and reality, tragedy and minnesong blend together. Similarly, the churches, gathering places of the townspeople and examples of the Romanesque Lombard style, also reflect the turbulent developments and the cultural streams that have

passed through this valley. One impressive example is the 10th-century church of **S. Maria Assunta** near Crespiano, with the old, long-deserted town crouching behind it. Unfortunately, the church has been changed for the worse due to constant "improvements" in recent years. One of the oldest examples of Romanesque church architecture in the Lunigiana is the **Chiesaccia**, which, together with a pilgrim hospice, was located by a one-time ford of the Magra, just across from the spot where the village of Lusuolo, with its characteristic terraces, stretches alongside a road on a mountain crest on the opposite bank of the river.

After gaining independence early, the valley lost it around 1300 and rapidly fell into insignificance, from which it has yet to rise. This has preserved the austere and charming beauty of Lunigiana and transformed it into a popular destination for

hiking excursions. You can get to know the impressive and constantly changing landscape step by step, following in the pilgrims' footsteps, so to speak; take, for instance, the wonderful round-trip route from Podenza to Pontremoli and back to Aulla.

The main arterial road for motorists with a little extra time, on the other hand, is the Cisa Pass road SS 62, from which numerous smaller roads lead off into the green valleys. It passes through **Aulla**, where the pilgrims to Rome stopped off to refuel before marching on to Lucca or undertaking the strenuous crossing of the Apennines, and through **Pontremoli**, the "keyhole to the Apennines," through which no traveler, whether emperor or soldier, bishop or pilgrim, could pass unseen. Before you head north and leave Tuscany, you have a chance to stop off at an old castle to visit one of Italy's most puzzling art collections: a museum of stelae containing prehistoric stone sculptures, ancient and yet seeming somehow modern.

Above: Waiting for the bus.

VERSILIA
Accommodations

VIAREGGIO: *LUXURY:* **Esplanade**, Piazza Puccini, 18, tel: 0584-53815. **Excelsior**, Viale Carducci, 88, tel: 0584- 50726. **Palace Hotel**, Via F. Gioia, 2, tel: 0584-46134. **Regina**, Viale Carducci, 64-66, tel: 0584-407440. *MODERATE:* **Bristol**, Viale Manin, 14, tel: 0584- 46441. **Liberty**, Lungomare Manin, 18, tel: 0584-46247. **Miramare**, Viale Carducci, 27, tel: 0584-48441. *CAMPING:* **La Pineta**, Via dei Lecci, tel: 0584-383397. **Paradiso**, Viale dei Tigli, tel: 0584-392005. **Viareggio**, Via Comparini, tel: 0584-391012.

TORRE DEL LAGO: *CAMPING:* **Bosco Verde**, Viale Kennedy, 5, tel: 0584-359631/359343. **Burlamacco**, Viale Marconi, 142, tel: 0584-359544.

LIDO DI CAMAIORE: *LUXURY:* **Villa Ariston**, Viale Colombo, 355, tel: 0584-610633. **Colombo**, Viale Colombo, 161, tel: 0584-619651. *MODERATE:* **Brunella**, Viale Pistelli, 102, tel: 0584-617258. **Gigliola**, Via del Secco, 23, tel: 0584-617141/618385.

CAMAIORE: *LUXURY:* **Il Contesso**, Loc. Nocchi, Via Nocchi, 27, tel: 0584-951775. *MODERATE:* **Cerú**, Loc. Gombitelli, V. Gombitelli, tel: 0584-971901.

FORTE DEI MARMI: *LUXURY:* **Augustus**, Viale Morin, 169, tel: 0584-787200. **Byron**, Viale Morin, 46, tel: 0584-787052. **Principe**, Viale Morin, 67, tel: 0584-787143. *MODERATE:* **La Versilia**, Via G. Pascoli 5/7, tel: 0584-787141. **Marsiliana**, Via N. Sauro, 19, tel: 0584-787151.

PIETRASANTA: *MODERATE:* **Grappolo d'Oro**, Loc. Strettoia, tel: 0584-799422/3. **Palagi**, Piazza Carducci, 23, tel: 0584-70249/70498. *BUDGET:* **Italia,** Via Oberdan, 9, tel: 0584-70175.

Restaurants

VIAREGGIO: **Gusmano**, Via Regia, 58/64. tel: 0584-31233. Speciality: spelt (whole wheat) with fish. Fine fish dishes, as well as Italian meat specialties; reasonable prices. Closed Tue. **Il Patriarca**, V.le Carducci, 79, tel: 0584-53126. One of the most famous restaurants in Versilia; prices are, accordingly, high. Closed Wed. **Tito del Molo**, Lungomolo del Greco, 1/3, tel: 0584-962016. Classic Tuscan meals, marvelously prepared. Closed Wed. **La Darsena**, Via Virgilio, 172, tel: 0584392785. Old fish trattoria near the harbor, reasonable prices. Closed Sun.

CAMAIORE: **Il Vignaccio**, P.zza della Chiesa, 5, Loc. S. Lucia, tel: 0584- 914200. Lovely setting, small menu with regional specialities. Closed Wed and Thu lunch. **Bernardone**, Via Pieve, 160, Loc. Bernardone, tel: 0584-951118. Traditional Lucchese cuisine. Closed Wed.

FORTE DEI MARMI: **Lorenzo**, Via Carducci, 61, tel: 0584-84030. Marvelous seafood, fairly expensive. Closed Mon. **Lo Squalo Charlie**, V. le Morin, 57, tel: 0584-86276. Inventive fish dishes, inventive (high) prices. Closed Tue and Wed lunch.

LIDO DI CAMAIORE: **Bagni Ariston**, V.le Colombo, 660, tel: 0584-904747. Good restaurant in a swimming complex, closed Sun eve and Mon.

PIETRASANTA: **Da Coppo**, V. Aurelia, 121, tel: 0584-70350. Traditional Tuscan-Lucchese food, closed Mon. **Sci**, Vicolo Porta a Lucca, tel: 0584-790983. Especially good: vegetable soup and cod. Very reasonable prices. Closed Sun.

Tourist Information

A.P.T. Versilia, Viareggio, V.le Carducci, 10, tel: 0584- 48881/2/3.

PROVINCE OF MASSA-CARRARA
Accommodations

MASSA: *MODERATE:* **Galleria**, V.le della Democrazia, 2 tel: 0585-42137. *BUDGET:* **Annunziata**, Via Villafranca, 4, tel: 0585-41023/810025.

MARINA DI MASSA: *LUXURY:* **Excelsior**, Via C. Battisti, 1, tel: 0585-8601. *MODERATE:* **Eco del Mare**, Via Verona, 12, tel: 0585-245200. *BUDGET:* **Bellamarina**, Via Zolezzi, 17, tel: 0585-240932.

CARRARA: *MODERATE:* **Michelangelo**, Corso F.lli Roselli, 3 tel: 0585-777161/2/3.

MARINA DI CARRARA: *LUXURY:* **Maestrale**, Via Fabbricotti, 2, tel: 0585-785371. *MODERATE:* **Mediterraneo**, Via Genova 2/h, tel: 0585-785222. **Miramare**, Viale C. Colombo, 23, tel: 0585-634743. *BUDGET:* **La Pineta**, Viale Colombo, 119 Bis, tel: 0585-633390.

Tourist Information

A.P.T. Massa-Carrara, Marina di Massa, V.le Vespucci, 24, tel: 0585-240046.

LUNIGIANA
Accommodations

FOSDINOVO: *MODERATE:* **Don Rodrigo**, Loc. Foseta, SS 446, tel: 0187-68861/68978.

PONTREMOLI: *MODERATE:* **Golf Hotel**, Via Pineta, tel: 0187-831573. **Napoleon**, P.zza Italia, 2/b, tel: 0187-830544.

Restaurants

PONTREMOLI: **Bussé**, P.zza Duomo, 9, tel: 0187-831371. Classic Lunigiana dishes, closed Fri. **Gino Bacciottini**, Via Ricci Armani, 4, tel: 0187-830120. Homemade sausage and ham, homemade pasta. Closed Thu.

Tourist Information

Pro Loco, Aulla, Via Gramsci, 1, tel: 0187-409960/409627. **Pontremoli**, P.zza del Comune, tel: 0187-831180.

THE MOUNTAINOUS HINTERLAND

GARFAGNANA

GARFAGNANA

Garfagnana, large magnificent forest. That is what the early natives called the fertile Serchio Valley that begins north of Lucca and is bordered by the Apuan Alps to the west and the Apennines to the north. Along the wild mountain streams running down the narrow side valleys, the ruins of small fortresses, Romanesque chapels and lonely monasteries are testimony to an eventful past.

The history of the valley goes back to the times of the Visigoths, Lombards and Franks, who fought with the residing feudal rulers over its ownership. In 1248 Frederick II decided to cede the area to the city republic of Lucca, which then lost it to the d'Este family from Ferrara in 1451. After this, a long period of peace ensued. Since 1847, the valley has belonged to Tuscany once again.

The Serchio Valley

If you're driving from Lucca through the lower, here still idyllic Serchio Valley, you have a choice of two routes: the national road SS 12, which takes you di-

Preceding pages: Farm woman in Bagni di Lucca. Left: Old watchtower in the Lunigiana.

rectly to Borgo a Mozzano where the Garfagnana begins, or a small road which leads along the right side of the river, past hamlets and Romanesque churches. The landmark of the small industrial town of **Borgo a Mozzano** is the 14th-century Magdalena Bridge (14th century), also called the Devil's Bridge, which arches steeply over the Serchio like the curve of a cat's back. Near Fornoli, the SS 445 branches off into the wild upper Garfagnana, while the SS 12 takes you to the Lima valley and to the mineral water spa town of **Bagni di Lucca**, sought out by everyone from Roman consuls to, in the late Middle Ages, the Tuscan countess Mathilde and Frederick II. Yet it wasn't until the Duke of Bourbon, Charles Louis (1824-47), discovered the curative powers of the thermal baths for himself that the little town became a fashionable resort; and it's in this period that its grand Neo-Classical monuments were built. On a side street which leads out of the city there are four Romanesque churches. Among them is one by Controne which had to be rebuilt several times because the main portal was buried in a landslide. Hikers should take the road up to the mountain village of Montefegatesi (2,753 feet / 842 m), from which a mule trail leads to one of the most impressive natural spectacles in Tuscany, the canyon of

Orrido di Botri, a narrow gorge in which golden eagles still nest.

Back on the SS 12, if you look up to your right you'll see, high above you, Crasciana, "the grandiose." Its landmark is, in addition to its fabulous palazzi, the campanile of San Frediano (10th century). After another six or so miles (10 km) on the SS 12, there's a right-hand turnoff to the castle ruins of Lucchio, a former outpost of Lucca which was located opposite the Florentine fortress of Popiglio. At first the construction workers lived in the stone-gray houses clinging to the mountain; later, these were tenanted by the castle guardsmen.

Now back to Fornoli, where the SS 445 begins, and leads to Ghivizzano, which sports, in addition to a castle and a Romanesque church, a *sassola*, or covered street. From here, a side road leads off through thick pine forests to **Coreglia**

Above: The Devil's Bridge across the Serchio in Borgio a Mozzano. Right: Tourists in Italy receive a friendly welcome.

Antelminelli, a pretty mountain village famous for its traditional plaster nativity figures. Some of these are displayed in a small museum in the Palazzo Rossi. Inside the 13th-century parish church S. Michele, there's a marble annunciation group and a beautifully-crafted gold crucifix from the 15th century.

Back in the Serchio Valley, the road on the opposite bank of the river leads to Fabbriche di Vallico. Here, you can still see old water wheels from the 10th century, which made the people's work easier and helped them to prosperity.

The center of lower Garfagnana is the silk town of **Barga**, which was under the jurisdiction of the bishops of Lucca and was fortified by Frederick Barbarossa in 1186. The town became part of Lucca 100 years later, only to go over to Florence in 1341. In the center of the old town with its steep, narrow alleyways rises the Cathedral of S. Cristoforo (12th century), a monumental edifice whose Romanesque-Lombard facade was once the broad side of a previous church from

GARFAGNANA

0   10   20   30   40 km

the 9th century. Egyptian alabaster panes filter the light which shines on a 1,000-year-old figure of St. Christopher, a marble pulpit (13th century) supported by lions, and terra-cotta reliefs from the Della Robbia workshop. From the forecourt of the cathedral you have a breathtaking view of the mountainous scenery below. Palazzi from the time of the Florentine occupation are tucked away in the winding alleys of the old city.

You have to cross the river once again to reach the **hermitage of Calomini**. This hangs on the steep face of a cliff like a balcony, and the Madonna is said to have appeared here around the year 1000. This place of pilgrimage was at first simply a chapel in the rocks, and later, in the 18th century, it was enlarged to a monastery. The road up to it begins at the pretty little town of Gallicano, where once stood one of the oldest baptisteries (7th century) in the Luccan region. At the end of the serpentine valley road near Fornovolasco, the stalactite cavern **Grotta del vento** might lure you in to visit its underground passageways. From Gallicano, it's not far to Molazzana or Cascio, where you can still see the old defensive the inhabitants put up after they'd rebelled against the d'Este rulers in 1613.

The small textile town of **Castelnuovo Garfagnana** owes its wealth to this very same d'Este family from Ferrara. It was to this family that the residents of the medieval fortress voluntarily pledged allegiance in 1429, because they had had enough of the Lucchese government. And this, the main town of Garfagnana, remained the administrative seat of the Este in Tuscany until the French occupation in 1796. From the storybook, 12th-century castle and the old city which developed within its walls, the Via Testi leads to the plain St. Peter's Cathedral from the 16th century. This, like the entire old city, was heavily damaged in World War II, and had to be rebuilt from the ground up. On Thursday mornings there's a bustling market in Castelnuovo – a good time to get to know the lively little town somewhat better.

209

Upper Garfagnana

The second part of the trip in Garfagnana is a bit more adventurous, since here the countryside is rougher, the mountains are higher and the roads more winding. From the river valley and the SS 445, a number of smaller valleys branch off, each concealing hidden beauties waiting to be discovered on foot, on horseback, by bicycle or by car.

There is, for example, the Via d'Arni, which leads from Castelnuovo to the Apuan marble quarries and continues on to a reservoir and the almost deserted town of Isolasanta. Where a pilgrim hospice once stood in the Middle Ages, hiking trails of various degrees of difficulty now cross through the virgin mountain country.

Just 5 miles (8 km) north of Castelnuovo lies Poggio, whose architectural

Above: Built into the cliff: the hermitage of Calomini.

treasure is the church of S. Biagio with its flat-topped campanile (13th century). On a small road once used by the Este for their own early postal service, you can reach the mountain nests of Vaglia di Sotto and Vaglia di Sopra in the Nature Preserve of Apuan. These villages, two of the oldest communities in Garfagnana, are situated on the banks of an artificial reservoir, from which emerges the spire of a church spire that stood in a section of town which was flooded in 1953. Shortly before Vaglia di Sopra, up above the road, there's a tiny hermitage built into the cliffs. This was founded by the 8th-century Scottish bishop Viano, who became a hermit in these secluded mountains.

On the other side of the Serchio Valley, between Camporgiano and Piazza al Serchio, is where both headwaters of the Serchio meet. Here, too, is the **dell'Orecchiella nature preserve**, 20 square miles (52 sq. km) in size, which, after successful reforestation, has again become home for a wide variety of animals.

There are two different ways to return to Castelnuovo: the direct route is along a high road past Corfino and Villa Collemandina. The latter, Romanesque church and all, was destroyed by an earthquake in 1920; the inhabitants painstakingly rebuilt the church, stone by stone. The other route leads through Orzaglia to Verrucole, where you can see the remains of a mighty castle on "Wart Hill." Along the rest of the way back to Castelnuovo, there's a whole string of Romanesque churches: S. Jacopo with its Baroque bell tower in San Romano; the 12th-century baptistery of Sambuca wedged between two cliffs; and a third one in Pian di Cerreto, of which only the Romanesque apse from the original construction remains.

Finally, one more excursion from Castelnuovo: take the SS 324 to **Passo delle Radici** (5,000 feet / 1,529 m) or to Alpe di San Pellegrino (4,970 feet / 1,520 m) where you can look out over the whole of Garfagnana. Along the way you pass the **Castiglione Garfagnana** fortress, strengthened with bulwarks, used by the Lucchese in 1371 to defend their island in the sea of Este possessions. Picturesquely situated on a ledge of rock, the scenic town, overlooking the entire Serchio valley, is a popular summer spot. The well-preserved old city and the 13th-century San Michele church with its fabulous Gothic-Romanesque facade of colored marble are certainly worth a look.

The next stop is **San Pellegrino in Alpe** (4,980 feet / 1,523 m), the highest inhabited town in the Apennines. What started out as a pilgrim hospice (14th century) later became a postal station and eventually made room to include a farming museum. This meeting-point of travelers from time immemorial is also the starting point for a number of marked hiking trails into the surrounding mountains. Brave motorists can return to Castelnuovo along the winding route of the old Via Vandelli, the first real road built in Garfagnana.

GARFAGNANA

Accommodations

Borgo a Mozzano: *MODERATE:* **Milano**, Via del Brennero, 9, Loc. Socciglia, tel: 0583-889191. *BUDGET:* **Il Pescatore**, Via 1. Maggio, 2, Ponte Pari, tel: 0583-99071.
BAGNI DI LUCCA: *MODERATE:* **Pensione Serena**, Via Paretaio, 1, Bagni Caldi, tel: 0583-86500. **Silvania**, Via Immagine, Loc. Lugliano, tel: 0583-805363. *BUDGET:* **La Frantoia**, Via Tovani, 28, tel: 0583-805339.
COREGLIA ANTELMINELLI: *BUDGET:* **Il Cacciatore**, Via Roma, 3/5, tel: 0583-78022. **Il Grillo**, Loc. Al Lago, tel: 0583-78031. **La Posta**, Via Antelminelli, 2/4, tel: 0583-78027.
GALLICANO: *MODERATE:* **Mediavalle**, Via Roma, 73A, tel: 0583-730074.
CASTELNUOVO GARFAGNANA: *BUDGET:* **Da Carlino**, Via Garibaldi, 13, tel: 0583-644270. **The Marquee**, Via Provinciale 14B, Piani Pieve, tel: 0583-62198. **Aquila d'oro**, Vicolo al Serchio, 6, tel: 0583-62259.
CASTIGLIONE GARFAGNANA: *BUDGET:* **Filippe**, State delle Radici, Filippe m. 1200, tel: 0583-649081. **Il Casone**, SS324, Passo delle Radici, Casone Profecchia, tel: 0583-649090. **Lunardi**, Loc. P.sso delle Radici m. 1525, Loc. Chiozza S. Pellegrino in Alpe, tel: 0583-649071.

Restaurants

CASTELNUOVO GARFAGNANA: **Da Carlino**, Via Garibaldi,15, tel: 0583-62045. Specialties: barley soup and trout from the Serchio. Class. Tuscan cuisine. Closed Mon.
CASTIGLIONE GARFAGNANA: **Il Casone di Profecchia**, Via Statale, 324, Loc. Il Casone di Profecchia, tel: 0583-649030. Former soldiers' accommodations from the 18th century; great Garfagnana specialties. Open daily.

Sights / Nature parks

Grotta del Vento, Fornovolasco, Loc. Trimpello. One-, two- or three-hour guided tours daily 10 am-noon and 3-6 pm (April 1-Sept 30). In winter, the grotto is open Sun and holidays only.
Parco Naturale dell'Orecchiella, rare plants and animals. Free admission. Guided tours are available.
Parco Regionale delle Alpi Apuane. Departure point for mountain tours and hikes in Castelnuovo Garfagnana, info: tel: 0583-644242.

Tourist Information

Province of Lucca: Servizio Turismo, Cortile degli Svizzeri, tel: 0583-4171.

CHIANTI WINE
From Quantity to Quality

In the 1960s bulbous, straw-covered bottles filled with Chianti wine, the characteristic *fiaschi*, flooded the shelves of supermarkets throughout the European Community. Back then, anyone who overindulged in too much Chianti in the evening ran the risk of experiencing a big fiasco the next morning – and the Chianti wineries, too, found that their fiaschi were something of a fiasco. In 1970, they produced a massive 240 million bottles, but they could hardly make the production pay off; the country was in the throes of radical social changes which were altering traditional structures of farming and methods of cultivation. Some problems of this era have held over to the present day, yet connoisseurs of good wine will find that they can always make new discoveries in Tuscany.

Tuscany's vast areas of arable land are comprised of a range of different soils and earth deposits, and the vintners who try their luck here are of equally diverse levels of expertise and have equally varied senses of responsibility with regard to the quality of their product. Over the past centuries the traditional vineyards with their alternating rows of grapevines and olive trees have practically disappeared; increasingly, the landscape is dominated by the monotonous ranks of vineyard upon vineyard, a byproduct of industrial production. These acres produce a veritable sea of wine each year. The products are of equally various quality and character – from pale supermarket swill to fruity and well-balanced, top-quality products.

Strictly speaking, the historic region of Chianti is a small triangular area bordered by Florence, Arezzo and Siena

Preceding pages: Excited spectators at the "Giostro del Saracino." Olive harvest. Left: Aging the noble grape.

(Chianti classico, Chianti colli fiorentini). Today, however, the cultivable areas for Chianti extend south beyond Montepulciano (Chianti Colli Senesi), west to Pistoia (Chianti Montalbano) and into the area between Pisa and Volterra (Chianti Colline Pisani). Chianti Rufina grows east of Florence. But not every Chianti is a Chianti; the "real," typical Chianti wines grow in the historic Chianti area and in the Rufina region.

"You are in the world of Gallo Nero," roadside signs inform you as you drive south of Florence. The black rooster, a trademark of the Chianti League in the Middle Ages, is today the trademark of the consortium that markets "Chianti classico." The beverage bearing this historic name is, however, a relatively recent invention. Not until about a hundred years ago did Baron Ricasoli, at his castle Brolio, hit upon the idea of blending red and white grapes: 75-90% Sangiovese, 5-10% Canaiolo and 25% white Trebbiano and Malvasia – proportions which the "DOCG" (*di origine controllata e garantita*) regulation stipulates today. Because of its white wine content, Chianti genuinely ripens early; the wine can be served as early as March 1st of the same year. However, a vintner's real expertise, or lack thereof, is demonstrated in his "Riserva" products, aged in a barrel for at least three years. A good Chianti can be recognized from its brilliant ruby red color; its fruitiness, its mild fragrance. Its proportion of white grapes give it a pleasant lightness despite its full body. Even in Tuscany, you can't be sure that every year will present you with a favorable wine-growing climate. Especially memorable was the excellent year 1990; other good years were '83, '85, '88 and '91.

The DOCG marking has only partly solved the problem of regulating the quality of Chianti. The yield per acre has been officially reduced, as has the percentage of white grapes in the mixture. The use of wines from other regions has

217

been restricted, but not forbidden everywhere; using other grapes, such as Cabernet, is permitted. The tangle of red tape and supervisory administrative bodies can surely accomplish a great deal, but there's one thing it still can't guarantee: a truly outstanding product from every vintner. Excellent Chiantis made according to the classic blend are produced by the same vintners who make first-rate wines from old varieties of Sangiovese grapes without the addition of any other variety. In every well-known wine-growing town you can get more information about local products at any *Enoteca*, and go on to taste them for yourself.

The fate of Ricasoli, the "inventor" of Chianti classico, and his vineyard illustrates the situation of Chianti vineyards today. Sold to a beverage group in 1974, the vineyard was run into the ground, to be reclaimed by the Ricasoli family some

Above: Wine is also sometimes mass produced. Right: It's such grapes as these that yield the Vino Nobile di Montepulciano.

years ago in a state of almost total ruin. The family is now trying to regain their former reputation. Another committed producer, Giovanella Stianti of Castello di Volpaia, is demonstrating one way to achieve success. She cultivates her vineyards "ecologically," without the use of artificial fertilizers and pesticides, and systematically cultivating old grape varieties while preserving the tradition of mixed cultivation with olive trees. In addition to her traditional Chianti classico, her Coltassala from Sangiovese grapes or her Balifico have been commended.

The same can be said for family businesses such as the small Fattoria Vigna Vecchia in Radda, run by Franco Beccari. In addition to his Chianti classico riserva, his Raddese is superb. Other vineyards which produce high-quality Chianti wines include Castellare and Castello di Fonterutoli, both near Castellina; Podere Il Palazzino near Gaiole; Vecchie Terre di Montefili near Greve; and Fattoria Isole e Olena in Barberino Val d'Elsa.

It is also worth visiting some of the of the less well-known Rufina wineries in the Sieve Valley, whose wines are robust and solid. Between Florence and Pistoia is the small wine-growing region of Carmignano, where an excellent red wine is pressed from four classic Chianti grapes and an admixture of Cabernet Sauvignon.

The Vino Nobile di Montepulciano from the south of Tuscany is, on the other hand, produced like a Chianti; but the Montepulciano wines come out rather poorly in comparison with the best Chiantis. It's not far from here, in the Montalcino area, that the unique Brunello is produced. In the 19th century, the Biondi-Santi wine-growers began cultivating a wine from Sangiovese-Grosso grapes, aged in oak barrels. A Brunello needs at least four years to ripen. Since the wine has recently become fashionable, countless suppliers have flooded the market, often with wines that don't quite

conform to the strict principles of Biondi-Santi that made Brunello famous and guarantee its distinctive character. Accordingly, you should be that much more critical when considering these top wines. A few reliable vintners include Poggio Antico, Poderi Costanti in Colle al Matrichese, and the Fattoria of Nello Baricci in Colombaio di Montosoli.

In Chianti and other regions of Tuscany, vintners are experimenting with new grape varieties and types of wine. Yet these rather expensive products, often oriented toward a French taste, seem to lack the typical Tuscan element that characterizes a good Chianti. Nevertheless, committed and experimental young oenologists have come up with some surprisingly good wines in the past few years, often from areas previously thought of as mediocre. Examples of these are the excellent Sassicaia from Bolgheri and the award-winning red wine from the Fattoria Sorbaiano in Montecatini Val di Cecina in the Montescudaio region, west of Volterra. There is

also a popular Vino frizzante, sold under the bland name of Matre and produced by the cooperative of Capalbio from Malvasia and Trebbiano.

The region's white, ordinary table wines taste good at local wine festivals, but they neither travel nor keep well. The Fattoria Buonamico and the Carmignani families in Montecarlo near Lucca produce good white wines; and there's also an excellent white in Pomino, east of Fiesole. The better-known white wines made from the Vernaccia grape around San Gimignano are generally rather mediocre; one of the few exceptions is the Vernaccia of Fattoria Ponte a Rondolino. A *Bianco* is also produced around Cortona and far south near Pitigliano.

Finally, you shouldn't pass up the opportunity to take along a bottle of Vin Santo, an excellent dessert wine similar to sherry. Remember – it is difficult to find truly good products. A few reliable examples are Avignonesi in Montepulciano, Castello di Volpaia or Isole e Olena in Barberino Val d'Elsa.

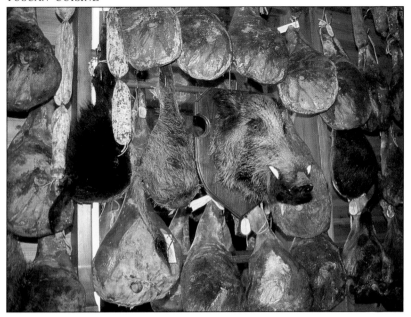

THE CUISINE OF TUSCANY

The same is true of Tuscany as of Italy in general: every region, every area has its own cuisine, based on whatever the local forests, fields, or waterways happen to offer. For visitors, this is a guarantee that what you're served arrives fresh and without additives at your table.

In general, one can say that the traditional Tuscan cuisine is free of unnecessary refinement. It's simple cooking, a little on the rough side, hearty, and strongly spiced so that it goes well with the unsalted bread that's served in abundance with every meal. The number of typical Tuscan recipes is rather limited. Olive oil is always a major ingredient; wild herbs, such as fennel or sage, are generally popular; and the region is known for its hearty soups and stews. On the coast, there's plenty of fish available;

Above: Wild boar delicacies. Right: A typical snack. Far right: Harvesting tomatoes can be a laborious task.

predominant in the country's wooded interior are game dishes and different kinds of mushrooms. Vegetables are eaten everywhere, and every region has its own particular local specialty.

The following is an attempt to introduce a few of these specialties and shed some light on how they're prepared.

Let's begin in northern Tuscany, in the green valleys of Garfagnana, where rough grains such as barley and spelt are cultivated and used to produce hearty soups. Another typical soup here is made of cornmeal (*Infarinata*), a thick stew enriched with beans, bacon, and various vegetables, which is especially popular in the mountain country on cold winter nights.

Along the coast, fish is served in every imaginable manner. Particularly well-known are the *triglie alla livornese* from the coast of Livorno, which has the most fish of any area of Italy. For this dish, otherwise known as "Red mullet, Livorno style," the fish are simmered slowly in a sauce of tomatoes, garlic and

herbs, and served in the pan. Equally well-known, and equally popular, is the spicy, creamy fish soup that goes by the name of *cacciucco*.

Every visitor to Florence is familiar with the word *bistecca*. This wonderfully tender, tasty piece of beef comes from the white Chianina cows from the Chiana valley, which are bred solely for this rather tragic purpose. "Tragic" because the young animals of this fast-growing breed are slaughtered at the age of between six and seven months, and are confined exclusively to their stalls for the entire span of their brief lives. But their meat, cooked on the grill and drizzled with fine olive oil, is simply a poem.

Typical of the area around Florence, but popular throughout Tuscany, are the white beans called *fagioli*, served in soups or as a side dish, drizzled with olive oil and perhaps garnished with a couple of slices of onion. A simple but tasty dish is *pappa al pomodoro*: old bread is softened in water and then mixed into a thick tomato soup.

Maremma is a region particularly blessed in its fertile earth, which, since the draining of its swamps about a century ago, has produced fruit and vegetables in abundance. The leanness of past years, however, can be seen from such holdovers as *acquacotta*, which translates as "cooked water," and proves on examination to be a soup of onions, eggs, vegetables, olive oil, and toasted bread. Served with this a white Pecorino wine which is so excellent in this region that it's allowed to have its own protected label (DOC).

In the forests of the hinterland there's an abundance of game, mushrooms, and chestnuts. Truffles are found in parts of the Maremma, and wild boar, above all, is served in every trattoria in a wide variety of dishes: roasted, as ham or salami, or as *salsiccia* (sausage). And on the coast here, too, is plenty of fresh fish, which in the evening, after your swim, you can buy directly from the men on the fishing-boats that have just come in for the night.

ARTS AND CRAFTS

To see Florence differently, for once! Not, in the usual manner, to follow the stations of the great artists, the painters, sculptors, or architects, but rather to seek out the *artigiani*, the artisans. Since the Middle Ages, they have ensured that Florence be known far and wide for its crafts and applied arts; together with the merchants, they helped ensure the city's reputation and wealth.

By the end of the 12th century, the city's artisans were already forming guilds to help regulate production and trade. And these guilds quickly came to exercise political power, something demonstrated, for example, by the Weavers' Revolt of 1378, which helped a member of the still-unknown Medici family to take political office for the first time. At the same time, the guilds acted as commissioners and patrons of public projects, thereby playing an important role for the city's cultural and artistic development.

Wandering through Florence, you encounter traces of this past everywhere. Take the church Orsanmichele, a former granary which the guilds transformed into their temple and meeting-place. Countless streets and piazzas bear the names of old guilds or professions; the *Palazzo dell'Arte della Lana*, the guild house of the wool merchants, still stands on the Via Calimala; and many houses still bear the coats-of-arms of various professions over their doors.

The oldest guild in Florence was, in fact, that of the Calimala; its name derives from the street running between the old marketplace, now the Piazza Repubblica, and the Mercato Nuovo, where the members of the guild had their shops. Later, these wool traders moved over to the first square; at the end of the 13th century, they had more than 300 manu-

Right: Alabaster fruit or eggs – there's something in Volterra to suit every taste.

facturers available to them and employed about a quarter of the city's population. The guild of Por Santa Maria, which at first included only dealers in dry goods and goldsmiths, didn't become powerful until the silkmakers joined its ranks; most valuable product of the latter was brocade cloth, which was in great demand. The patterns on these fabrics were designed by such artists as Lippi, Botticelli and Ghirlandaio. Among the so-called "higher" guilds were those of the moneychangers, the judges and notaries, doctors and pharmacists; the "middle" guilds included butchers, shoemakers, blacksmiths, tanners, stonemasons and carpenters. Other professions were lumped together in the "lower" category.

On your excursion into this Florentine past, you'll notice that the borders between artisans and artists often blur. Art and artisan guilds, *arte e arti*: even the Italian language doesn't make much of a distinction. Our separation of art as an intellectual, spiritual expression as opposed to the mechanical workmanship of artisans is a relatively modern development. In the days of Leonardo da Vinci, art wasn't produced in studios, but rather in workshops; painting and sculpture counted as "applied," rather than "fine," arts. Such artists as Michelangelo, Giotto, or Ghirlandaio were simply the best in their guilds. Sculptor Andrea Verrocchio created monumental sculptures, but also banners for tournaments; the painter Botticelli earned extra money by decorating dowry chests; and Donatello, like nearly all of the sculptors of his day, trained not as a sculptor, but as a goldsmith.

Today, throughout Florence, you can watch the descendants of these great masters, recipients of artisan wisdom that have been passed down from generation to generation, as they work wood, stone or metal according to the original old methods. They are masters of the traditional techniques, know all of the ins and outs of their trade, and can make old

things look new or new things old. For a long period, Florence's artisans contented themselves with merely copying the venerated objects of the past; today, however, it's once again difficult to draw the distinction between artist and artisan. These women and men, often true masters of their trade, are again employing traditional techniques in conjunction with modern shapes and forms: the resulting objects are true works of art(isanship).

Don't, however, put off paying a visit to a traditional workshop. Even though there are still masterful artisans, industrial production is, inevitably, taking over, and the traditional techniques are slowly dying out. And fewer and fewer young artisans are coming along to take up the torch. But for the time being, production continues, both in Florence and throughout Tuscany.

There's a particular flurry of activity in the streets around Santa Croce and Santo Spirito, neighborhoods which it was once advisable to frequent only in broad daylight. Legion small workshops here build new furniture or restore old pieces; carve and gild picture frames; repair musical instruments; weave or sew fabric; throw ceramics. The air is filled with the smells of clay and glue, paint and wax. In the alleyways to the left and right of the Arno, too, you can find artisans who make objects to order or ably repair broken porcelain heirlooms with patience and skill. Some have even achieved world renown, such as the woodcarver Bartolozzi on Via Maggio, who with the help of a few photographs was able to recreate the choir pews of the Benedictine monastery of Monte Cassino, after it was destroyed in World War II.

And before you know it, your tour has become a shopping expedition. One typical souvenir of Florence is stone inlay work. With the old technique of *pietre dure*, a paste of powdered gum resin, marble and shell is used to create marvellous patterns in stone. There are also true artists among the ranks of potters, who use their wheels to create marvelous traditional or modern ceramics.

223

On the Ponte Vecchio, you can see the monument which the old guild of the goldsmiths erected to their great master Benvenuto Cellini – perhaps in part to remind themselves of the great creative heights to which members of their profession can rise. Where today gold is melted, shaped and soldered was, until the 16th century, a base for the city's butchers. Because of the stench of their rubbish, which they threw into the Arno, these were forced to clear the site and move further out of town. Near the water, too, are the leather tanneries, where, now as then, leather is tanned, cut, gilded, chased, and transformed into elegant boxes or book-covers.

If you'd like to see how *carta marmorizzata*, the marbled paper so typical of Florence, has been produced for centuries, you can go to Giannini on the Piazza Pitti and watch the bizarre patterns forming atop a tank of water. In the neighboring quarter of San Frediano is the *Antico Setificio Fiorentino*, where marvellous silk fabrics are produced on traditional looms.

But it isn't only in the city where fine artisanship to be found: it's spread throughout the region. You don't have to go all the way to Venice, for instance, to find fine hand-blown – or mouth-blown – glass. Since the Middle Ages, the secrets of this art have been handed down from father to son (or daughter) in the Colle Val d'Elsa. There's supposed to be a "Benvenuto Cellini of crystal" at work here, carving patterns in the glass as if telling a story (Boreno Cigni on the Viccolo delle Fontanelle).

In Cortona, too, the artisan traditions date back to the Middle Ages: the old city is scattered with carpenters, furniture restorers and blacksmiths, still in demand all over the world by virtue of their abilities. And ceramics fans flock to this old Etruscan city for the typical sunflower pattern featured on its pottery.

Above: Florentine artisanship continues to enjoy an excellent reputation. Right: Old copper pots.

Carrara, of course, centers around its marble; in marble-working, the fine line between art and craft becomes particularly difficult to draw. In Coreglia Antelminelli, on the other side of the Apuan Alps, smaller accessories are modelled from plaster. The local museum documents the history of this trade.

If you're looking for basket-weaving or raffia work from Tuscany – a Florentine hat or bag – you may strike it lucky in Fiesole, in the Caldine neighborhood, on Via di Coverciano. But there are hardly any *trecciaiole*, or women who braid the fine straw, left in Tuscany. Even the hand-plaited *fiaschi* from Greve in Chianti, the round-bellied wine bottles in straw casings, are few and far between. But here, in the heart of Chianti, one old Etruscan tradition has been preserved: blacksmithing, or metal-working. Here, on the road between Greve and Figline, lives the last basket-weaver in Chianti, Ferruccio Ferrucci, born in 1909.

Impruneta is virtually synonymous with fired earthenware. Even the Renaissance master Brunelleschi favored tiles of these material, and used them in the construction of his masterpiece, the dome atop the Cathedral in Florence. Today, the principal product of the kilns seems to be decorative flower-pots.

Lucca, on the other hand, has been able to guarantee the quality of its silk and gold products for centuries. Like their hated rivals, the Florentines, Lucca's citizens based their prosperity on their abilities as artisans and merchants. If you want a real pipe carved from a tree root, you'll have to go into the Maremma, to Massa Marittima, where you can also purchase hand-made lutes.

Pescia attracts visitors with its large flower market and with handmade copper wares. If you have the time and can speak Italian, the Maestro Giovanni Donnini, by the Porta Fiorentina, will doubtless be more than happy to explain to you the secrets of his trade.

Before it's altogether too late and people have quite forgotten the traditional artisan methods, the town of San Gimignano, where cabinet-making and embroidery are the main crafts, has opened a museum of these trades. Handmade lace and crossbows are the signature products of Sansepolcro, city of Piero della Francesca. In Sesto Fiorentino, on the other hand, is produced the fine porcelain of Richard-Ginori or heavier handmade ceramics, crafted on the potters' wheels, in a range of shapes and patterns, both traditional and modern.

What's the difference between a Florentine, Neapolitan and Sardinian knife? In Scarperia, the knife capital north of Florence, you'll surely be able to find an expert who can give you the answer. And in Volterra, you can see that Tuscany's artisan traditions still bear an Etruscan stamp. After visiting the museum with antique alabaster urns, you can go into the shop of a modern craftsman and see how he, today, still works this "light stone" from the belly of the earth.

TUSCANY'S CULTURAL LANDSCAPE

The village of Monticchiello, south of Siena, had problems. In fact, emigration to the cities is an ill suffered by many towns in the region. In the 1960s, the people steadily departed, houses stood empty, the land lay fallow. The number of village residents dropped by one-half. Those who remained behind were afraid that they, too, would be forced to give up their living space, and have to turn it over to city slickers and strangers.

Since 1967, however, Monticchiello has taken steps to help itself with its *Teatro Povero*, or poor theater. The residents chose spoken drama as a means by which to defend themselves against this development, to give themselves a new sense of community. They write the plays themselves and are also the actors and actresses in the performances, which are held every year at the end of July and the beginning of August. No one really remembers why exactly they hit upon theater, all those years ago. Perhaps it was because there was a long tradition of folk theater in Tuscany, including marionette plays, spring festivals, rhymed verse performed in song. The first production was devoted to the historic theme of the eternal struggles between Siena and Florence: costume theater. But then the Montichiellese hit upon their own, true form: representing their own problems as a way of seeking to establish a new sense of identity. The famous Milanese stage director Giorgio Strehler has found the appropriate name for this form of theater: *autodramma*.

Drama has brought the residents of Monticchiello together again, and they've also been able to prove that the horizons of the province may be rural, but don't have to place any limitations on creativity.

Right: Open-air performance of the Teatro Povero in Monticchiello.

Monticchiello's Teatro Povera is only one of many open-air summer cultural events held throughout Tuscany between June and September, when the regular theaters are closed for the summer. The natural beauties of this countryside are already a work of art in themselves, a work, moreover, which has been refined through the years into a marvelous play of contrasting lines, colors and proportions by the hands of the farmers; during this time of year, the landscape becomes the backdrop for a wealth of musical and theater productions, a veritable explosion of every sort of cultural activity, state or private.

During the Middle Ages and the Renaissance, it was painters, sculptors and architects, such as Leonardo da Vinci, Piero della Francesca, Michelangelo Buonarotti or Filippo Brunelleschi, who worked to create all of the incomparable works which continue to attract millions of visitors to Tuscany's museums, churches, and monasteries.

Today, on the other hand, the central focus of Tuscany's cultural landscape has shifted to the performing arts and *cultura popolare*, culture of the people.

Throughout the province, cloisters are being restored, undergrowth cleared from old ruins, churches cleaned out, or a village square simply declared to be a cultural venue, in order to make room for every conceivable sort of spectacle. The summer festivals have various forms and contents and are of equally varying degrees of quality. There are improvisational theaters and traditional plays, avant-garde and ultra-conservative productions, plenty of mediocrity, but also some productions of real quality which have a great deal to offer audiences. In some places, the performances remain simply a colorful mixture of theater, music and dance, a little of everything, something for everyone. Some of the organizations, however, have managed in a remarkably short space of time to make

their events veritable Meccas for artists and spectators.

Tuscany's summer calendar begins in May with the *Maggio Musicale Fiorentino*, Florence's Musical May. This oldest of all Italian music festivals has been attracting fans of the classical modern to Florence with its first-rate performances for more than 60 years. In the past, you could hear all of the great orchestras here, the very best conductors (Bruno Walter), singers (Maria Callas), and works; there were opera productions that set standards for years to come (Verdi's *Macbeth*), staged in historic settings by legends of the stage (Gustav Gründgens).

In recent years, however, the Maggio Musicale has lost a bit of its erstwhile glamour. This is partly because every city of any size is trying, these days, to get its own festival up and running. But also partly to blame are the power-hungry politicians, who are all too fond of filling the festival's administration with their own (political) allies.

Not quite as spectacular, but another reason for classical music fans to come to Tuscany in July, is the *Estate Fiesolana*, the Cultural Summer of the city of Fiesole. In the town's Roman amphitheater and in the cloister of the Abbey of Badia Fiesolana, audiences watch films, music, dance, or theater performances.

For the entertainment of bathing guests from mid-July to the end of August, Versilia offers the festival *La Versiliana* with a number of theater and dance performances as well as concerts.

At nearly the same time, and not far away, is the *Festival Pucciniano* in Torre del Lago, where every year the great composer Giacomo Puccini is commemorated in the town where he composed some of his most important operas. These are performed in magnificent stagings on a large open-air stage built over the lake.

These large festivals, of international renown and with very high budgets, are the landmarks of Tuscany's cultural summer; but specialists and simple fans are often even fonder of the legion smaller festivals and series throughout the countryside, which truly bring the province's theater and musical landscape to life.

At the beginning of July, for example, theater-goers in the province of Florence have an important date in the Etruscan city of Volterra with the Volterrateatro, where classical, modern and even children's theater is presented in the city's loveliest squares.

You can hear contemporary tones in June and July at the Festival delle Collini in the Medici's summer palace in Poggio a Caiano. Street theater fans and anyone who likes street musicians, or buskers, should check out the picturesque little town of Pelago near Pontassieve at the beginning of July.

In Florence itself, there are two private organizers who insure – not only in summer – that there's always a musical tidbit or two on the program. Responsible for classical music in general and chamber music in particular is the *Associazone Amici della Musica*, an exclusive union of music-lovers which has been around since 1919. No less serious music is on the program of the *Centro Flog*, dedicated to researching and documenting folk traditions and music. Its showcase is the *Festival Musica dei Popoli*, held from late June to early July, which presents music of peoples from around the globe.

And while we're on the subject of ethnic music, one should really mention the largest blues festival in Italy, the three-day *Bluesin* held in Pistoia at the beginning of July. Classical-music lovers, however, may prefer to attend the so-called Pistoiese Culture Summer in July, held in the gardens of the town's old villas.

In the neighboring province of Lucca, in the silk center of Barga, there's an

event for modern music from France and Italy; while the spa town of Bagna di Lucca takes the minds of its bathing guests off their aches and pains with chamber music, theater performances and ballet between July and September.

Highlight of summer's cultural calendar in the province of Pisa is the festival *Pisa Estate*, which offers excellent theater and music events. At about the same time Castiglioncello, in the province of Livorno, is a gathering-place for all fans of modern dance theater.

Musica nel Chiostro, a series of concerts in the cloister of Santa Croce in Batignano in the province of Grosseto, is one of many praiseworthy private events which have come into being thanks to the love of a foreign artist, in this case the Britisher Adam Pollock, for Tuscany's landscape and culture. Every summer, Pollock presents musical works which are rarely, if ever, performed elsewhere at this small festival.

Not far away, near Capalbio, there's another remarkable project, the bizarre sculpture park by the French artist Niki de Saint-Phalle in the garden of the artist's own summer house. The park, which resembles a colorful fairy-tale garden, is popular with children as well as adults. Visitors can enter freely in the months of June and July. And anyone who likes traditional folk theater should stay in the neighborhood, here in the Maremma, at the end of July for the festival in the Etruscan city of Sorano.

For more than 50 years, the *Accademia Musicale Chigiana* has presented a select series of chamber concerts, orchestral concerts, or operas in Siena in July or August. At the same time, the city hosts a kind of jazz summer school with evening concerts, known as *Siena Jazz*.

The province of Siena, in fact, which also contains the theater village of Monticchiello, has cultural tidbits of one form or another to offer all summer long. In Castelnuovo Berardenga, for example,

Right: Popular culture depicted in Monticchiello's Teatro Povero.

classical music is presented, while the Abbadia San Salvatore on Monte Amiata offers theater and musicals.

Bruscello, the traditional form of local peasant theater, is presented in Montepulciano's main square, where it has to share facilities with an extraordinary cultural undertaking, the Cantiere Internazionale d'Arte. Together, students and artists create avant-garde works in theater and music workshops, and ultimately present them before audiences. Founder and leading light of the festival is the well-known German composer Hans Werner Henze.

In the province of Arezzo, there are no fewer than three unusual musical events: the *Concorso Polifonico Internazionale "Guido d'Arezzo,"* a competition in which choruses of all different waters vie with one another; an organ festival in the monastery of San Francesco in La Verna, where you can hear organists from throughout Europe; and a festival in nearby Sansepolcro, where unpublished chamber music from every nation is performed before an interested public. And all of this is only an incomplete listing of the region's multi-faceted cultural calendar.

Before leaving this topic, one should also make mention of another welcome variation of Tuscan culture. For several years now, museums have been founded throughout the region which are devoted to documenting peasant life. These are often financed privately and initiated by foreign guests who comb the area for grains of lost or vanishing tradition. In the wake of initiatives of *cultura popolare*, folk culture, such as the *Teatro Povero* in Monticchiello, interest has grown and is growing on the region's long-neglected past.

Particularly noteworthy among these museums are the Farmer's Museum in Gaville near Figline, the Museum of Folk Culture in Palazzuolo sul Senio, the ethnographic center in the Bisenzio valley, and, last but not least, the Ideale Museum of Leonardo da Vinci in Vinci, the artist's home town.

BREAD AND CIRCUSES

Driving in summer through the Tuscan countryside, you'll see bright posters plastered across tree trunks or the walls of houses announcing impending *sagra*: *Sagra del Tartuffo, Sagra di Tortellini, Sagra del Cinghiale*. The name of this church festival announces a whole schedule in itself, for a *sagra* has, basically, one purpose: to offer the rural population and any city visitors who happen to be around on a given weekend the chance to sit at long wooden tables, eat local specialties, and thereby forget the long winter. To help along this processing of forgetting, the proceedings are fueled with plenty of local wine. And because a *sagra* is always a great opportunity to meet neighbors and friends under the open sky and spend a couple of convivial hours together, there's usually a band in attendance to provide dance music.

Sagras, like the festival of a patron saint hosted by a given congregation or the party festivals of the old Italian Communist Party, the ever-popular Festa dell'Unità, have long been a focal point of village life and a highlight of the year; but if you look for some old tradition underlying this widespread custom, you're doomed to disappointment. Rather, sagras are a child of popular culture, born in the postwar era when, seeking a new identity of their own, young people in the country began to express themselves more creatively within their landscape or community, social surroundings and countryside. It wasn't that there had previously been a dearth of popular culture in Tuscany; the region looks back on a long history of folklore traditions, some of them deriving from a mixture of heathen customs and religious rites, often seasonal, that are still celebrated enthusiastically throughout the

Right: In autumn, locals gather at chestnut festivals.

area. But many of these traditions were abandoned for a time, not to be pulled out of mothballs and reanimated until the 1960s. Today, only a few other regions of Italy have such a vivid awareness of their own authentic folklore and festivals as does Tuscany.

The annual festival calendar begins on January 6 with a children's festival which centers around the *Befana*, a friendly witch who gives children, according to how they've behaved in the course of the preceding year a reward in the form of a small gift or punishment in the form of a lump of coal laid before the doors of their bedrooms. The next important folklore event is carnival season, which in days gone by was often the only chance a young peasant girl had to go out dancing and look around for a husband. High point of Tuscany's carnival celebrations are the parades in Viareggio with colorful, allegorical floats and imaginative choreography. At the same time, in many village squares, there are *bruscello*, a grotesque-erotic form of peasant theater centering on the subject of fertility.

During Holy Week, the proceedings are far more decorous. There are penitential processions and passion plays – in, for example, the town of Grassina near Florence, where the residents reenact the life and suffering of Jesus in the course of the night before Good Friday.

On Easter Sunday, the Florentines meet in front of the Cathedral to participate in a religious Easter ceremony, the *Scoppio del Carro*, and watch how, with the help of a clay pigeon, the "holy fire" is ignited on an oxcart. This tradition reaches back to the days of the Crusaders.

Tuscan through and through is the *Canto del Maggio*, an old song festival which ushers in the spring, particularly in the coastal regions. On the night of April 30, a group of young people, known as the *maggiolanti*, go singing and dancing from house to house, which is supposed to ensure a good harvest. In the Lunigi-

ana and Garfagnana, a local version of this tradition, the *Maggio Drammatico*, is a mixture of tradition and folk theater which links the dualities of winter and spring, good and evil to historic events, and presents them in earthy verses.

Lucca, too, has its religious-folkloric ceremonies. On September 13 the *Volto Santo*, the early medieval figure of Christ from the Cathedral, the origins of which are obscured in a web of legend, is borne through the city in a festive torchlight procession.

Christmas in Tuscany has a tradition all its own, although today this has followed the lead of the rest of the Western world and degenerated into the normal consumer orgy of gift-giving under a Christmas tree adorned with lights. Once, however, it was a *ceppo*, or triangular rootstock, which played the central role on Christmas Eve; this was decorated with fruits and laurel leaves, sprayed with wine, and finally burned slowly in an open fireplace in a mixture of religious ritual and praise to the wine god Bacchus.

In city apartments without fireplaces, the *ceppo* was imitated by a pyramidal set of shelves, in which presents and sweets were set. Another part of the Christmas tradition here is the viewing of the various Nativity scenes and crèches that are set up throughout the region: old and new; comprised of living figures, such as the one in the Grossetan town of Montorsaio, where the entire village population enacts the Christmas story on Christmas Eve; and even, in a grotto in Porto Santo Stefano, under water.

In the ranks of Tuscan festivals and holidays, the historic games of various towns have a very special position. These are generally magnificent costume pageants, albeit often with imaginative rather than historic costumes, which are supposed to reawaken the population's sense of its history and its past. Usually, they are accompanied by splendid parades or linked to a banquet or feast. One major impetus for such popular entertainments is the tourist traffic which they encourage; but the games are taken very

seriously by their protagonists as well as by the local spectators. In recent years, such pageant-games have seen a veritable Renaissance throughout Tuscany.

A typically Tuscan element of these games is that they're virtually all competitions, a fact which probably indicated an inherent characteristic of the Tuscan soul. Of the "*maledetti toscani,*" the accursed Tuscans, as the writer Curzio Malaparte termed his fellow-countrymen, it's said that they amuse themselves best in pairs. As soon as a third party enters the picture, people immediately take sides and start amusing themselves at the cost of their opponents. What appears to tourists and visitors to be an entertaining costume party often develops into deadly earnest for the people who are actually involved. Not infrequently, someone comes out of the games with an ear torn off or a broken arm. This somewhat du-

Above: You have to start young if you want to be a good flag-waver. Right: After the Palio, the Sienese gather at huge banquets.

bious form of entertainment may have its origins in the fact that the Tuscans, in the course of their eventful past, were nearly always engaged in various acts of war, and that a kind of bloodthirstiness has been preserved in their descendants.

Take, for example, the *Calcio in Costume* in Florence (June 24), a wild free-for-all between two teams over a ball. This is a kind of football game played in historic costumes, although feet are mainly employed to inflict damage upon the anatomy of members of the opposing team. This may have made sense in 1530, when the Florentine men challenged the Imperial troops who were occupying the city to a "game." For the Florentines, the prize of victory was the privilege of being allowed to collect food supplies. Today, however, there really isn't any justification for the kind of brutality that one sometimes sees on the playing field.

Another tradition dating back to the 16th century are the *Giostra del Saracino* held on the last Sunday in August on Arezzo's Piazza Grande. This is another

competitive game in which riders from different quarters of the city joust with lances against a puppet, the "Saracen," who hits back with a firm blow if you don't hit him exactly in the middle.

In the medieval *Gioco del Ponte* in Pisa (last Sunday in June), strong men struggle to push, pull or shove each other off a bridge into the Arno. The former maritime republic presents another spectacle, the *Regatta Storico di S. Ranieri*, a rowing regatta on the Arno on June 17, in honor of the city's patron saint.

Also dedicated to a saint, Bernard, are the *Balestro del Girifalco* (May 20 and the second Sunday in August) in Massa Marittima, a competition between crossbow archers shooting at falcons, which dates back to the Middle Ages and was resumed in 1959. And it's for St. Jacob that Pistoia holds its *Giostra dell'Orso* (July 25), an equestrian tournament with roots in the 13th century. After a picturesque parade, twelve riders tilt with their lances at two stylized figures of bears. This tournament is the climax of

the "Pistoiese July," a festival combining cultural, athletic and folklore events.

In Sansepolcro, the *Palio della Balestra* has been held for the last 600 years. On the second Sunday in September, crossbow archers compete with rivals from the Umbrian town of Gubbio, in the name of St. Aegidius. In the month of May, the costumed archers from Sansepulcro parade over to Gubbio, where the opposing team formally challenges them to the contest. The participants' costumes are copied from the clothes depicted in old frescoes, and the weapons they use actually date from the 14th century.

Unchallenged queen of Tuscany's games is the *Palio* in Siena (July 2 and August 16), a horse race on the Piazza del Campo. An uninitiated visitor could easily come away with the impression that the fanatical Sienese would be perfectly able to take the death of horses and riders in stride if only the riders representing their city neighborhood succeeded in capturing the contested banner, the *palio*, and thus the victory.

HIKING IN TUSCANY

Hiking is the most romantic and perhaps also the most intensive way to travel. A hiker is part of the landscape, and he takes it in actively with all his five senses. Travelling on foot, you approach towns, peoples, or sights gradually, at a human pace. Meetings and chance encounters take place which would be impossible for someone travelling by car, cut off from his surroundings. A hiker's route generally bypasses overcrowded spots and leads through solitary landscapes which have preserved their original, natural qualities, and allow real insight into the land's true character.

Tuscany is an ideal country for hiking. And this mode of travel is actually the best way to discover this region. The land is, in many places, like a giant garden; its winding paths, uphill and down dale,

Above: Tuscany – ideal country for riding holidays. Right: After all those hills, a little refreshment is in order.

keep yielding up new vistas or opening out on unexpected panoramas.

Tuscany is a comfortable country for hiking, as well. The trails are not overly difficult or demanding; they're suited for walkers of all ages and all levels of physical condition. The climate is mild – apart, of course, from the hot summers and cold winters – and you can plan your trip hour by hour or map out a route that will take you several days. You can embark on a walk around one of the smaller villages, which often lie on hilltops; you can walk from one town to the next; or you can avoid civilization altogether and plunge into the region's unspoiled nature. Overnight accommodation of all kinds is available at every turn: in farmhouses or village inns, in hotels in the larger cities, or campgrounds throughout the countryside. In mountainous regions, there are even mountain huts.

If you'd like to plan out your hiking route carefully before you set out, the tourist offices in every town can furnish you with a wealth of material. In addi-

tion, there are plenty of books available with various routes, tips, and background information. A few such titles are listed in the "Guidelines" section of this book.

Tuscany, of course, isn't for hikers alone. Another intimate way to explore and experience this magnificent landscape with its gentle colors, intense smells and unbelievable tranquility is on horseback. "Tranquility" is a better term to describe the absence of civilization than "silence," for it's hard to believe the cacophonous din of bird song, especially in spring, that rises from the dense maquis undergrowth which provides the birds with an ideal natural habitat. This is punctuated with the cries of the pheasants which flourish here, and which are popular targets for the hordes of passionate sport hunters who flock to the countryside in season.

Another popular target are the wild pigs, although these certainly don't seem much bothered by the hunters; they've procreated at an alarming rate all over Tuscany, and have become a real nuis-ance. At night, they force their way into farmers' gardens and vineyards and help themselves to fruit and vegetables. The payoff for this is that, especially in the wooded parts of the region, you can find all kind of delicious wild boar specialties...

If you opt to take a car along the narrow, notably winding and often very steep mountain roads, you'll encounter, especially after working hours or on weekends, what at times seems a constant stream of cyclists in bright jerseys, either grimacing and battling with their slender racing bikes up a steep incline or zooming down again without much evident care for approaching traffic. If you're not as ambitious as these cyclists, and would like to explore Tuscany *en plein air* and yet at a slightly faster pace than a pedestrian, you may find a bicycle the perfect way to go. There are all kinds of possible tours at all levels of difficulty – although be warned that nowhere in Tuscany is the land altogether flat. But that's exactly why it's so lovely.

FOREIGNERS IN TUSCANY

"The land where the lemons blossom..." Since Goethe's famous Italian Journey, or even earlier, the Apennine Peninsula has been a Paradise for all those who seek to rediscover the romantic Italy of yesteryear. For the English, the works of Shelley and Byron had a similar effect. Writing down their observations and experiences, these poets unwittingly unleashed an avalanche. First individually, then in groups, today *en masse*, tourists from around the globe converge on Italy, and seem particularly drawn to Tuscany. After all, this region is Mediterranean without being too foreign; its cuisine is southern without threatening the digestion; and its people, its inhabitants are southern, temperamental, spirited, and yet "somehow civilized."

The first great wave of vacationers broke over Tuscany in the 1960s. It was this which leveled the way for the onslaught of mass tourism. Today, package tourists to Florence are herded along the well-trodden routes – Cathedral, Piazza Signoria, Ponte Vecchio – after which they're taken off, in the afternoon, to photograph the skyline of San Gimignano and the Leaning Tower of Pisa.

Then there were the academics, intellectuals, and other scholars, who have for centuries come south for purposes of study, their gaze trained firmly on the past. For a long time, these travellers to the temples of art overlooked the fact that it could also be fun to mingle with the people of the region. Today, however, young people come to Florence, Pisa and Siena not only to learn about the sun-drenched Renaissance culture, but to learn the art of *saper vivere*.

In the 1970s, more and more travellers arrived for whom the second-most im-

Right: Dream of many visitors to Tuscany – fixing up an old house in a gorgeous setting as a holiday home.

portant holiday reading material, after the Blue Guide or Baedeker, was their checkbook. These people bought themselves a plot of vacationland and thereby inscribed themselves into a long tradition of English aristocrats and intellectuals who were already buying up villas in the hills around Florence by the turn of the century, there to remain among themselves in an imported, British atmosphere. If an Italian did set foot in one of these salons, he was likely to be a member of an old Florentine family – for the local aristocracy, at least, knew a bit of English and had a proper feeling for the importance of afternoon tea.

The modern holiday settler, however, is more likely to hail from Zurich, Oslo or Munich, and is probably a university professor, filmmaker, or therapist. A well-paying job enables him to retreat for a few months every summer into his simple Tuscan country house, so that he can "find himself" anew. These summer guests embark well-armed on their search for the meaning of life. They're usually fluent in the local language, seek out contact with Italians, and generally love all things Italian: the wine, the food, the clothes, the lifestyle. And when autumn begins and the rains start, they return, rested and content, to their comfortable city apartments north of the Alps.

For a while, a few modern romantics even tried to flee the pressures of an achievement-oriented society by retiring here altogether. They could be spotted at local markets in colorful, hand-knitted garments, trying to sell cheese made of ewe's milk or painted pottery of their own design. Later, they invented imaginative self-help seminars for like-minded people. Their illusions of the joys of a primitive life, however, gradually exploded one by one like soap-bubbles. They learned to fear cold winters in damp houses, or the Italian tax authorities. They learned, too, that today it's impossible to live without a steady monthly

income, preferably from one's own country – even in Paradise.

The Italianophilic summer guests who own property here will doubtless remain faithful to "their" Tuscany. They have a great time here, and they're tolerated by the locals. After all, they spend their money in the local shops and at the bar, and don't miss a single *sagra*, or local summer festival. They ask for help and advice in pruning their olive trees and grapevines – for, of course, a price – and help gather in the grape harvest – for free.

The Tuscans themselves look with equanimity, sometimes with a bit of amusement, but generally with distance upon these comings and goings. Certainly they're happy that guests bring money into the local economy. The rural population is glad to see decrepit houses being bought up and restored. They have the greatest respect for anyone who doesn't shrink back from hard work in the stony soil. And as the population here has watched for centuries wave after wave of foreigners coming through, be they pil-grims, merchants or soldiers, they're not particularly impressed, much less intimidated, by this peaceful invasion.

As for foreigners who live and work in Tuscany, such as myself – that's a whole subject unto itself. Many of them came here hoping to discover the Italy of Antiquity, and ended up colliding head-on with the actual Italy of today.

"You live with Italy as you would with a lover: today quarreling mightily, tomorrow in adoration," Schopenhauer noted pithily during one of his stays in Florence. Anyone who wants to make a long-term commitment to stay here has to be aware that he'll need all his strength and energy to reach a compromise with the country. There's no room here for imported illusions, habits, expectations, and other baggage. Nor is there any place for halfway measures. If you prefer things a little calmer, you'd do better to stay in a place like Germany, where life, according to Schopenhauer, is "like life with a housewife, without great anger, but without great love."

FRESCOES
The Television of the Renaissance

We, the children of the television generation, think that the concept of conveying information through pictures is a terribly modern innovation. But it really isn't all that new. Six hundred years ago in Tuscany, pictures were already being used as a medium to communicate the experiences of the then-contemporary world. And for a modern visitor, these pictures can be a key opening up a door to the history of the cities and their culture, which remain fascinating because they still have so much to say to us today.

In 1338, the painter Ambrogio Lorenzetti was commissioned to decorate the Sala della Pace in Siena's Palazzo Pubblico with frescoes. This room was the meeting-chamber of the Council of Nine, a body which passed laws that regulated

Above: Effects of the Ideal Government: Ambrogio Lorenzotti's fresco in the Palazzo Pubblico in Siena.

the city's life down to the smallest detail. These laws were written down in the Tuscan dialect, and lay in the town hall to be read by any citizen who wished to do so. In 1339, both Lorenzetti's frescoes and a new body of laws were completed. And the painter's frescoes can be seen as a kind of illustration of these legal texts.

At that time, the visitor entered the room through the old entrance in the corner of the central wall. The two frescoes which he saw above him if he turned his head depicted the victory of Justice on the right, and, on the left, her defeat. The right-hand image shows a majestic woman on a throne; on the left, she is lying bound on the floor, and her scales are broken. The visitor, then, can decide between these two alternatives, and the consequences of his decision are immediately illustrated: peace or war. These subjects are treated in detail in the rest of the frescoes.

The bad, unjust government leads to a state of tyranny. The city decays, the streets are unsafe, the workshops plun-

dered. Murder, thievery and rape are shown next to allegorical figures of arrogance, greed, betrayal, cruelty, and war. Fear rules the entire country. Roads, bridges, and farmhouses fall into decrepitude, and armed men march over the fields.

Under the good government, however, the ideal of the Council of Nine in Siena, the city and the surrounding countryside flourish. The city overflows with goods, the people are dressed elegantly, and everywhere you see people working, learning, and building (the frescoes offer an excellent illustration of the building techniques that were then in use). Even the countryside is depicted in graphic detail; you can easily recognize the Arbia valley. Fields and vineyards are well-tended, and the roads are crowded with travelling merchants. A winged image of security overlooks the scene.

And the allegorical figures at the sides represent the virtues of peace, strength, intelligence, courage, temperance, and justice.

"Talking pictures" is the term one art historian coined for Lorenzetti's frescoes. And there are comparable images in Pisa's Camposanto, in the chapel of Santa Maria Novella in Florence or the municipal and administrative buildings of a number of smaller cities. These are impressive pictorial narratives of Tuscan civic culture in the 14th century. The frescoes convey a certain social ideal and organize the experiences of the viewer into an order corresponding to the world view of the epoch in which he lived. This order is a form of knowledge, of understanding.

When you've looked your fill and are back out on the Campo sipping a cup of espresso, you may suddenly feel you've been transported back into the 14th-century city republic. And later, when you're sitting at home in front of the evening news and watching images of war, assassination, and other catastrophes, you may close your eyes and think back to the images you saw in Siena. And all at once, you, too, may begin to understand.

Nelles Maps ... get you going.

MANILA

PHILIPPINES

VIETNAM, LAOS CAMBODIA

SOUTH EAST ASIA

Road Atlas

INDONESIA

NELLES VERLAG

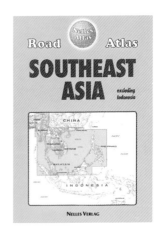

Road Atlas

SOUTHEAST ASIA excluding Indonesia

NELLES VERLAG

- Afghanistan
- Australia
- Bangkok
- Burma
- Caribbean Islands 1 / Bermuda, Bahamas, Greater Antilles
- Caribbean Islands 2 / Lesser Antilles
- Central America
- China 1 / North-Eastern China
- China 2 / Northern China
- China 3 / Central China
- China 4 / Southern China
- Crete
- Egypt
- Hawaiian Islands
- Hawaiian Islands 1 / Kauai

Nelles Maps

- Hawaiian Islands 2 / Honolulu, Oahu
- Hawaiian Islands 3 / Maui, Molokai, Lanai
- Hawaiian Islands 4 / Hawaii
- Himalaya
- Hong Kong
- Indian Subcontinent
- India 1 / Northern India
- India 2 / Western India
- India 3 / Eastern India
- India 4 / Southern India
- India 5 / North-Eastern India
- Indonesia
- Indonesia 1 / Sumatra
- Indonesia 2 / Java + Nusa Tenggara
- Indonesia 3 / Bali
- Indonesia 4 / Kalimantan

- Indonesia 5 / Java + Bali
- Indonesia 6 / Sulawesi
- Indonesia 7 / Irian Jaya + Maluku
- Jakarta
- Japan
- Kenya
- Korea
- Malaysia
- West Malaysia
- Manila
- Mexico
- Nepal
- New Zealand
- Pakistan
- Philippines
- Singapore
- South East Asia
- Sri Lanka
- Taiwan
- Thailand
- Vietnam, Laos, Cambodia

TRAVEL INFORMATION

TRAVEL PREPARATIONS

When to Go

Tuscany is "in season" all year long. More than four million foreign and Italian tourists, who have more than 120,000 beds in hotels and pensions at their disposal, flood into Florence and other popular tourist centers throughout the year – above all on short package tours on holiday weekends. If possible, try to avoid planning a trip to Tuscany over Easter, Pentecost (Michelmas), or Christmas. It can also be unbearable in the cities in the oppressive heat of summer; at this time, you're better off following the lead of the Tuscans themselves, who set aside their work in July and August and take refuge at the seaside.

Another alternative are the cooler regions up in the mountains, where you can go off for marvelous hikes, but where you'll find that there's still, often as not, plenty of diversion for lovers of art and culture.

The mild, Mediterranean climate makes Tuscany particularly marvelous in spring and autumn. As most visitors, however, think the same way, it may be quite difficult to find lodging in these seasons. It can also happen that a visitor in April/May or October/November may be surprised by a sudden cloudburst. Seldom, however, will you encounter a protracted period of bad, rainy weather, such as you might expect to find north of the Alps.

Art lovers, more than anyone else, are well advised to travel in winter, when the museums are likely to be empty of people. The countryside, too, has a special attraction all its own at this time of year. At higher altitudes, however, January may see temperatures around freezing level, and the old stone buildings can get extremely cold. Particularly in mid- to low-priced accommodations, the heating is often inadequate to the winter weather.

If you want some time to get to know Tuscany rather than merely stopping in for a superficial visit, you should plan to stay for at least three weeks. If you don't have that much time, then limit yourself to fewer destinations; for Tuscany is a country which demands time, effort, and a sense of adventure if you want truly to get to know it.

Clothing

Light summer clothes are always fine, but in spring and autumn you should be sure to bring along a warm pullover and some rain gear. In winter, you'll probably need warm wool clothing. And it's not a bad idea to take along a blanket or a sleeping bag, which may stand you in good stead as extra bedding in old country estates or hotels and pensions in the lower price category.

When setting out to visit churches and monasteries, make sure you're wearing suitable clothing: no shorts and no miniskirts, and keep your shoulders covered. If you don't follow this code, they may not let you in. Italians set store by dressing well and, above all, properly. Even in beach towns, therefore, don't run around in your bathing suit unless you don't mind being followed by disapproving glances.

Suggested Reading

A selection of books for pleasure, preparation for your trip, or further background on what you'll encounter:

Abrams (publisher), Renaissance and Mannerist Art.
Barzini, Luigi, The Italians.
Berenson, Bernard, The Florentine Painters of the Renaissance; The Passionate Sightseer.
Burckhardt, Jacob, Civilization of the Renaissance in Italy.
Fischer, Heinz-Joachim, Tuscany (Prestel Guide).
Forster, E.M. A Room with a View.

Fruttero, Carlo/Lucentini, Franco, The Secret of the Pineta.

James, Henry, Italian Hours; Portrait of a Lady; short stories.

Lawrence, D.H., Etruscan Places.

McCarthy, Mary, The Stones of Florence.

Murray, Peter, The Architecture of the Italian Renaissance.

Origo, Iris, The Merchant of Prato.

Pater, Walter, The Renaissance.

Tuscany: Facts & Figures

Tuscany is the fifth-largest of the twenty regions of Italy. It measures about 8,876 square miles in area (23,000 sq. km) and is divided into ten provinces: Arezzo, Florence, Grosseto, Livorno, Lucca, Massa-Carrara, Pisa, Pistoia, Prato (since 1993) and Siena.

The largest cities are Florence (in October, 1991, the population was officially recorded at 402,316), Livorno (population ca. 167,445), Prato (160,000) and Pistoia (103,500).

Quite some time ago, Tuscany ceased to be primarily an agricultural region: today, only some 10% of the population live from agriculture, although the figure is 20% in the provinces of Siena and Grosseto. The main crops are grains and feed plants, wine and olives; but there's also some cultivation of fruit and vegetables. Additional agricultural products are meat, ewe's-milk cheese, and tobacco.

Some 60% of all Tuscans are employed in industrial fields (engineering, textiles industries, shoe-making, woodworking and chemical industries) or support themselves by artisan skills, usually practiced in small or even family businesses. Trade and service fields (mainly in the tourist industry) support about one-quarter of the population.

One-tenth of the tourists in Italy head for Tuscany; of these, about 35% are foreigners, 40% Italians, and 25%, believe it or not, Tuscans.

GETTING THERE

By Plane

Tuscany's international airport is located in Pisa (Galileo Galilei); from here, trains and buses of the Linie Lazzi run to Florence every hour. Florence has its own little airport (Peretola), but there are very few direct flights. At the moment, Peretola is mainly accessed by domestic connecting flights, but there are plans to expand it in the near future. From abroad, you can also fly into Milan or Rome and continue on from there into Tuscany by train.

A few smaller planes fly to the little airport La Pila in Marina di Campo on the island of Elba; there are direct connec tions from Munich, for example, or from Innsbruck.

By Car

From central Europe, if you're coming through Germany and Austria, you can get to Tuscany by taking the Autobahn A 22 and going by way of Bozen, Verona and Modena. From there, the A 1 leads on via Bologna to Florence. If you're coming from the south (Rome), the A1 will also bring you to Florence, but from the other direction.

If you're driving in by way of Switzerland, pick up the A 1 in Milan and follow it to Modena. You can also opt for the route from Milan-Parma, from where you can take the A 15 over the Cisa Pass to La Spezia and then get onto the A 12 to go further south. From Viareggio, the crossland route A 11 (Firenze-Mare) runs through Lucca and on to Florence.

If you're coming from France, follow the A 12, which leads from Genoa along the lovely, scenic Ligurian coast and then follows the Versilia to Pisa or Livorno.

You're required to pay a toll for the privilege of travelling on an Italian expressway. From the Brenner Pass to Florence, the charge right now (1994) is about 45,000 lire.

On stretches where there is a particular risk or likelihood of traffic tie-ups, automatic information tables keep you continually informed about current traffic conditions.

By Train

Some of Tuscany's larger cities (Massa-Carrara, Pisa, Livorno, Grosseto, Florence, Arezzo) are located on the main Italian train lines, and therefore have direct connections to a number of European cities. A number of trains end at the dead-end station of Santa Maria Novella in Florence; trains which go on from Florence stop at the station Campo di Marte in the eastern part of the city. If you want to travel to your final destination by taking a local train from one of the larger cities, then you'd better bring plenty of patience, as most of these trains really do stop at every station. This leisurely pace can, on the other hand, allow you to get a real sense of the countryside and get into the relaxed swing of Tuscan life.

By Bus

There aren't any regular international bus connections to Tuscany, but a number of private bus companies offer package tours lasting several days or even weeks to Florence and Tuscany from major cities in Central Europe.

Getting Around

If you're planning a tour of Tuscany's cities and know where you'd like to go, it's wisest to travel by plane or train. Most of the old city centers are closed to car traffic, parking lots can be few and far between, and furthermore most of the sights, which are generally grouped together within a city center, are easy to reach on foot. Good public transportation within the cities, furthermore – that is, public buses – make it quick and easy to get to slightly out-of-the-way destinations.

But if you'd like to get to know the country, and aren't prepared to hike or cycle an inordinate amount, you're practically obliged to go by car, which will give you the freedom to seek out small villages and hidden corners. Another advantage of going by car is that it gives you more room to transport wine, oil, and any other specialties you might want to stock up on along the way.

Of course, you can always rent a car (or motorcycle) in Tuscany, as well. All of the major rental car companies have branches in Florence and the region's other large cities. It's considerably cheaper, certainly, if you make a reservation before you go.

There are also two main bus lines in Tuscany, operated by the transport companies SITA and Lazzi Fratelli. In addition, smaller local buses service individual cities and the surrounding villages. You can buy tickets at the bus company offices or in bars and kiosks in town.

PRACTICAL TIPS

Accommodations
Hotels

Hotels and Pensions in Italy are classified or categorized by stars (* to *****). This system, however, doesn't take into account the location, possible noise, or atmosphere. Still, you can assume that a three-star hotel will provide solid comfort at moderte prices. Anything over that is luxury class or first category, in which you should expect to pay around 350,000 (single) and 550,000 lire (double) or 150,000 (single) and 200,000 lire (double). In the lower price classes, accommodations can range from friendly little family hotels to run-down dumps.

All in all, you can expect that in tourist centers such as Florence, Lucca and Siena you'll have to pay more than you would elsewhere. Prices must be posted in the room and at the reception desk; breakfast is only included if the guest has asked for it. Usually, it's better in any case to forget about the (usually rather indifferent) hotel breakfast and pick up a cappuccino and a fresh *cornetto* (roll, croissant) in the nearest bar. Some hotels, certainly, are starting to go over to the custom of serving a full, Central European breakfast buffet.

There are reasonably-priced, and often especially lovely and peaceful, accommodations in a number of old monasteries, where the food is often very good, as well. Sometimes, however, unmarried couples will not be allowed to share a double room in these facilities. Complete hotel listings are available from A.P.T. offices or from local tourist information.

Youth Hostels

If you hold an international youth hostel membership card, you can sleep cheaply in Italian youth hostels (sometimes you don't even need a card). It's a good idea to call ahead, and essential if you're travelling in a group of more than five people. For further information, contact the Associazione Italiana Alberghi per la Gioventù in the Palazzo della Civiltà del Lavoro, Quadrato della Concordia EUR, 00144 Roma, tel: 06-5913702.

Camping

Most campgrounds in Tuscany are only open from April to September or October. You can make reservations at Federcampeggio, Casella Postale 649, 50100 Firenze, tel: 055-882391. There, or at a local bookstore, you can also get a guide to campgrounds in the region.

Airlines

Offices in **FLORENCE**:

AIR FRANCE, 9, Borgo SS. Apostoli, tel: 055-284304/05 or 219798
ALITALIA, 1, Vicolo Oro, tel: 055-27881
BRITISH AIRWAYS, 36/R., Via Vigna Nuova, tel: 055-218655/216769
KLM, 2, Piazza Antinori, tel: 055-2381035/282993

LUFTHANSA, 2, Piazza Antinori, tel: 055-2381444
TWA, 4, Via Vecchietti, tel: 055-284691/2396856/2382795
Offices in **PISA**:
AIR FRANCE, Aeroporto Galilei, tel: 050-21482
ALITALIA, 21, Via Puccini, tel: 050-48025/501570; Aeroporto Galilei, tel: 050-20062
LUFTHANSA, Aeroporto Galilei, tel: 050-500151/501132
Offices in **CAMPO NELL'ELBA**:
INTERNATIONAL FLYING SERVICES, Aeroporto La Pila, Marina di Campo, tel: 0565-977937/38.

Banks

Opening hours: Monday-Friday 8:30 am-1 pm and about 3-4 pm. At the train station S. Maria Novella and at the airport Galileo Galilei in Pisa, the exchange counters are open longer, and are alos open on Saturdays. Many hotels will change money for you, but the exchange rate is often much less favorable than it may be in exchange offices or banks. It's still cheapest to get the cash you need from automatic bank tellers with international card capacity, which are available in most mid-sized and large cities.

You can only cash Eurocheques at a bank, and they have to be filled out in lire by the teller. Many hotels and shops also take credit cards.

Bathing

Tuscany has a wealth of mineral springs, most of which were already known in Antiquity. Today, the largest baths are Chianciano Terme and Montecatini Terme, but there are a dozen or so smaller mineral baths. You can get information materials from the tourist offices. Here are a few addresses and telephone numbers:

Bagni di Lucca: Villa Ada, tel: 0583-867757 / 87223 / 867756; 11, Piazza S. Martino, tel: 87221.

Chianciano Terme: Via Rose, tel: 0578-68111 / 60622.

Monsummano Terme: Grotta Giusti, Via Grotta Giusti, 171, tel: 0572-51008; Grotta Parlanti, Via Francesca Nord, 108, tel: 953029.

Montecatini Terme: Viale Giuseppe Verdi, 41, tel: 0572-7781; Viale Bustichini, tel: 78503.

San Giuliano Terme, Via Niccolini, 29, tel: 050-818005 / 818100.

Terme di Bagno Vignoni, Via Dante, 35, tel: 0577-887365.

Breakdown Service
ACI (Automobile Club Italiano): 116

Bus Companies
SITA: Florence, Via S. Caterina da Siena, 15r, tel: 055-211487; **Lazzi Fratelli**: Florence, P.zza Stazione, tel: 055-211245; Lucca, 135, Via Catalani, tel: 0583-419822; **ACIT**, Pisa, P.zza S. Antonio, 1, tel: 050-29413/501038; Livorno, Via C. Meyer, 57/59, tel: 0586-800566/807096; **RAMA**, Grosseto, 12, Via Topazio, tel: 0564-456745

Car Rental (*Autonoleggio*)
FLORENCE (area code: 055): **Avis Autonoleggio**, Via Andreotti, 44, tel: 355552; 128/R. Borgo Ognissanti, tel: 289010; **Europcar**, 53, Borgo Ognissanti, tel: 2360072/73; **Europcar Italia**, 1, Via Agnelli, tel: 644252; **Hertz italiana**, 33/R., Via Finiguerra, tel: 2398205/282260; **Maggiore Autoservizi**, 11/R., Via Finiguerra, tel: 294578, via Termine, 1, tel: 311256.

AREZZO: (area code: 0575): **Avis Conc. SIVOC**, 1/a, P.zza della Repubblica, tel: 354232; **Europcar Inter Rent**, 34, Via Varchi, 23168; **Autonoleggio Marcozzi**, 1/a, Pzza. della Repubblica, tel: 23866

GROSSETO (area code: 0564): **Maremma Tours**, 25, Via Topazio (in the industrial zone) tel: 451261

LIVORNO (area code: 0586): **Autono-leggio Hertz**, 63, Via Mastacchi, tel: 400491; **Avis Autonoleggio**, 49/51, Via Garibaldi, tel: 880090; **Maggiore Autoservizi**, 31/33, Via Fiume, tel: 892240

LUCCA (area code: 0583): **ACI Lucca Service**, 59, Via Catalani, 53535; **Giglio**, 4, Pzza. Giglio, tel: 492698

MASSA (area code: 0585): **Autonoleggio, Viale Roma**, 354, Loc. Marina di Massa, tel: 241360

PISA (area code: 050): **Liberty Rent**, airport, ACI office, tel: 49500; S. Frediano a Settimo, tel. 701034; **Avis**, 3, Lungarno Guadalongo, tel: 42327; airport, tel: 42028;

Europcar Italia, Via Aeroporto, tel: 41017; **Hertz Italiana**, airport, tel: 49156/49187; **Maggiore**, airport, tel: 42574

SIENA (area code: 0577): **Avis Autonoleggio** 36, Via Martini, tel: 270305 / 49275; **Hertz**, 10, Via XXIV Maggio, tel: 45085

Consulates
In FLORENCE (area code 055)
Austria, Via die Servi, 9, tel: 2382014; **Belgium**, Via dei Servi, 28, tel: 282094; **Denmark**, Via dei Servi, 13, tel: 211007; **Finland** , Via degli Strozzi, 6 (2. Stock), tel: 293228; **France**, Piazza Ognissanti, 2, tel: 2302556; **Germany**, Lungarno Vespucci, 30, tel: 294722; **Great Britain**, Lungarno Corsini, 2, tel: 284133 / 212594 / 287449 / 289556; **Luxemburg**, Piazza Bellosguardo, 11/12 and Via Bartolommei, 4, tel: 473219; **The Netherlands**, Via Cavour, 81, tel: 475249; **Norway**, Via G. Capponi, 26, tel: 2479321; **Spain**, Via G. La Pira, 21, tel: 217110; **Sweden**, Via Scla, 4, tel: 2396865; Switzerland, Piazzale Galileo, 5, tel: 222434; **Turkey**, Via Nazionale, 7, tel: 294893; **USA**, Lungarno A. Vespucci, 38, tel: 2398276 / 217605 and Lungarno A. Vespucci, 46, tel: 216531 / 294921.

Emergencies
Carabinieri: 212121

Police and Emergency (automobile accidents): 113

Farmhouse Holidays
(*Agriturismo* and *Turismo Verde*)
Nowhere else do you have so many chances to spend a relaxed, back-to-nature holday as you do in Tuscany. Countless former or still-working farmhouses offer reasonably-priced accommodation, often with a chance to help out in actually working the land and usually with rates for the whole family. If you want, you can also pay a small fee and have meals included as part of the package. Meals are taken family-style, and usually consist of good solid home fare made of the farm's own products.

For addresses and further information, contact the individual tourist information offices.

Ferries
You can get the ferry schedule for boats between the mainland and the islands of the Tuscan Archipelago from the following agencies:

ISOLA D'ELBA:
TOREMAR, 57100 Livorno, Via Calafati, 4. tel: 0586- 896113; 57037 Portoferraio, Calata Italia, 22, tel: 0565-918080; 57025 Piombino, Piazzale Premuda 13-14, tel: 0565-31100; 57038 Rio Marina, Banch. dei Voltoni, 9, tel: 0565-962073; 57036 Porto Azzurro, Banchina IV Novembre, 19, tel: 0565-95004; 57030 Cavo, Via Appalto, 114, tel: 0565-949871.
NAV.AR.MA. Lines, 57025 Piombino, Piazzale Premuda 13, tel: 0565-221212; 57037 Portoferraio, Viale Elba, 4, tel: 0565-914133/918101.
ELBA FERRIES, Piombino, tel: 0565-220956; Portoferraio, tel: 0565-930676.

ISOLA DEL GIGLIO:
TOREMAR, 58013 Isola del Giglio, Loc. Porto, Via Umberto I, tel: 0564-809349;

58019 Porto Santo Stefano, Piazzale A. Candi, tel: 0564-814615;

ISOLA DI CAPRAIA:
TOREMAR, 57032, Isola di Capraia, Via Assunzione, tel: 0586-905069.
Sample prices for the trip to Elba:
Piombino-Portoferraio (Jan 1 to June 30) Fare per person: 8,000 lire; per car (depending on size): 36,000-63,000 lire. Hydrofoil, per person: 16,000 lire. From July 1-Dec 31 the fare is about 1,000-2,000 lire (per person) and 6,000-7,000 lire (per car) more expensive.
For the trip to Giglio:
Porto S. Stefano-Giglio (Jan 1-June 30), fares per person: 8,000 lire, per car: 36,000-63,000 lire.

Information
Branches of the Italian State Tourist Office **ENIT**
in Canada: 3 place Ville Marie, 56 Plaza, Montreal H3B 2E3, tel: (514) 866-7667;
in the USA: 630 Fifth Avenue, New York, NY 10111, tel: (212) 245-4822;
in Tuscany (A.P.T. or Pro Loco): addresses and phone numbers are listed in the "Guidepost" sections at the end of every chapter.

Lost and Found
(*Uffici oggetti smarriti*)
You can get the addresses of lost and found offices from local tourist offices, at the town hall, or from various police offices (Vigili urbani). Lost property offices are open mornings only from 8 or 8:30 am to about 1 pm. If you've left something lying in a public bus or lost something on the train, go to the responsible authority (the railroad, the bus company, or the ferry line).

Markets and Congresses
Flower markets: in Florence, Thursday mornings on Via Pellicceria. Every year at the end of April/beginning of May

on the Piazzale degli Uffizi, there's a huge sales show of spring flowers.

In Pescia, Tuscany's largest flower market is held Monday-Saturday from 6:30-9:30 am (Via Amendola).

Flea markets are held Monday-Saturday in summer, Tuesday-Thursday in winter on the Piazza dei Ciompi in Florence and Thursday mornings on the Piazza Cavour in Viareggio. Monday afternoons and Tuesday-Saturday you can go to the US Market in Livorno (Piazza XX Settembre) to buy everything which American GIs stationed near town want to sell. You can get, for example, cheap parachutes, which the farmers spread out under their olive trees to make it easier to collect the olive harvest.

In Florence, every year from the end of April to the beginning of May, the International Artisan Congress (*Mostra Internazionale dell'Artigianato*) is held in the Fortezza da Basso. Distributors come from throughout Italy and from 30 other countries. For information, call 055-49721.

In September on the main square in Greve in Chianti, there's an annual wine congress for all of Europe, at which private individuals can stock up as well. There are permanent wine exhibitions in the Medici fortress in Siena and in the Fortezza of Montalcino.

Medical Assistance

If you can present form E 111 entitling you to international medical treatment, **USL** (*Unità Sanitaria Locale*) centers will treat you free of charge. It's a good idea, however, to look into special travel insurance, particularly if you'd like to ensure a slightly better level of care.

In emergencies, call First Aid (tel: 118) or *Pronto Soccorso* at the hospital nearest you.

Museums

Opening hours of museums are not regulated in Italy, and therefore tend to change frequently, which makes it difficult to state anything definite here. Most museums are closed at midday, from around 1-3 pm, and some are only open in the morning. Many museums are closed on Christmas Day, January 1, Easter Sunday, and May 1.

To ensure that you don't end up standing in front of a locked door, phone ahead to check the opening hours, or ask at the local tourist office.

In September 94, admission fees for Italian museums were divided into three categories. The largest – including the Uffizi in Florence – now cost a flat fee of 12,000 lire. Entrance to less spectacular establishments costs 8,000 lire, while the smallest museums charge 4,000 lire. In most cases, this has meant a price increase of up to 50%.

Nature Parks and Huts

CARRARA (MS), area code 0585:
CAI Carrara, Loc. Campocecina, tel: 841972.

CASTELNUOVO DI GARFAGNANA (LU), area code 0583
Parco delle Alpi Apuane, Piazza Erbe, 1, tel: 644242 and Via Fulvio Testi, 9, tel: 644478.

GROSSETO, area code 0564:
Parco Naturale della Maremma, Piazza Combattente Alberese, 17/d, tel: 407098 and Loc. Pianacce Alberese, tel: 407111.

MASSAROSA (LU), area code 0584:
L.I.P.U., via Pietra Padule, 2, Massaciuccoli, tel: 975567.

MINUCCIANO (LU), area code 0583:
Donegiani G., Rifugio Orto di Donna, tel: 610085.

PISA, area code 050:
Parco Naturale Migliarino San Rossore Massaciuccoli, Via Aurelia Nord, 4, tel: 525500.

STAZZEMA (LU), area code 0584:
Del Freo, Foce di Mosceta, tel: 778007.
Forte dei Marmi all'Alpe della Grotta, Alpe della Grotta, tel: 777051.

Opening Hours

In general, stores are open Monday to Saturday from 8:30 or 9 am to 12:30 or 1 pm, afternoons from 3:30, sometimes as late as 4 or 5 until 7 or 8 pm. In Florence and in the main tourist centers, some stores have started abandoning the midday lunch break; and in large beach towns such as Viareggio and Forte dei Marmi, you can even take a shopping tour on Sundays.

Pharmacies

Opening hours of pharmacies are no different from those of other stores. For information about opening times on Sundays and holidays, call 110. In Florence there are a few pharmacies with 24-hour-service:

All'Insegna del Moro, 20/R, P.zza S. Giovanni, tel: 055-211343

Comunale 5, 5, Piazza Isolotto, tel: 710293

Comunale 13, Stazione S. Maria Novella, tel: 289435

Molteni, 7/R., Via Calzaiuoli, tel: 289490

Post Office

Opening hours: Monday to Friday, usually from 8:15 am-1:30 pm, Saturdays until 12:30 pm. In provincial capitals and vacation centers, post offices may be open throughout the day.

Apart from post offices, you can buy stamps in bars and tobacco shops. A letter sent abroad usually takes about 5 days to reach its destination.

Shopping

Tuscany is a true shoppers' paradise for anyone looking for original souvenirs, high-quality *objets d'arts*, jewelry and antiques, or culinary delicacies.

Florence is clearly the shopping center of the region. For elegant fashion, the best place to look is the Via dei Tornabuoni, the Via degli Strozzi and the Via dei Calzaiuoli. There are also countless young boutiques, leather and shoe shops throughout the old city as well as on the other side of the Ponte Vecchio. Here, in the alleyways around Santo Spirito, you'll find most of the city's traditional artisan workshops and restorers. The Ponte Vecchio itself is a center for gold- and silversmiths. The famous *carta marmorizzata*, marbled paper colored according to centuries-old techniques, is another product of a traditional Florentine craft which you can buy all over the city, including the square of the Duomo. The lovely old pharmacy of Santa Maria Novella, Via della Scala 16, sells creams and soaps, liqueurs and perfumes made according to traditional recipes handed down by the Dominican monks.

But outside of Florence, as well, there's a tempting range of unique gifts and souvenirs. In Lucca, for example, you can get marvelous hand-woven silk; while in Impruneta and Mercatale, south of Florence, there are hand-made ceramic pots for plants and flowers, as well as hand-made earthenware tiles.

Arezzo is famous for its antiques shops. The first weekend of every month sees a huge antiques market on the Piazza Grande and in the surrounding streets of the Old City, where you can buy furniture, pots and pans, silverware, etc. In Florence, too, there's a good address for antiques and odds and ends: the Piazza dei Ciompi, where you can look by weekdays or on the last Sunday of every month. There are other interesting markets for collectors in Lucca (next to the cathedral, third weekend of each month), Viareggio (Piazza Manzoni, last weekend of the month), Pisa (Loggia dei Panchi, second weekend of each month), Fiesole (courtyard of the seminary of San Francesco, second Sunday of the month, except July and August), Carrara (Piazza Gramsci, first weekend of each month, best if you're trying to sell something) and Pistoia (old factory grounds at Breda, second weekend of each month).

Volterra is known for its alabaster; countless workshops in the town produce a variety of objects either copied from old models or in wholly new forms. There's a lot of kitsch sold here, but if you seek out the smaller shops in the old city you may find something pretty or original. In the city center, there's also a sales outlet for the Union of Artisan Alabaster Workers on the Piazza dei Priori 5, tel: 0588/87590.

Culinary delicacies are to be found throughout Tuscany. Some typical offierings include the baked goods and spicy cakes, such as *panforte* from Siena, a dense kind of fruitcake prepared with honey and almonds, or the *Biscotti di Prato*, hard little cookies flavored with almonds and anise, which are a popular dessert, especially when they're dunked in Vin Santo.

In Greve, as well as in the Maremma, a number of sausages are made out of the meat of wild boars. Typical Tuscan cheese is generally made of ewe's milk (*pecorino*), and can be found mainly in the Crete and the Maremma.

You can purchase olive oil directly from the producer at many regional farmhouses. If the label announces that it's *Olio extra vergine d'Oliva*, and the contents are slightly cloudy and greenish, then you know it's of the very highest quality and worth the generally high price. Particularly famous is the oil from around Lucca, but fabulous olive oils also come from other olive-growing areas around Tuscany.

Many monasteries have pharmacies or sales outlets where they sell their own olive oil, honey, herbal liqueurs, and cosmetics products, all prepared by the monks or nuns according to traditional recipes.

Taxi

Florence: 4390
Livorno: 210000
Pisa: 541600

Telephone

You can call from public telephone booths with coins, *gettoni* (telephone tokens), or telephone cards. Many bars have a public telephone you can use (you'll know it by the yellow telephone symbol posted by the door). The Italian phone company SIP (which is wholly independent of the post office) has some public rooms in larger towns which are fitted out with several phone booths, from which you can also make international calls.

Most public telephones today have slots for coins, gettoni, and telephone cards. You can buy telephone cards at tobacconists or kiosks for 5,000 or 10,000 lire.

International country codes (dialling from Tuscany)
to the USA and Canada 001
to England 0044
to Holland 0031
Directory assistance (domestic): 12
Directory assistance (international): 15

Tipping *(mancia)*

Tips are included in hotel and restaurant bills, but it never hurts to round up and add 5-10% of the total as a *mancia*. In bars, service is not included, so you should leave a 15% gratuity behind. Porters, too, expect you to round up; and you generally leave 500 lire in toilets and public bathrooms. At the cinema or the theater, it's common practice to give the usher 500-1000 lire.

Trekking

For information about trekking tours, apply to the tourist office of the area you're interested in.

AUTHORS

Ulrike Bossert, Project Editor and co-author of this book, studied German literature and Romance languages and literature in Heidelberg, with a special focus on italian literature. After several courses of study in Italy, she now works as a freelance television journalist and author in Munich. She is editor of the Italian editions of Nelles Guides. She was the Project Editor for the *Nelles Guide to Rom*e, for which she wrote several articles herself, and translated Italian-language contributions into German.

Christiane Büld Campetti comes from the Westphalian town of Gronau. She studied German and Dutch in Münster and Amsterdam, and has worked for 10 years as an editor for the Bayerischen Rundfunk. For the past 6 years, she has lived with her Florentine husband in an old farmhouse near Florence. From there, she provides the Munich radio with reports about country and people, and special coverage of Italian and specifically Tuscan cultural events.

Dr. Stephan Bleek studied history, political science and sociology in Munich, and has worked for years as a television journalist and film author for Bavarian Television. Because one of his focuses is cultural history, he often goes to Italy, particularly to Tuscany. He contributed the articles on the frescoes in Siena and on Tuscan wine.

PHOTOGRAPHERS

Archiv für Kunst und Geschichte Berlin 10/11, 15, 21, 22, 25, 27l, 29, 30, 31, 32, 33, 34l, 34r, 35, 36, 37, 38/39, 40, 48, 56, 61, 64, 78, 133
Archivio arcivescovile capitolare, Lucca 23

Bleek, Stefan 26, 42, 54, 60, 65, 68, 73, 79, 92/93, 94, 98, 102, 106, 110, 114, 122, 123, 124, 128, 144, 146, 147, 151, 152, 155, 165, 166, 167, 182, 187, 192, 195, 199, 219, 221l, 234, 235
Bondzio, Bodo 46/47
Bossert, Ulrike 224
Campetti, Fabio 75, 153, 201, 202, 206, 210
Christ, Manfred 16, 24, 27r, 69
Ender, Klaus 66, 117
Fischer, Peter 58, 67, 89
Focke, Andreas J. 20, 126, 134, 135, 138/139, 156, 157, 162, 164, 232
Galikowski, Elisabeth 140
Gruschwitz, Bernd F. 116, 161, 204/205, 208
Helbig, Konrad (Mainbild) 163
Holzbach, Renata / Bénet, Philipp 1, 44/45, 55, 62, 97, 108/109, 129
Janicke, Volkmar E. 103
Kirchgessner, Markus 175
Krause, Dorothee 184
Krimmer, H. (Voller Ernst) 57
Pfeiffer, Gerd 145, 160, 237
Poblete, Jose F. 14, 19, 41, 50, 59, 71, 72, 74, 76, 83, 85, 87, 115, 119, 130, 132, 170/171, 176, 178/179, 189, 191, 196, 197, 212/213, 214/215, 221r, 225
Reichmann, Hermann 104
Scala, Instituto Fotografico Editoriale, Antella (Firenze) 12, 28, 238/239
Schraml, Oskar (Foto Amberg) 63, 112, 188
Schultz, Anja 51, 70
Stadler, Hubert 99, 125, 127, 148, 150, 154, 158, 159, 216, 231, 233
Stuffler, Jeanette 8/9, 82, 88, 209l, 218
Stuhler, Werner 18, 86, 131, 172
Tetzner, Marina 180
Teatro Povero di Monticchiello 227, 229
Thiele, Klaus 100, 185, 220
Thomas, Martin cover, 43, 223